THE SPORTING WIFE

THE

SPORTING WIFE

Edited by Barbara Hargreaves

A Guide to Game and Fish Cooking

H. F. & G. WITHERBY LTD.

First paperback edition, published 1976
by H. F. & G. Witherby Ltd.
5 Plantain Place, London, SE1
Reprinted (with minor amendments) 1978
Reprinted (with minor amendments) 1979

ISBN 0 85493 121 X
Printed photolitho in Great Britain by
EBENEZER BAYLIS & SON LTD.
THE TRINITY PRESS, WORCESTER, AND LONDON

INTRODUCTION

Since publication of *The Sporting Wife* and *The Compleat Angler's Wife* there has been an increasing interest in cooking game and fish in more varied and imaginative ways.

Apart from the many new recipes sent to me since publication of the first two books, there were also many people who suggested that it would be more convenient to have game and fish cookery together in one volume. So here are the two books combined, both extensively revised with a large number of new sections and recipes added.

There could be no more fitting dedication to this book than to all those interested and enthusiastic cooks who have contributed to this volume: to Kathleen Thomas and Suzanne Beedell who helped so much with the earlier books; and for recipes in this volume to Susan Brownlow, Margaret Costa, Ann Gore, Thérèse Grosvenor, Susan Stirling and Brigid Witherby.

I am much indebted to Mary Norwak for writing the section on *Home Freezing of Game and Fish* and Sidney Spencer for very kindly supplying the section on smoking fish at home. There are many others who have helped in various ways and where they have supplied a recipe an acknowledgement appears beneath, and to all, many thanks. The information on Condition and Age of Game Birds is reprinted with kind permission of The Game Conservancy, Fordingbridge from their booklet *How to Distinguish Sex and Age in Gamebirds* (1965).

Finally, a word about the illustrations. Most of the period engravings illustrating this book are the work of either Thomas Bewick (1753-1828) or William Dickes (1815-1892).

Thomas Bewick, renowned for his illustrations to the *Quadrupeds* and the *Birds*, worked during the reign of George III. Pre-eminent among wood engravers, he combined a superb eye for detail with a prowess at his art which has made him one of the really great illustrators.

William Dickes practised as a wood engraver in the mid-nineteenth century. His sensitive and delicate line work deserves to be much better known than it is at present. His engravings are frequently signed with his initials.

NOTE TO PAPERBACK EDITION

The opportunity has been taken to make some revisions, and add a few new recipes. I wish particularly to thank Mary Norwak for providing additional information to her chapter on *Home Freezing of Game and Fish*, Kathleen Falkus for her recipe on page 180, and Hugh Falkus for the quotation on page 178 from his book *Sea Trout Fishing*.

BARBARA HARGREAVES

CONTENTS

PART THREE

PART ONE
GAME

CONDITION AND AGE OF GAME BIRDS

Shooting men like to record the proportion of young birds in the bag—certainly partridges—as it gives them an indication of the success of the previous breeding season. In poor reproduction years it warns them when they are in danger of shooting next year's breeding stock.

In the kitchen it will be as well to know whether a bird can be roasted or whether it must be destined for the casserole.

Two GENERAL TESTS. While young gamebirds may be distinguished from old ones by many different methods in the early part of the shooting season, there are only two tests which apply to most species throughout the whole of the shooting season.

All young gamebirds have a small blind-ended tube opening on the upper side of the vent. This tube, commonly known as the *bursa*, is believed to play some part in disease control. In all species it becomes much reduced or may close completely when the bird reaches sexual maturity, and the presence of a normal bursa is a certain test for a young bird. In ordinary hands the bursa test should not be attempted on live birds.

The second method (which unfortunately cannot be applied to the pheasant) is to examine the two outer primaries or flight feathers. In the partridge the pointed, lance-shaped tips of these feathers distinguish the young bird from the old,

[11]

which has blunt-ended outer primaries. It should be mentioned that when feathers are wet, even blunt-ended ones can look pointed.

Young pheasants cannot be distinguished by this means, since, in contrast to other gamebirds, *all* the juvenal flight feathers are moulted. Partridge and grouse moult only eight of the ten sharply pointed juvenal feathers, and retain the outermost pair for approximately a year.

GREY PARTRIDGE. In September and early October the familiar dark beak, yellowish legs and relatively soft bones of the young birds will readily differentiate them from the grey-beaked, grey-legged and hard-boned adults, but later in the season the simple flight feather test is to be recommended— the pointed primaries (two outer feathers) indicating a young bird. In September a few partridges in their second year may *not* have moulted these sharply pointed primaries of the juvenal plumage, but these feathers will be faded and abraded to such an extent that the bird will be easily recognised as old.

The bursa test may be applied with a matchstick, burned at one end so that it is narrow but not too sharp, or the quill of a flight feather. With very gentle pressure the probe should penetrate about half an inch in a young bird, while in old birds the bursa will either be completely closed or, in some cases, open for only $\frac{1}{4}$ in. It is unlikely that the busy keeper or shoot-owner will have the time to use the bursa test on a couple of hundred birds at the end of a day's shooting, but it is useful for small numbers and for otherwise doubtful specimens.

RED-LEGGED PARTRIDGE. The bursa is approximately the same depth in young birds as in the partridge ($\frac{1}{2}$ in.) Another method of ageing redlegs is to inspect the two outer primaries —not for shape but for colour markings. The young bird has these two flight feathers tipped with a cream colour; sometimes other primaries not yet moulted will also show this cream coloration.

PHEASANT. The bursa test is relatively easily applied to both cock and hen pheasants. The bird should be laid on its back on the palm of the left hand while the thumb is used to bend back the tail and expose the vent. The opening of the bursa of a young bird will be seen to lie inside the opening of the vent on the side nearest the tail. In young birds the depth of the bursa will be approximately 1 in. In old birds the bursa may close completely (when the site of the opening is often marked by a slight bump) or remain open for about $\frac{1}{4}$ in; very rarely up to nearly $\frac{1}{2}$ in. This is the only method for distinguishing young *hen* pheasants from old ones: early in the season young cocks may be separated from old ones by their blunt and relatively short spurs. Later in the season, surprisingly enough, the spurs of early-hatched young birds can be as long and as sharply pointed as some old ones! The only certain means of distinguishing young from old, therefore, is again the bursa test.

GROUSE. The presence of a bursa and the more sharply pointed extremities of the two outer primaries are reliable means of distinguishing young from old throughout the season. In the early part of the season the last primary to be moulted (the third from the outside) is also usually only partly developed and considerably shorter than the feathers on either side. Even for some time after it has grown out this third feather will have a 'new look' about it. In August many other characteristics may also be used for rapid age distinction. The inflexibility of the lower jaw, the hardness of the skull and the presence of claw scars are indications of an old bird.

THE GAME CONSERVANCY, FORDINGBRIDGE

CHAPTER ONE

PARTRIDGE
QUAIL
PHEASANT
GROUSE
BLACKCOCK
PTARMIGAN
CAPERCAILLIE

Partridge

"It is a fact that people really believe no part of a partridge is ever taken away after being set before him. Neither bones nor sinews remain: so fond is he of the brown bird. Having eaten the breast, and the juicy leg and the delicate wing, he next proceeds to suck the bones; for game, to be thoroughly enjoyed, should be eaten like a mince-pie, in the fingers. There is always one bone with a sweeter flavour than the rest, just at the joint of the fracture: it varies in every bird according to the chance of the cooking, but, having discovered it, put it aside for further and more strict attention. Presently he begins to grind up the bones in his strong teeth, commencing with the smallest. His teeth are not now so powerful as when in younger days he used to lift a sack of wheat with them, or the full milking-bucket up to the level of the copper in the dairy. Still they gradually reduce the slender skeleton. The feat is not so difficult if the bird has been well hung."

"ROVING ABOUT A GREAT ESTATE" RICHARD JEFFERIES

The native Grey or Common partridge, having diminished to an alarming degree throughout Britain is now becoming more plentiful. In the south and east the "Frenchman" or Red-Legged partridge, imported 200 years ago when over-shooting threatened the British stock, is just as common. When a partridge is young its feet and legs are bright, the beak supple and, most important of all, the wing feathers, particularly the first flight feathers, are pointed, although these disappear at the moult. Young birds need hanging for only 3 to 4 days, old birds a little longer. Casserole old birds.

Provided the birds are not dried out by underbasting and overcooking, and are young to start with, there is no sub-stitute for a roast partridge!

Spit-roast Partridge (young birds)

2 partridges.   Some rashers of bacon.
Little melted butter.

Pluck, draw and truss the partridges in the same way as you would a chicken. Season with pepper and salt. Tie thin rashers of fat bacon on the breasts and roast on a spit in front of a bright fire—an old and trusted recipe says, but to-day you could use one of the new oven spits, if you have

[17]

one, for 30 minutes, basting frequently with melted butter. Straw potatoes and a little cress are all that need be served with roast partridge.

Salmis of Partridge

Some partridges.	Bunch of herbs.
¼ lb. streaky bacon	Salt and pepper.
cut thick.	Piece of ham or slice
Butter.	of thick bacon.
2 shallots.	1 glass red wine.
Nut of butter. 1 oz. flour.	Juice of half a lemon.

Truss the birds as for roasting and cut the streaky bacon into inch squares. Put these pieces in a saucepan with an ounce of butter and fry till they begin to turn colour. Now dip in your birds and fry and turn them for 10 minutes, then take them out and allow them to cool. With a sharp knife (the older birds will need this!) carve off the wings, legs and breasts and skin and trim them and put aside. Chop up the carcases and return them and the trimmings to the stewpan, to which you have added a couple of chopped shallots, sweet herbs, pepper, salt, a slice of ham, with as much stock made by boiling the giblets as will cover the whole, and simmer for a couple of hours. Strain and completely cool it. Remove all fat, add a glass of red wine, and the pieces of partridge and again warm gradually to simmering point.

For the Sauce

In a separate small saucepan melt a piece of butter and add flour to it, then pour in a little of the gravy and the juice of half a lemon. Stir this well and turn the whole into the salmis,

[18]

which then thickens to the right consistency. Pile the portions of the bird in the centre of a dish and pour the sauce over them. Serve with sippets of dry toast.

Casserole of Partridge and Cabbage (*for older birds*)

A brace of partridge. $\frac{1}{2}$ lb. chipolata pork
2 onions. sausages.
2 carrots. 1 medium savoy cabbage.
4 oz. streaky bacon in $\frac{1}{2}$ pint good stock.
one piece. Thyme and parsley.
Butter. Salt and pepper.

Partridge pieces served in rich sauce. It takes a little trouble, and, on and off, all day to get through the cooking and cooling. Allow half an hour before serving to finish off the sauce and reheat the meat.

Rather a "country style" dish, containing lots of vegetables. Easy to make with simple ingredients. Can be made long before the meal is to be served and left in the oven without spoiling.

Cut the onions and carrots into rings and sauté them in butter. Brown the partridges in the same butter. Cut the cabbage in quarters and cook it in boiling water for about 6 minutes with the bacon. Drain and squeeze it and cut the rind off the bacon. Cut cabbage and bacon into smaller pieces. Now put half the cabbage in a casserole, season lightly, and lay on it the partridges, bacon and vegetables. Season again, adding a pinch of thyme. Pour in stock and cover with the rest of the cabbage. Close down the lid tightly and cook in a slow oven for 2 hours. Grill the sausages lightly and add for the last half hour of cooking.

To Dish. Heap the cabbage in the middle of a large dish, put the partridges on top and the bacon and sausages round. Sprinkle with a little chopped parsley.

[19]

Partridge in a Pot *(young or old birds)*

2–3 partridges.   ½ lb. butter.   Stock.
Sherry.

Easy to make, simple ingredients, this dish is in fact improved by keeping, and for those without a Home Freezer, a fine way to cook a main meal well ahead of time. Rich and tender stewed partridge, but the birds remain in one piece.

Prepare the birds as for roasting, season them inside and put a lump of butter in each. Put into a casserole with some good stock. (1 chicken bouillon cube, dissolved in boiling water, will substitute.) Add more seasoning according to taste, (the sherry) and add about ¼ lb. more butter. Cover with cooking foil or double greaseproof paper, or use a casserole with a close-fitting lid—and put in a slow oven for 1½–2 hours, until the birds are tender. They must be completely covered with stock and water, and when cold the butter will form a seal on top. Do not uncover until they are to be eaten. Then re-heat. They will keep for several days. Garnish with red-currant jelly and parsley.

Partridge Pie *(various aged birds)*

2 partridges.	2 hard-boiled eggs.
½ lb. veal.	1½ oz. butter.
½ lb. bacon.	6 mushrooms.
Parsley.	½ lb. pastry.
Salt and pepper.	1 gill stock.

Rather more ingredients, but again, simple enough to make, and fit for a king or a hungry family, or guests who like robust food. Can be cooked beforehand and served cold.

Cut each partridge into 4 pieces. Melt the butter in

a pan, put in the birds, and fry them lightly. Cut the veal and bacon into thin slices, line a pie dish with these slices, put on them the pieces of partridge, season with salt, pepper, chopped parsley and mushrooms, then put over them another layer of bacon and veal. Cover the pie with the pastry, and bake for about 1 hour in a hot oven. When done, fill up with stock, and serve either hot or cold.

This recipe for partridge pie is particularly useful if you have several birds of unidentifiable age. If some of the birds are known to be old the pieces should be simmered gently in a medium oven until the meat just comes off the bones, before putting on the pastry. Then bake in a hot oven for 25 minutes.

Cold Partridge Spliced (*older birds*)

1 old partridge.　　　　　Lemon juice.

2/3 tablespoonsful rum.　Lettuce hearts.

Very simple, but the rum just gives it that different touch.

Roast or pot-roast the bird, being careful not to get it too dry if using the former method. Cut it up into the usual joints immediately, and put all these while still warm into a deep dish containing a couple of tablespoonfuls of rum. Cover the dish and let the pieces, which should be turned from time to time, remain in the rum until next day. Then drain them, but not too thoroughly, of whatever little rum the pieces have not absorbed, sprinkle a very few drops of lemon juice on them, and dish them surrounded by a salad of the hearts of lettuces.

Braised Partridge with Celery Sauce (*young bird*)

2 partridges.	1 onion.
Pork rind.	2 bay leaves.
1 carrot.	1 sprig thyme.
Salt and pepper.	$\frac{1}{2}$ pt. white stock.
Celery sauce.	

A good simple dish with plenty of vegetables, but needs to be prepared and brought straight to the table; there won't be much chance to leave it while it cooks!

Singe, draw, wipe and truss two partridges with their wings inside. Lay a piece of pork rind in a saucepan, adding one carrot and one onion, both cut in slices, two bay leaves, one sprig of thyme, and the two partridges. Season with one pinch of salt and half a pinch of pepper. When they have assumed a good golden colour on the hot stove, moisten with half a pint of stock, then put the saucepan in the oven, and allow to cook for 20 minutes. Dress them on a serving dish, untruss, pour a pint of hot celery sauce over, (see page 308) and serve.

Boiled Partridge (*young bird*)

1 young partridge.	Thin rashers of fat
Vine leaves.	bacon.
Salt.	

The vine leaves may present a problem, but are essential. The flavour is delicate rather than rich.

Partridge roasted, and even á la crème, are superior to it, but if you have a young partridge just hung so and cook it in this way, you will capture a fleeting fragrance unflavoured by butter or cream. Salt the bird lightly inside and out. Wrap it first in vine leaves and then completely in thin rashers

[22]

of fat bacon. Boil it for 35 minutes in plain, unsalted water, and then at once plunge it into iced water, where it must remain only just long enough to get cold. Then unwrap, serve with a plain lettuce salad.

AMBROSE HEATH

Rebhühner mit Sauerkraut (*young* *birds*)

3 partridges.
¼ teaspoonful salt.
⅛th teaspoonful pepper.
6 strips bacon.
3 tablespoonfuls butter.
1 crushed juniper berry.
1½ lb. sauerkraut.
1 teaspoonful sugar.
2 tablespoonfuls butter.

3 medium-sized carrots, quartered.
6 baby onions or shallots.
2 tablespoonfuls hot water.
1–2 teaspoonfuls flour.
1 tablespoonful cold water.
½ cup sour cream.
1 cup dry white wine or champagne.

You and your guests must like sauerkraut to enjoy this dish which comes up with a most definite "German" flavour from the juniper berries and the wine and sauerkraut. The method given here for cooking the sauerkraut is a simple one, but if you know how to cook the stuff using the rather more complicated German or Austrian methods, do so; the dish will be even better.

Rub salt and pepper inside and on back of each cleaned bird. Tie 2 strips bacon around each breast of partridge. Melt butter in heavy iron pan and fry partridges until brown on all sides. Put in the crushed juniper berry, the carrots and onions. Cover and simmer slowly until birds are tender. Baste with hot water from time to time.

[23]

To make Sauce

Strain gravy and mix flour with cold water to a smooth paste, add the gravy to the pan and fold in the sour cream. Season with salt if needed. Allow to boil and thicken. Cut partridges in half and arrange on a hot platter. Serve gravy separately.

Cook sauerkraut by putting in a saucepan with the butter and add a little water and sugar. Cover and simmer for ½ hour. Add wine and continue cooking until tender and the liquid is reduced. Serve in a covered dish. Also serve fluffy mashed potatoes.

"WORLD WIDE COOK BOOK" PEARL METZELTHIN

Perdrix à La Purée de Lentilles (older birds)

2 old partridges.	4 ozs butter.
2 large onions.	1 glass white wine.
4 carrots.	1 glass stock.
1 lb. brown lentils.	2 cloves.
2 cloves garlic.	

Simple solid and nourishing country style dish, spicy but not rich. Tender whole partridge in thick lentil puree sauce.

Clean and truss the partridges and put into a pan just big enough to hold them, pack round with a large sliced onion and 2 or more carrots cut in rounds. Add 3 or 4 oz. butter. Cook in the oven, basting frequently. When the birds have taken colour, pour over them a glass of white wine and let it reduce by half, add seasoning and a glass of stock, cover and finish cooking over a low flame.

Prepare a purée of 1 lb. brown lentils which have been soaked overnight, an onion stuck with two cloves, 2 cloves garlic, 2 carrots and salt. Cover with water and simmer for 2 hours, and when quite soft put through a sieve. Mix the purée with half the sauce from the partridges, work it over a fire until the purée is smooth and of the right consistency. Serve on a dish with the purée all round and the rest of the sauce poured over. These quantities are for 6 birds.

Norman Roast Partridge

1 partridge (youngish).
Fat bacon.
Butter.
¼ calves' liver.

4 cooking apples.
1 glass brandy or calvados.
2 oz. breadcrumbs.

Typical Norman dish flavoured with apples. Easy to make and fine for a dinner party, especially if flamed at the table. If you have a suitable dish in which to roast and serve the birds, use it; the apples will remain undisturbed before serving, and the whole lot will come to the table very hot so that the brandy or calvados will make a spectacular fire.

Fry the liver with the partridge liver, mince and mix with breadcrumbs and season the bird with this filling. Peel and core the apples and place in a roasting tray. Wrap partridge in bacon and place in the middle of the tray and brush over all with melted butter. Cook for 15 minutes in pre-heated oven at 400 degrees. Gas 8. Just before serving, pour brandy over bird and light.

Pakistan Spiced Partridge (*Teetur Qorma*)

4 partridges (any
aged birds).

4 cloves garlic.

1 onion.

4 cloves.

6 ground peppercorns.

3 cardamom seeds.

1 small piece ginger.

1 dessertspoonful roasted
coriander seeds.

½ pint curd (or yoghourt).

¼ teaspoonful saffron
soaked in water.

6 oz. butter.

Salt and chilli pepper to taste.

Curried partridge. Its a matter of having the right spices. Those who specialise in curries will have them, but some are not in common use. However, any good delicatessen sells these ingredients and if you buy them for the first time for this recipe, you will go on using them for others, they are so good. Like all curries, serve this with rice, poppadoms, chutney and any side dishes or "Sambals" you care to make.

Crush 1 clove of garlic and mix it with 1 pint water. Wash the birds in this and then in well-salted water. Dry. Prick with fork and rub with salt. Thinly slice the onion and fry in butter till soft but not too brown. Drain the onion and pound to a paste with the garlic, coriander seeds, pepper-corns and ginger. Mix with the curd, or yoghourt, and beat well, adding salt and chilli pepper to taste. Reheat the fat, fry the partridges until browned all over and gradually stir in the curd. Add the cloves and cardamom seeds and saffron. Cover the pan and cook over gentle heat until the birds are tender. Serve hot. This recipe may be used with any type of game bird and is especially good with pigeons.

"A COOKS TOUR" ROBIN HOWE

Partridge with Mushrooms *(any-age bird)*

2–3 partridges.   Butter.

$\frac{1}{4}$ lb. mushrooms for each bird and $\frac{1}{4}$ lb. extra.

$1\frac{1}{2}$ oz. butter. $\frac{1}{2}$ pint stock.

$1\frac{1}{2}$ oz. flour.   2 glasses sherry.

Seasoning.

A variation on roast partridge.

Clean and prepare the birds. Cook all but $\frac{1}{4}$ lb. of the mushrooms in a little butter with plenty of seasoning. Stuff each bird with mushrooms, filling the body cavity. Cook in an open casserole in a good oven, 400°F., for 20 minutes.

To make Sauce

Melt the butter, add flour and let it cook a little, then add stock and sherry, cook until thick, test for seasoning.

Pour this sauce over the birds and put back into the oven, let simmer for 45 minutes. For this you will need to reduce oven temperature or put on lower shelf. Serve with plain boiled potatoes and a green vegetable.

Partridges à la Wellington

2 young partridges.   Bunch of mixed herbs.

Thin slices bacon. $\frac{1}{4}$ lb button mushrooms.

$\frac{1}{2}$ lb small button   2 heads of chicory.

    onions.   Salt and pepper.

Butter.   1 beef stock cube.

Flour.   Green pepper.

1 pt cider or white wine.

Rich casseroled whole partridges. Not difficult and can be cooked ahead of time and reheated. This dish, with its wine and green peppers and chicory, has a sharpish taste which is out of the ordinary. Good for a dinner party.

Prepare the birds for braising and place in a casserole or deep fire-proof dish. Cover the breasts with rashers of bacon. Put two ounces of butter in the dish, and then add the onions and mushrooms evenly round the birds. Add the bunch of herbs and the chicory (whole). Cover the dish and cook over a low gas for fifteen minutes. Sift a little flour over the birds, and add the stock cube dissolved in a tablespoonful of water. Add the cider (or wine) and cook in a quick oven for about an hour, basting frequently. Make a bed of mashed potato on a serving dish, and place the birds on this, surrounded by the vegetables, garnish with pieces of raw green pepper, and pour the sauce, which should be reduced until it is fairly thick, round the dish.

Partridge Casserole (old birds)

1 bird.	$\frac{1}{4}$ lb. mushrooms.
Butter.	4 shallots or 1 small
4 ozs. bacon.	onion.
Salt and pepper.	Bay leaf.

$\frac{1}{2}$ pt. dry red wine.

Casserole of old birds, redeemed by the wine. Good family food or dinner party course for those who like food simple. Can be made ahead of time.

Flour the bird and brown it in the butter on all sides. Put the bird and butter into a casserole or fireproof dish and add the chopped bacon mushrooms and shallots which should have been sautéd lightly in butter. Add bay leaf and salt and pepper and the wine, and cook in a slow oven till tender.

[28]

Little Mousses of Partridge in Sherry Sauce

1 large old bird.
1½ tablespoonsful sherry.
4 yolks of egg.
4 whites of egg.
Shredded gherkins.
Red chillies.

¼ pint Bechamel sauce. (see p. 315)
Salt and pepper.
1½ tablespoonsful thick cream.
Butter, salt and pepper.
Hard-boiled egg whites.

½ lb. mushrooms.

Here is a fussy one with lots of ingredients, and lots of fiddling about. Suitable for a dinner party but it will take all the cook's attention right up to the time of serving and there should be no interval between the mousses being cooked and eaten. But gorgeous!

Take all the raw meat from the carcase, pound it, sieve it, mince it or put it through your electric blender till it is smooth. There should be a quarter of a pound or more. Add to it the bechamel sauce, the sherry, salt and pepper, the raw egg yolks and the cream, and blend all together. Whip the egg whites very stiff and fold into the partridge mixture. Butter the insides of enough small moulds and put a mixture of chopped gherkins, hard-boiled egg whites and red chillies (just a little, they are very hot) in each. Fill the moulds with the partridge mixture and stand in a pan containing boiling water to three parts of their depth. Watch the water reboil and let the contents poach with a lid over for about eighteen minutes. Meanwhile sauté the thinly sliced mushrooms in butter with a little salt and pepper. Place the mushrooms on a serving dish and turn the little mousses out onto this. Pour sherry sauce around and serve immediately.

2 partridges.   1 sound hard cabbage.

Chicken stock cubes.   Tablespoonful ground rice.

2 oz. bacon or ham.   Salt and pepper.

Country-style thick soup, quite delicious and filling, a meal in itself in fact. Simple ingredients, but takes a little time and trouble to make.

Trim and quarter the cabbage. Put in a saucepan with salt and enough cold water to cover it. Bring to the boil, then remove it and wash it in cold water. Put it back into fresh boiling water and cook for 15 minutes. Drain and squeeze out all water, and put it into a big casserole or fireproof dish with three pints of stock made with stock cubes. Cook slowly till tender. Then remove the birds and take off the meat in fillets to serve in the soup. Strain the cabbage from the stock and put the carcases back into the stock to boil for half an hour, adding more water if necessary. You should have three to four pints. Put the cabbage through your blender, or a sieve, and add the stock and the ground rice previously moistened with some of the stock. Reheat all this purée, stirring constantly until it thickens.

Dice the bacon and fry it till crisp, and add it and the fillets of partridge meat to the soup just before it is served.

Stuffed Oven-roast Partridge

2 young birds.   2 oz. bacon or ham.

2 oz. bacon rashers. $\frac{1}{4}$ lb. mushrooms.

Butter.   4 juniper berries.

Another variation on roast partridge. Possibly the nicest of all.

Prepare the birds for cooking. Blend together the 2 oz.

chopped bacon or ham, the livers of the birds, the mushrooms and the juniper berries, and season well with pepper
and salt. Stuff the birds with this mixture. Smear the birds
all over with butter and put bacon rashers on the breasts.
Put in a covered roasting tin and cook in a medium oven
till tender, basting frequently. Serve with roast potatoes or
game chips, watercress, and Brussel sprouts.

Quail

In general appearance it is *much like a very small, delicately-built Partridge*, which it also resembles in flight if flushed, but its presence is more often detected by the *characteristic note of the male* than by the bird being seen. The general effect is more sandy than in Partridge. If flushed it flies low and for a short distance only, but it is reluctant to fly and in its regular haunts, with ample cover of grass or plants, is seldom put up except by dogs. Found in family parties or bevies in autumn and on migration, but is not otherwise notably gregarious.

Call of the male is a liquid "quic, qui-ic" usually repeated several times. It is heard by night as well as day and usually from the latter half of May through June and July.

Quail are delightfully fat, tender and succulent, with a wonderful flavour. They used to be very common in Great Britain, but live netting (halted by law in 1937) and shooting reduced the population drastically. The quail is now a fully protected bird in Great Britain, and it is therefore illegal to shoot them. They can, however, be obtained for eating from quail farms and from high-class poulterers.

Quail with White Grapes

4 quail.	2 tablespoons flour.
3 oz. seedless grapes.	4 tablespoons butter.
2 tablespoons blanched	$\frac{1}{4}$ pint dry white wine.
sliced almonds.	2 tablespoons lemon
Salt and pepper.	juice.

Quail in a delicious sharp mediterranean sauce.

Clean the quail and rub well with salt and pepper and flour. Melt the butter in a thick pan and sauté the birds in it until they are nicely browned. Add the wine and lemon juice and continue cooking slowly for 15 to 20 minutes. Add the grapes and almonds and cook for a further 5 to 10 minutes, or until the birds are tender.

Quails en Casserole

6 quails.	2 yolks of eggs.
1 small cupful of milk.	3 or 4 chicken livers.
2 oz. butter.	6 slices of bacon.
1 handful	1 small cup of Madeira
breadcrumbs.	sauce. (See page 298)
Salt, pepper, parsley.	Nutmeg.
1 bay leaf.	Shallot.

Rather a fiddly recipe, but the result is very special, a rich casserole.

[33]

Prepare the quails for stuffing. Put the milk, butter, bay leaf, salt and pepper to taste and a little grated nutmeg in a saucepan and bring to the boil. Stir in the breadcrumbs and simmer them for 10 minutes. Remove the bay leaf and stir in the egg yolks. Cut up the chicken livers, and sauté them in butter in which the finely chopped shallot has been blended, season with pepper and salt and put through the electric blender or sieve. Mix this purée with the bread-crumbs, etc., and stuff the birds with this. Wrap each quail in a thin slice of bacon, place them in a casserole with the rest of the butter, and cook them in a slow oven for $\frac{1}{2}$ an hour. Pour off the fat, add the sauce, and cook until tender.

Roasted Quail

4 quails.	4 vine leaves.
4 slices of fat bacon.	4 croutons of toast.
Gravy.	Fried breadcrumbs.
Watercress.	Butter for basting.

Classic roasting recipe, perhaps the best way.

Prepare the birds for roasting and brush with warm butter, cover each breast with a vine leaf and tie a piece of bacon over each vine leaf. Roast or spit roast for 12 to 15 minutes, basting frequently with the hot butter. When cooked remove string. Serve the bacon and vine leaves if liked, and put the birds on the toast, which should be dunked in the dripping tin to mop up the bastings. Garnish with watercress, serve with gravy and breadcrumbs.

Pheasant

"I aimed at the head—knowing that it would mean instant death, and would also avoid shattering the bird at so short a range; besides which, there would be fewer scattered feathers to collect and thrust out of sight in a rabbit bury. A reason why people frequently miss pheasants in cover-shooting, despite of their size, is because they look at the body, the wings, and the tail. But if they looked only at the head, and thought of that, very few would escape. My finger felt the trigger, and the last increase of pressure would have been fatal; but in the act I hesitated, dropped the barrel, and watched the beautiful bird."

"THE AMATEUR POACHER" RICHARD JEFFERIES

Pheasant must be hung, but for how long depends upon individual taste, the weather, storage conditions and the condition of the bird. If it has not been shot clean it will not need to hang so long. In average weather a week is long enough, in frosty weather the bird may hang longer. Unhung pheasant is little more than a tasty chicken, correctly hung it will taste incredibly rich and gamey.

To decide the age of a cock bird look at his spurs. First-year spurs are short and rounded, second-year spurs are short and pointed, old birds have long pointed spurs. Young hen birds have soft feet and light feathers. Hen birds are usually tenderer than cock birds. See also page 13.

Roast Pheasant (*young bird*)

Pheasant (preferably a young hen).	1 oz butter. Little flour.
Pepper and salt.	Some slices of fat bacon.

Provided the bird is kept well basted and not overcooked, there is nothing to beat plain roast pheasant. It is easy and quick to cook.

Draw and truss the bird as you would a chicken; season with pepper and salt inside and out. Dredge the breast with flour and brown it in sizzling butter. Then tie some thin rashers of fat bacon over the breast. Place in a covered roasting tin or wrap in foil and cook in a medium oven for 45/60 minutes. Then remove the lid or the foil, baste well and allow to cook until nicely browned, for about another 20 minutes, turning the oven up if necessary. Serve with mashed chestnuts or braised celery, or, classically, with bread sauce, butter fried breadcrumbs, brussels sprouts and roast potatoes. Make a good game gravy or one of the sauces for game detailed in Chapter Sixteen.

Roast Pheasant with Mushrooms (*preferably young birds*)

1 pheasant.	1 dozen mushrooms.
2 oz. butter.	Salt and cayenne.
	Some fat bacon.

Variant of roast bird, with field mushrooms. A combination of tastes for the most discriminating!

Prepare the pheasant in the usual way, then cover each side of the breast with small rashers of fat bacon. Wash and skin the mushrooms; if they are large, then cut them into halves or quarters. Also add 1 oz. butter, ½ teaspoonful salt and a few grains of cayenne. Stuff the pheasant with these. Cover the whole of the breast with a thickly buttered piece of paper. Let it roast for 45 minutes, basting several times. Remove the paper and roast 10 minutes longer. Serve with gravy and bread sauce.

The mushrooms should preferably be fresh field ones; cultivated ones never have quite the same flavour.

Pheasant Pie (*with left-over pheasant*)

Pheasant. Salt. Butter. 1 shallot.
Cooked spaghetti, about 1 oz. per person.
Cayenne pepper.

More pie than pheasant, a good way to use up leftovers for family eating, or just a change from a surfeit of them.

Cut up the left-over flesh of either roast or boiled pheasant into fairly small pieces and brown them in butter, with the addition of a little cayenne pepper and salt. Remove this and keep it hot. Chop one shallot and brown that in butter and mix with the pheasant. Add this to a sufficient quantity of cooked spaghetti, according to the size of the pie-dish you are using. Mix well together, put into a pie dish, covering with flaky pastry, and bake in a quick oven till the pastry is nicely browned.

This is a good way of using small quantities of left-over birds which otherwise wouldn't make a meal. Add some good gravy to the mixture.

[37]

Pheasant Pâté (*for using up scraps*)

Cooked pheasant—free of all bones, sinews and skin.

½ weight of pheasant of fat ham.

Very finely mince pheasant and ham together—preferably using a Moulinette. Season highly with salt and freshly ground black pepper. Melt one ounce butter for every 4 ozs. of mixture—add 1 desertspoon brandy for every ounce of butter and pour into pheasant and ham—mix well. Serve with toast. Will keep well in refrigerator for 3 or 4 days or for 10 days to 2 weeks if sealed with clarified butter.

ANN GORE

Lincolnshire recipe for Pheasant (*young bird*)

1 pheasant.	Stock or water.
1 onion.	4 tomatoes.
1 carrot.	½ lb. mushrooms.
Salt and pepper.	1 tablespoonful chopped
4 oz. dripping.	parsley.

Pieces of young pheasant in a vegetable sauce. Very English, tasty but not herb or spice flavoured.

Cut up a tender pheasant, peel and shred an onion and a carrot. Melt the dripping in a pan, add the carrot and onion and fry for 5 minutes, stirring with a wooden spoon. Place the pieces of pheasant in this, with a little salt and pepper, and fry for another 5 minutes, stirring all the time; add 2 tablespoonfuls of flour and cook for 3 more minutes, gradually adding 1½ pints of stock and stir till it boils. Cut 4 tomatoes in quarters and ½ lb. peeled mushrooms, 1 tablespoonful chopped parsley; add these to the contents of the pan and simmer for half an hour. Set the pheasant in the centre of a hot dish, pour over the sauce and garnish with mushrooms.

[38]

This will only be really successful with a young bird; it is a well-known fact that the poacher takes only the best young birds and this is a Lincolnshire poacher's recipe.

Stewed Pheasant with Onions (*old bird*)

Simply stewed old pheasant in a sharpish, creamy onion sauce.

1 old pheasant.	Yolks of 2 eggs.
Some small onions,	2 tablespoonfuls butter.
shallots or 1 large	2 tablespoonfuls flour.
chopped onion.	Salt, pepper and a squeeze
$\frac{1}{2}$ cup cream.	of lemon.

Cut an old pheasant into pieces, cook slowly in a small quantity of water with a dozen small onions, shallots or chopped onion. Remove the pheasant to serving-dish as soon as it is tender, and when the onions are soft drain from the stock and reduce to about 1 cupful. Make the sauce of 2 tablespoonfuls butter and the same of flour, and the stock can now be added with half a cup of cream, then add the yolks of 2 eggs, salt, pepper and a squeeze of lemon juice to taste. Pour the sauce over the pheasant and onions and serve very hot.

Stewing a pheasant by this method makes the oldest of birds very tender. It's also a good way to cook the, legs of any pheasant, young or old.

Norwegian Pheasant (*young bird*)

1 young pheasant.	3 oz. butter.
Dessertspoonful plain	3 tablespoonsful cream.
flour.	

A slightly different way of cooking the bird which is neither roasting nor stewing, but will tenderise it well and produce a tasty bird in creamy sauce.

Place the pheasant on the fire in a thick-bottomed stewpan with 1½ oz. butter and let it simmer with the lid on for half an hour. Roll a dessertspoonful of flour in 1 oz. butter and a little salt. Add 3 tablespoonfuls cream and shake the mixture well together. Put it in the pan and let it stand for 5 minutes. Place the pheasant on a large round of toast spread with butter and the bird's liver (if possible, the liver of another pheasant as well). Strain the sauce through a fine wire sieve and pour over the bird.

"FIFTY WAYS OF COOKING A PHEASANT" ELSIE TURNER

Pheasant Soup (*your oldest and toughest bird*)

1 old pheasant.	1 onion.
1 head celery.	3 leeks.
Parsley.	Salt and pepper.

A clear leek and pheasant soup, an excellent first course for dinner.

Set the pheasant in a pan with enough water to cover it, a little salt, onion, and the celery. Simmer slowly for about 2½ hours, remove the bird and strain the stock. Allow to cool, carefully skimming all fat. This should now be beautiful clear stock, into which you put the leeks and a little white flesh of the pheasant, both cut in very thin slices. Boil together for about half an hour quite slowly till the leeks are soft, and throw in a little finely-chopped parsley before serving.

"FIFTY WAYS OF COOKING A PHEASANT" ELSIE TURNER

Cutlets of Pheasant (*young birds*)

1 large pheasant.   Fine brown breadcrumbs.

1 beaten egg.   Frying fat.

Salt and pepper.   Espagnole sauce.

Pieces of pheasant cooked rather like Wiener Schnitzel and served with rich sauce. A little fiddly to cook well, but not difficult.

Cut up the bird and remove all bones from joints. Season each piece nicely and flatten, trimming into shape and folding the skin under, sewing up if necessary. Dip each piece thus prepared first into beaten egg, then in breadcrumbs. Fry in deep fat or, if preferred, sauté gently in hot butter, until well cooked. If frying fat is used, it should not be too hot or the insides of the fillets will be underdone. Serve with fried parsley and Espagnole or any preferred hot rich sauce (see Chapter Sixteen, p. 298), handed separately.

"GUIDE TO GOOD FOOD AND WINES" ANDRÉ SIMON

Faisan à la Choucroute (*old bird*)

1 old pheasant.   1 thick slice streaky

1 glass white wine.   salt pork.

Sauerkraut (see pages 23-4).

A simple way of using up old birds provided you like sauerkraut. To make it a little more tasty (and more complicated) cook, after braising, as per the recipe Rebhunnher mit Sauerkraut in the Partridge section.

After braising a pheasant until nicely coloured, add to the pan a sufficiency of good sauerkraut. Add salt pork and a glass of white wine. Cook gently until all is done and serve together with boiled or steamed potatoes.

[41]

Pheasant with Apples *(young bird)*

1 young pheasant.	3 tablespoonfuls of
4 oz. butter.	cream.
8 medium-sized cooking	A little salt, pepper and
apples.	sugar.

A sweet, creamy and rather Norman way to serve pheasant, unusual, and very easy, but not a bit like an English traditional recipe.

Heat 3 oz. of the butter in a sauté pan and brown the pheasant on all its surfaces. Peel, core and chop small the apples.

Melt the rest of the butter in an earthenware casserole and sauté the chopped apples in it with a pinch of sugar. When they are a little softened, put the pheasant on top with the juices from the sauté pan and then pour the cream over the bird. Put the lid on the casserole and place it in a moderate oven for about 45 minutes. Add the seasoning and serve.

"GUIDE TO GOOD FOOD AND WINES" ANDRÉ SIMON

Fagiano al Madera. Pheasant Cooked in Madeira *(any-age bird)*

1 pheasant.	$\frac{1}{2}$ an onion, chopped.
4 slices fat bacon.	1 stick celery, chopped.
2 slices ham, chopped.	1 teaspoon parsley, chopped.
1 diced carrot.	1 oz. butter.
Salt and pepper and	1 wineglassful Madeira.
nutmeg.	1 wineglassful stock.

This one isn't traditional either, but the result is delicious. Whole pheasant pot roast in wine sauce.

Pluck and draw a pheasant, and stew with bacon, chopped ham, onion, celery, parsley, carrot and butter with pepper and

[42]

salt and a dash of nutmeg. Cook slowly together until pheasant begins to brown, then add Madeira and stock. Cover the pan and cook for about 45 minutes or until tender. Place bird in a hot dish, strain the fat from the sauce, sieve and pour over the bird. Garnish with croûtons of fried bread (see recipe on page 152).

Pheasant à la Viennet

½ lb cold pheasant diced.	2 large onions diced.
Salt and pepper.	Bouquet garni.
1 pint milk.	2 oz. flour.
1 gill cream.	2 oz. butter.
2 oz. grated Parmesan cheese.	2 hard-boiled eggs.

Cheese sauce (see page 300).

Pheasant pieces stewed and then made into a cheese and egg pie. Takes a little time but can be made well beforehand and cooked up just before serving. Good family dish.

Put the pheasant pieces and the onions into a pan and cover with cold water, add a pinch of salt and bring to the boil. Drain and rinse and reheat in milk with herbs for 15 minutes. Remove the herbs. In another pan make a roux with the butter and flour, then add the liquid from the pheasant and onions to this gradually, stirring all the time. When this has thickened, recombine with pheasant and onions, add the cream and the cheese. Butter a deep fireproof dish and put in first a layer of this mixture, then a layer of hard-boiled egg, and so on until all is used. Cover the lot with a layer of thick cheese sauce (see page 300) and put the dish into a quick oven until the top is nicely browned. This recipe can be used also for rabbit and chicken.

1 young pheasant.   Butter.

10 oz. thick cream.   2 sweet apples, diced.

1 wineglass (small) Calvados (brandy or whisky).

A Norman recipe, using the combination of apples and (preferably) Calvados, to produce a very special dish which is very easy to cook.

Melt the butter in a heavy enamel or earthenware deep fireproof dish, on top of the stove, and brown the pheasant on all sides. Let it cook in this for about 40 minutes, moistening with a little Calvados, and being careful that the butter does not burn. Joint or carve the bird and put it on a serving dish and keep it warm. Pour the rest of the Calvados into the gravy in the pan which should be hot and bubbling, and set light to it. When the flames have died add the cream and stir till the gravy thickens. Dice the apples and sauté in butter, and serve with the pheasant.

Pheasant à la Garfield

1 pheasant.	18 button onions.
Pepper and salt.	1 oz. butter.
Bay leaf.	1 lemon.
Thyme.	3 mushrooms.
Parsley.	1 teaspoonful plain flour.
1 tablespoonful chutney.	1 chicken stock cube or
Small tomatoes.	game stock.

Pheasant pieces in a rich sauce with plenty of little onions in it, a few more ingredients than some, but still not in the least complicated.

Take the meat from the bird and boil up the carcase for stock. Cut the meat into pieces and season it well. Chop

[44]

the liver small and put it, with the meat and herbs, the onions and the butter, into a pan and sauté well for about 10 minutes. Then add the flour, chutney and stock (1 pint) and let it simmer for three-quarters of an hour until the gravy is thick. Sauté the small tomatoes lightly in butter. Make a circle of mashed potato on a dish and pour the pheasant mixture into the middle. Garnish with the tomatoes and serve. This recipe does for any remains of game.

Pheasant au Vin

2 young birds.	1 pint red burgundy or
Butter.	home-made red wine.
Olive oil.	12 small onions.
Plain flour.	White sugar.
¼ lb. mushrooms.	Salt and pepper.

Like coq au vin, rich, gorgeous and easy. First-class main course for any important meal, it's really just a very rich pheasant casserole.

Chop the shallots and pheasant livers together and put half into each prepared bird. Heat two tablespoonsfuls of olive oil and an equal amount of butter in a heavy pan and sauté the birds all over till nicely brown. Then put them into a casserole. Pour the wine into the remains of the butter, add the chopped mushroom stalks and let it all cook till the liquid is reduced by half. Make a roux with butter and flour and thicken this gravy. Meanwhile cook the onions in boiling salted water until tender and drain them. Then glaze them by cooking them slowly in a tablespoonful of melted butter mixed with a tablespoonful of sugar. Sauté the mushroom tops in a little butter. Put the onions, mushrooms and sauce in the casserole with the pheasants and cook slowly, with the lid on, till tender.

[45]

Left-over pheasant.	Flour.
2 oz. butter.	Salt and pepper.
Curry powder.	Three tomatoes.
Fried onions.	Four tablespoonsful
Red chillies.	tomato purée.
Croutons.	Chopped parsley.

One way of using up cold pheasant, comes up very hot and tasty and not swimming in liquid. Excellent savoury course, or supper dish.

Dip the pieces of cold pheasant into flour, and put in a frying pan with the melted butter, salt, pepper and curry powder. The amount of curry powder depends on the amount of pheasant and your taste, but should be at least a tablespoonful. Fry till brown, then add the tomatoes and tomato purée. Add a little stock if the mixture is too dry, but it should not be made too liquid. Dish up garnished with fried onion rings, red chillies and croutons of bread fried in boiling fat, drained and sprinkled with parsley. Good for any cold game or poultry.

Pheasant Pie à la Française

1 pheasant.	Short pastry.
Pepper and salt.	Thyme.
2 oz. mushrooms.	Bay leaf.
1 shallot.	Parsley.

1 tin Plumrose liver pâté.

All this takes quite a bit of time, but the pie has to be made some time ahead of being eaten, so that it can set. There is a lot to do, and a lot of ingredients, but the result is very special indeed—a very rich pie in short pastry. Not really difficult, but the good cook will get everything right—pastry, filling, and gelatine.

Butter a square tin and line it with short pastry a quarter of an inch thick. Joint the pheasant, and slit each joint open, making quite large flaps. Mix together all the herbs, seasonings, mushrooms and shallots, and the chopped liver of the pheasant. Put them through your blender if you have one. Season all the slits in the joints with this mixture, and then place a piece of pâté as big as a chestnut in each slit and fold the flaps back over. Pack all the pieces in the pie, and put on a pastry lid, leaving a small hole in the middle so as to be able to put gravy in when the pie is cold. Put buttered greaseproof round the tin, standing up three inches, and cover the pastry with a piece of wetted paper. Cook the whole for one and a half to two hours, slowly, wetting the top paper frequently so that the pastry does not get too brown. Allow it to cool completely then fill it up with the gravy below.

Gravy

Carcase of bird.	Butter.
Onion.	Thyme.
Salt and pepper.	Parsley.
Gelatine powder.	Bay.
1 quart chicken stock (made	Marjoram.
with stock cubes).	

Chop up the bones and fry them in butter with the sliced onion, herbs and seasonings. After fifteen minutes add the stock, and let simmer for three-quarters of an hour until the stock is reduced to the amount you will need to fill the pie. Strain it and remove the fat. Then add sufficient powdered gelatine to set the stock (see instructions in gelatine packet) and pour it into the pie. Leave the pie to set in your fridge for a day before turning out ready to serve.

[47]

Faisan Sauté aux Champignons (*young bird*)

1 young pheasant. 12 button mushrooms.

2 oz. butter. 1 glass Madeira.

1 tablespoonful oil. Seasoning.

Much the same as the last only the pheasant is jointed and the mushrooms add another flavour. Easy, but rather special.

Joint the pheasant. Melt half the butter in a sauté pan, and add the oil. When it is hot, put the pheasant in and quickly brown it on all sides. Cover the pan and cook over a low heat until done (approx. 25–30 minutes). 5 minutes before the end of the cooking, add to the pan the 12 button mushrooms which have been cut in a series of spokes from centre to edge with a sharp knife.

Pile the joints up on a hot serving dish, surround with the mushrooms. Remove excess fat from the cooking liquor. Pour in the Madeira. Raise the heat, scrape the pan well and adjust the seasoning. Pour it over the pheasant and serve at once. Braised chestnuts (see recipe on page 153) are nice with this dish.

Grouse

The birds should be hung for from 3 to 10 days according
to age (see page 13) and weather conditions. Wipe them out
with a cloth after drawing, don't wash them. Grouse can
dry out during cooking, so should be well basted, or wrapped
in bacon. They must not be overcooked, and twenty to
thirty minutes is usually long enough for roasting.

Cranberry or rowanberry jelly goes well with grouse, and
some people use whortleberries or bilberries to stuff
the birds.

Roast Grouse (*young bird*)

1 grouse.   Herbs—as available.

Salt and pepper.   Some rashers of bacon.

Little butter.

Traditional way to roast grouse. Just needs care and attention and the result is classic.

Pluck, singe, draw and truss as you would a chicken. Season inside and out with salt and pepper; insert a nut of butter and a sprig of lovage, if available, but no bay leaf, thyme nor any strongly scented herbs. Put a layer of thin rashers of fat bacon over the bird's breast and roast in a hot oven for 20–30 minutes, according to the size of the bird. It must not be raw or "rare" but slightly underdone; not "blue" but pink. Baste frequently during cooking with bacon fat or rum butter; remove bacon, dredge lightly with flour and put back in the oven for a very little time to brown the breast. The liver allowed to half cook inside the bird may be pounded and seasoned, then spread upon a square of toast, with the crusty ends left off; this piece of toast is slipped under the bird to catch the gravy that drops from it during cooking, and the bird is dished on this piece of toast.

Cold Terrine of Grouse (*old and damaged birds*)

4 birds and livers.   Garlic salt—if liked.

Parsley and thyme.   2–3 rashers fat bacon.

Delicious game pâté, but like all pâtés the secret is in the texture. If you do have an electric mixer or blender which will really break down the meat before sieving, all the better.

Take some slices off the breasts and put aside. Fry and pound and pass through a fine sieve the remainder of the flesh with the livers, a little parsley, thyme and bacon. Line a glass ovenproof dish with bacon and fill with alternate layers of these breast slices and forcemeat. Add stock, seasoned with garlic if you like the flavour, otherwise a good gravy stock, and season. Cook until quite tender, after which, if necessary, add a little more stock. When set, turn it into another dish and cover with jelly or warm butter.

"GUIDE TO GOOD FOOD AND WINES" ANDRÉ SIMON

Terrine of Grouse (*old birds*)

2 old grouse.	Glass of sherry.
3 oz. diced bacon.	1 bay leaf.
1 pint stock.	2 oz. chopped mushrooms.
Sprig thyme.	1 oz. butter.
1 teaspoonful gelatine.	1 onion.

Potted grouse, perfect with a good salad. This takes a bit of care as use too much liquid and the jelly will not set. Experience will teach you the exact amount.

Roast grouse for 10 minutes, allow to cool, and remove breasts. Place carcases in a saucepan. Fry 1 slice onion with the diced bacon and add this to the grouse with the stock and sherry. Simmer very gently for 1 hour. Allow to cool, then remove flesh from birds and mince. Strain off 2 cups stock, add the bay leaf and mushrooms and thyme and boil for 10 minutes, then dissolve 1 teaspoonful gelatine and 1 oz. butter in it. Cut the breasts of the grouse into thin slices, coat them with minced grouse and sandwich together by twos. Place in an earthenware casserole and pour in the boiling liquid, but remove the thyme and bay leaf. Stand in a tray of water and cook at 350 degrees. Gas 4. Press with a weight overnight and serve the next day.

2/3 old grouse.	4 oz. butter.
2 oz. grouse livers.	1 lb. belly pork.
4 wineglasses of sherry.	Salt, pepper.
2 raw egg whites.	Bay leaf.
2 young grouse.	Thyme.
Stiff flour and water paste.	Piece of fat bacon.

Gorgeous potted grouse, but it takes a bit of time and trouble to make. Some cooks think it is old fashioned to use flour and water paste as a sealing lid, and not foil, but it does keep the heat and the flavours in well and it is not that much trouble.

Take the meat from the old grouse, the belly pork and the grouse livers and chop it all small then put it through a blender or pound it till it is smooth. Put into a basin with seasoning and finely chopped herbs, and 2 wineglasses of sherry and the egg whites. Blend all well together.

Take the breast fillets from the young grouse, salt them lightly and steep them in the rest of the sherry. Line a terrine or jar with some of the smooth paté, then put in a layer of the breast fillets, then paté, then fillets, till all is used up. Then sprinkle the top with sherry, and cover it with a piece of fat bacon. Put a piece of buttered greaseproof paper over the bacon and then an inch-thick layer of white flour paste. Stand the jar or terrine in a pan containing hot water to three-quarters the depth of the jar or terrine. Put it on the stove until the water boils, then place in the oven to simmer slowly, uncovered, for an hour and a quarter. Let the terrine cool, then remove the flour paste and the paper and pour clarified butter over the top of the paté. Let it set, put the lid back on, and keep in the fridge till needed.

Broiled Grouse, with Bacon (*young birds*)

Salt and pepper.   2 fat grouse.

Olive oil.   Maître d'Hôtel butter.

6 thin slices broiled bacon.

This traditional recipe can be adapted to modern methods. Sauté the birds in a heavy pan, on top of the cooker, using extra oil or butter if necessary.

Singe, draw, and wipe nicely two fine fat grouse. Split them in two through the back without separating the parts; lay them on a dish, and season with a pinch of salt, half a pinch of pepper, and a tablespoonful of sweet oil. Roll them in well, then put them to broil on a brisk fire for seven minutes on each side. Prepare a hot dish with six small toasts, arrange the grouse over, spread a gill of Maître d'Hôtel butter (see recipe on page 153) on top, and garnish with six thin slices of broiled bacon, then serve.

Braised Grouse (*old birds*)

Old grouse.   Stock.

Carrot.   Onion.

Celery.   Cornflour.

This is a good rich casserole with the birds kept whole, and not swimming in sauce. Good family dish.

Clean, truss and season the required number of old birds, and fry till brown in bacon fat. Put them into a casserole with a small quantity of stock, a piece of carrot, onion, celery, and braise for 2 hours, adding a small quantity of stock or water if required. Thicken the sauce with cornflour. Dish with vegetables in the centre.

"A HIGHLAND COOKERY BOOK" MARGARET FRASER

Grouse.   Butter.
Rowanberries or wild raspberries.

By most people's standards this is over hung, and the dish
will be very gamey; however it is delicious if you like game
that way. Not a recipe to try on those whose tastes you do
not know. The fruit ingredients may take some getting if
you don't live in the part of the country where they grow.

Leave grouse to hang for at least a fortnight. After plucking,
trussing and dressing, stuff with butter and rowanberries, or
better still with the little wild raspberries of the mountain-
side. The juicy fruit melts almost away during cooking (25
minutes in hot oven), but the melted, spicy, buttery juice is
all the gravy required.

Grouse en Casserole (*old birds only*)

4 Grouse.	Flour, pepper and salt.
2 medium sized	1 dozen carrots.
onions.	Game stock, or Game soup
10 oz. butter.	would do.

Melt 6 oz. butter in large pan with lid. Slice and fry onions
lightly. Put grouse in to brown. Add a little water and the
carrots. Put lid on and simmer gently for two hours. When
cooked, remove grouse from pan and put the onions and
carrots through liquidiser or sieve.

Make a sauce with 4 oz. of butter, enough flour to thicken,
add stock until smooth but not too thin. Add liquidised
vegetables, pepper and salt to taste. Cut grouse in halves or
quarters, put in casserole, pour over sauce, re-heat to serve.

MRS. WILLIAM STIRLING OF KEIR,
COOK, MRS. ALICE THOMSON

Grouse Pie (*young and old birds*)

2 grouse.	Salt, pepper and herbs.
½ lb. pie-crust pastry.	Few yolks hard-boiled eggs.
Game forcemeat.	Few slices raw ham.

Good rich game pie, no problems about this recipe.

Cut up a brace of grouse, each of them in five parts, and season with pepper and salt. Mask the bottom of a pie dish with a layer of game forcemeat (see recipe on page 149), on which place the pieces of grouse; sprinkle over a little cooked fine herbs; fill the cavities between the pieces with a few yolks of hard-boiled eggs, and place on the top of the grouse a few slices of raw ham; pour in good gravy, to half the depth, cover the pie with pastry, and put it in a moderate oven for 1½ hours.

Salmis of Grouse (*any-age birds*)

2 grouse.	1 tablespoonful plain flour.
Stock.	2 wineglassfuls red wine.
2 lemons.	1 beef stock cube.
¼ lb. mushrooms.	Cupful water.
1 tablespoonful	Salt and pepper.
dry mustard.	Nutmeg.
1 tablespoonful butter.	Chopped parsley.

Grouse pieces served in rich sauce. Not difficult, but takes care and a bit of tasting as you go along to get it just right.

Half roast or braise a brace of grouse, then joint them and place the pieces in a pan with sufficient good stock to cover them. See this is well seasoned and simmer gently for 15–30 minutes, according to age of birds.

Remove meat from stock and cut them into joints, returning all juices to the stock. Add the wine, beef stock made with a little water, and juice of the lemons then crush the livers

[55]

and giblets and add these together with seasonings, spices and mushrooms, and pour the lot over the jointed grouse. Cook until the whole is very hot but not boiling and then thicken with beurre manie (see page 153). Sprinkle with parsley.

Grouse Soufflé

Cold grouse.   1 oz. butter.
2 handfuls boiled   Seasoning.
    rice.   3 eggs.
1 tablespoonful meat glaze, dissolved in a little stock.

Rather special and unusual soufflé. Expert soufflé-makers will like this one. Of course use your electric blender or mincer if you have one, but the meat must be broken right down.

Remove the meat from the bones of the grouse, pound well with the butter, rice, and glaze; season well and rub all through a wire sieve, then mix in the yolks of the eggs, add the whites, beaten very stiff, steam gently for 1 hour, and serve with brown sauce.

MRS. ELLISON, THE VICARAGE, WINDSOR

Ptarmigan

Ptarmigan is not the finest of game birds to eat and it seems rather a shame to shoot this comparatively rare high mountain resident, but if you must, cook it as grouse, or roast it simply as below.

Roast Ptarmigan

2–3 ptarmigan.   Butter for basting.
1 slice bacon for each bird.

Let the birds hang for 3–4 days; when plucked, drawn and trussed, tie over each breast a slice of fat bacon, and roast in a moderate oven for 30–35 minutes, basting very frequently with butter. When almost cooked, remove the bacon, dredge lightly with flour, and baste well to brown the birds. Serve on toast, which should be previously put into the dripping tin to catch the gravy that drops from the birds. Serve with bread sauce, gravy and breadcrumbs fried in butter.

Blackcock

Blackcock may be cooked according to most grouse recipes as it is a member of the grouse family. Check its age in the same way as grouse.

Blackcock—Roast

1–2 blackcock.   Vine leaves or cabbage leaves.
Some thin rashers of fat bacon.

Simple standard recipe for roasting the birds.

Secure thin rashers of bacon over the breast of the trussed bird with skewers or string—and some fresh vine leaves if available or cabbage leaves. Roast on one of the new oven-spits if you have one. Baste frequently and allow from 45 to 60 minutes according to the size of the bird. If no spit is available, cook in a moderately hot oven, as you would a chicken, basting frequently. Serve on thick slices of buttered toast with clear gravy and bread sauce.

Fillets of Blackcock Financière

2 blackcock	1 glass sherry or Madeira.
3 slices of bacon.	12 button mushrooms.
½ pint of brown sauce.	1 medium onion.
¼ pint of stock.	1 small carrot.
Salt and pepper.	½ turnip.

Fillets of blackcock in a splendid rich sauce. Doesn't take too long and makes a main course for a special dinner.

Cut the birds into neat fillets, slice the vegetables, place them in a sauté pan with the stock, add the slices of bacon, lay the fillets on the top of them, cover closely with well-buttered paper or foil, and cook gently for about 30 minutes. Make a brown sauce, and add to it the mushrooms which have previously been sautéd in a little butter, and the wine, season to taste, and keep hot until required. When the fillets are done, arrange them on a hot dish, strain the sauce over, and garnish with the mushrooms, and, if liked, the bacon cut into dice and grouped round the base.

Capercaillie

Capercaillie, a member of the grouse family, but as big as a small turkey. Because it lives on pine needles, its flesh tastes highly resinous, and although one enjoys this flavour in the occasional glass of 'retsina' or in Greek food, it doesn't improve Capercaillie. Only eat young birds, because they are not quite so permeated with the taste; remove the crop immediately the bird is shot, clean it as soon as possible and soak it overnight in milk, drain and soak again in vinegar and water for 10 hours before cooking.

Roasted Capercaillie

For 6-10 persons.

1 capercaillie.	Butter.
¼ lb. beefsteak.	Good gravy.
1 or 2 slices of bacon.	Bread sauce.
Water-cress.	Fried breadcrumbs.
Salad oil.	Salt and pepper.

Slightly different, as it includes beefsteak to improve the flavour.

Prepare and truss the bird in the same way as a roast chicken. Put the beefsteak inside the bird; it greatly improves the flavour and can afterwards be used for a cold meat dish. Cover the breast with slices of bacon, and roast in a moderate oven for about 25 minutes per lb. weight, basting frequently. When three-quarters cooked, remove the bacon, sprinkle the breast lightly with flour, and baste well to give the bird a good appearance. Serve on a hot dish garnished with water-cress which has been seasoned with salt and pepper and a little salad. Gravy, breadsauce and breadcrumbs accompany this dish.

Roast Capercaillie (*young bird only*)

1 young hen capercaillie.	Softened butter, as required.
Salt and pepper to taste.	Chestnut or sausage stuffing.
Flour as required.	1 cup chicken stock.

Rub bird all over with salt and pepper. Dredge with flour. Rub with softened butter. Stuff if liked. Skewer opening. Place on a rack in a baking tin with a cover. Cover breast with fat bacon. Place stock in bottom of tin. Roast in a fairly hot oven, 425°F., for 10 minutes, then lower to 300°F. Baste well with stock and dripping. Cook till almost

[61]

tender, then remove lid of pan and fat bacon. Baste well and roast till breast is brown. Total roasting time should be 20–25 minutes per lb. Serve with game gravy (see recipe on page 149) and bread sauce. Garnish with watercress and little bundles of asparagus dipped in seasoned melted butter.

"FAMILY COOKERY" ELIZABETH CRAIG

"... *See! Through the gloaming*
The Young Morn is coming,
Like a bridal veil round her the silver mist curled,
Deep as the ruby's rays,
Bright as the sapphire's blaze,
The banner of day in the East is unfurled.

The red grouse is scattering
Dews from his golden wing,
Gemmed with the radiance that heralds the day;
Peace in our Highland vales,
Health on our mountain gales—
Who would not hie to the Moorlands away!
Far from the haunts of man
Mark the grey Ptarmigan,
Seek the lone Moor cock, the pride of our dells.
Birds of the wilderness!
Here is their resting place,
Mid the brown heath where the mountain-roe dwells.

Come then! the heather bloom
Woos with its wild perfume,
Fragrant and blithesome thy welcome shall be;
Gaily the fountain sheen."

[62]

CHAPTER TWO

PIGEON ROOK

Pigeon

There is no close season for pigeons as they are classed as vermin. Most shoots are organised in spring and autumn so that is when you will get most birds, but they are such a plague that they are shot at all times and are always available. They should always be hung head downwards for a while, immediately after being killed, and bled so that the flesh will not be too dark. Pigeons off corn land are always best as they carry more fat.

Pigeons are dry birds and it is important to keep them moist and to baste with plenty of fat while cooking. They are a great nuisance to prepare if you have to pluck them, seeming to have an amount of feathers entirely disproportionate to the amount of meat they carry. If you have plenty of birds and are sick of the sight of them, just pluck the breasts and cut out the meat with a sharp knife and use only these for any of the pot or casserole recipes.

Roast Stuffed Pigeon (*unidentifiable-age birds*)

Allow 1 bird per person. Sausage meat, 4 oz. per bird.
Breadcrumbs.   Fat for roasting.

This one takes a little time and trouble but does ensure tender meat, not too dry.

Prepare the birds and put them into a steamer, cook for 2–3 hours and leave to get cold. When cold, make a shallow cut across the breast of each bird and pull the skin gently off, being careful not to pull the flesh as well. Stuff the birds with the well-seasoned sausage meat, brush with dripping and dredge with breadcrumbs. Have some fat very hot in a baking tin, put the birds in this and bake for about an hour, basting frequently. Serve with good gravy made from the water in which the birds were steamed, a green vegetable and mashed potatoes.

The birds can be used any time after twelve days, but this involves advance planning if you wish to serve them at a special meal. The result is gamey and tasty, but not everyone likes this.

Pot Roast Pigeons (*any-age birds*)

Allow 1 bird per person.   1 oz. butter.
                1 teaspoonful mixed herbs.

Simple pot roast, which will produce tender birds tasting of fresh herbs. Doesn't take much trouble and won't spoil by remaining in the oven till you are ready.

Prepare the birds as for roasting. Dip in well-seasoned flour. Have 1 oz. butter very hot in a large saucepan, brown the birds in this, add a small teaspoonful mixed herbs, put on a close-fitting lid, and cook slowly for about 1½ hours. Serve with the liquid in the pan, slightly thickened, as gravy; bread sauce and chips.

Pigeon Pie *(any-age birds)*

Use 5–6 pigeons.
8 oz. medium-quality steak.
8 oz. pastry crust.
Seasoning.
Little good gravy.

Country recipe, not highly flavoured, tastes as much of steak as it does of pigeon.

Joint the birds so that each one yields 4 joints, 2 breast joints and 2 leg joints, put the rest of the carcases to stew in a little water, to use for the gravy.

Cut the steak into small thin pieces each about the size of a tablespoon, line a pie dish with these slices, then lay the pigeons on top, cover with water, add plenty of seasoning, cover with greased paper and put in a medium oven and allow to simmer for 1 hour. Take out the dish, have ready a good pie-crust pastry, cover the pie with this. Brush the top with beaten egg, and put back into a hot oven, bake until the pastry is golden brown.

Mix a dessertspoonful of cornflour with a little cold milk, add a cupful of the hot bone stock, and allow to thicken, season to taste, and when the pie is done, lift up the crust and add the thickened gravy.

Jellied Pigeons *(old birds)*

3–4 pigeons.   1 oz. gelatine.
Seasoning and herbs.

Good with salad, or for picnics. The art is in getting the gelatine and stock proportions just right so that it sets well.

Joint the birds, skin them and cook in a very little well-seasoned water with the herbs added, until the meat falls from the bones, this will take about 1½ hours. Take all meat from bones, test again for seasoning, dissolve the gelatine in some of the stock used for cooking the birds, pack the meat into a wetted mould and pour over it the stock. Add a little gravy browning, if necessary. Leave to set, then turn out and serve with watercress.

Terrine of Pigeon

6–8 pigeons.	Pepper (plenty of) and salt.
2 oz. butter.	Generous teaspoon made
2 oz. fat bacon.	mustard.
$\frac{1}{2}$ crushed clove garlic.	1 cupful aspic jelly—or
1 tablespoon red wine,	$\frac{1}{2}$ oz. powdered gelatine
sherry or brandy.	dissolved in a cup of stock.
2 hard-boiled eggs.	A pinch of mixed herbs.

This one turns pigeon into something much more elegant, and although it takes a bit of time and a few more ingredients, is well worth the trouble.

Cut each pigeon's skin and lift from the back towards the front over the breast. Cut off the breast meat and remove the liver. Cut the meat and bacon into $\frac{1}{2}$-inch dice. Heat the butter in a large frying pan and cook the bacon for a minute or two. Add the cut-up pigeon and sauté for a few minutes, turning constantly with a fork. The pieces of meat should still be slightly pink inside.

Remove meat from the pan and put through a mincer or an electric liquidiser. Bubble the wine or brandy in the butter and mix in with the minced pigeon, add all the other ingredients and mix well. Pour into the bottom of an earthenware terrine which has been coated with a little aspic jelly. Press the eggs lengthwise into the mixture and leave in a cold place to set.

MRS. ARCHIE COATS

[67]

Pigeon Pudding

3 pigeons.	Rich pastry.
½ lb. good beefsteak.	Salt and pepper.
Yolks of three hard-boiled eggs.	1 beef stock cube.

For those who like their pastry steamed or boiled—pudding rather than pie—this is a pretty succulent way of serving pigeon. Can be made well beforehand and is a first-class family dish.

Line a pudding basin with suet crust pastry ½ inch thick. Put in the pigeons, and pack round with the beefsteak and chopped egg yolks, season well, and fill with stock to half the depth. Cover with pastry, and tie a cloth over the top. Boil or steam the pudding for three hours.

Pigeon Soup (*old birds*)

2 pigeons.	Fresh cream.
Pepper and salt.	1 pint milk.
1 dessertspoonful aniseed seeds.	2 pints water.

A soup with a very unusual flavour, not for aniseed haters! Takes a bit of fiddling with the carcases.

Simmer 2 pigeons in water and milk for 2 hours, adding a little more milk as and when necessary; season with pepper and salt and aniseed seeds. Take the birds out, remove the flesh from the breast and cut up in strips which return to the soup; pound all the other meat from the birds and make into quenelles, which are added to the soup at the time of serving. Add also some fresh cream and stir well in. This soup is known in culinary French by the name of Crême Colombine.

Pigeons with Cabbage (*old birds*)

1 large green cabbage. Salt and pepper.
2 pigeons.   Little parsley, thyme and a
3–4 rashers fat bacon.   bay leaf.
Butter.   Chicken stock cube.

Country-style recipe, easy, filling and tasty. Good for a hungry family, and it can be prepared well beforehand.

Blanch the cabbage in boiling water for 10 minutes. Drain and plunge into cold water, leave for 10 minutes. Drain well and press out as much water as possible. Line a greased fireproof dish with the chopped vegetable and the rashers of bacon. Season with salt and pepper and add the herbs, all except the bay leaf. Have some very hot butter in a pan and brown the prepared pigeons all over. Put the birds into the casserole, with the bay leaf, cover with a few more rashers of bacon, add stock and put on a close-fitting lid. Bring to the boil and allow to simmer for at least 2 hours. The birds can be cut in half and served straight from the bed of cabbage.

Braised Pigeons with Oranges

3 pigeons.   1 oz. flour.
¼ lb. mushrooms.   1 glass red wine.
3 small onions.   1 teaspoonful dried herbs.

For each person 1 small orange, 1 rasher bacon per bird.

Fairly rich casseroled pigeon with the added flavour of orange.

Dress the pigeons, and into the body cavity of each bird insert a small skinned orange. Cut down beside each breast with a sharp knife and into each cut insert a slice of fat bacon. Skewer skin each side of cut. Fry the birds lightly in lard or

[69]

butter, transfer to a casserole, then fry mushrooms and onions. Add the flour and the wine and cook until thick, add seasoning and the herbs. Pour all this over the birds in the casserole, put on the lid and cook for 2–2½ hours or until the meat is tender.

Pigeon Casserole (*young birds*)

3 young pigeons.   3 rashers fat bacon.
Butter.   Gravy.
3 small onions.   2 oz button mushrooms.
1 glass claret or   Cayenne pepper.
  homemade red wine.   Salt.

Casserole whole pigeons in a rich sauce.

Take 3 young pigeons trussed for boiling. Cover each with a strip of fat bacon, fry them in butter till nicely browned, drain them and put them in a casserole with just enough good gravy barely to cover them. Add green onions and mushrooms, together with a good glass of claret and a seasoning of salt and coralline pepper. Let the birds cook very slowly for three-quarters of an hour at the side of fire, and then when cooked serve up in the same casserole.

"FOOD FOR THE GREEDY" NANCY SHAW

Pigeons Cooked with Green Peas (*young birds*)

2 young pigeons.   ½ lb. fat bacon diced.
1 lb. green peas.   1 dessertspoonful sugar.
1 lettuce.   5 small onions.

Pot roast pigeons with lots of fresh green vegetable, this is a change from some of the rich, rather gamey recipes.

Take a couple of young pigeons and roast them for about 25 minutes in a casserole with fat bacon and a dessertspoonful of butter. After about 15 minutes cooking, season birds. While the pigeons are cooking, prepare the peas. Melt a tablespoonful of butter in a pot and then add green peas, sugar, a lettuce cut up, onions, cover the pot with a soup plate full of cold water, and this will prevent the evaporation of the juices of the vegetables while they cook. They will require to cook slowly for approximately 30 minutes; when done, add the sauce from the pigeons, thickened with a little flour. Serve the pigeons surrounded with green peas.

"BOUQUET GARNI" DAVID DE BETHEL

To Marinade Old Pigeons

To marinade meat or game means to cover it with a mixture of wine, herbs, spices, onions and vinegar for any period of up to 14 days. The effect of putting tough meat into this mixture is to break down the tissues and shorten cooking time.

Allow one bird per person. Vinegar.

½ bottle cheap red wine. Little sliced onion.

Cut up the birds and put them in a large earthenware jar or crock. Allow half as much vinegar as you have wine, mix the two, add the sliced onion, pour this over the cut joints. Leave for 12–14 days.

When wanted, remove the meat from the marinade, fry some sliced onion, then lightly fry the joints of meat, pack into a greased fireproof casserole, add a little flour to the fat in which you have cooked the birds, and then enough of the marinade mixture to make a thick sauce, pour this over the joints, and put the casserole in a fairly hot oven for about 2 hours.

Roast Pigeons (*young birds*)

Pigeons.   Bacon rashers.
                 Watercress.

Simple roast birds.

Once plucked and singed, cover the breasts with thin slices of fat, salt pork or bacon, truss up tidily, spread with fresh butter and roast in a rather sharp oven from 15 to 20 minutes, according to size of bird and degree of cooking required, removing the bacon slices half-way through the cooking to brown the breasts nicely. Baste well every few minutes, and, after removing trussing strings, serve either whole or cut in halves, with watercress and the strained gravy. Season nicely before serving.

Pigeons à la Catalane

2 pigeons (drawn and trussed).	4 rashers fat bacon.
2 oz. butter.	2 oz. streaky cut into strips.
1 glass dry white wine.	Bouquet garni.
1 glass stock.	2 cloves garlic.
Orange peel.	1 lemon.

1 teaspoonful tomato purée.

1 teaspoonful plain flour slaked in a little wine vinegar.

A Spanish recipe which takes a little more trouble than ordinary roasting, but is not difficult and produces a nice sharp sauce.

Tie the bacon rashers on the pigeons' breasts. Place the strips of streaky bacon and the butter in the bottom of a thick stewpan. When the bacon begins to brown, put in the pigeons. Brown well on all sides. Season and pour in stock and wine. Allow them to cook slowly 35 minutes to 1 hour.

Blanch the garlic for 10 minutes in boiling water. Drain and add it to the pan with the lemon cut into rounds, the bouquet garni and the strip of orange peel. When cooked, remove the pigeons. Slake the flour with the vinegar and add, with the tomato purée, to the liquor in the pan. Cook for 5 minutes, stirring well.

Remove the bacon from the birds and arrange them on a hot dish. Season the sauce to taste. Strain it over the pigeons. Sprinkle them with chopped parsley. Serve very hot.

Pigeons à la Normandie (*young birds*)

3 young pigeons (drawn and trussed).	1 glass thick cream.
	1½ lb. apples.
5 oz. butter.	Seasoning.

1 tablespoonful oil.

If you have a fireproof dish in which you could cook *and* serve this recipe, all the better, as the apples do tend to break up when being moved to a serving dish. It is a delicious Norman recipe. To make it superb, add a little Calvados to the cream, just enough to flavour it.

Wipe the pigeons. Heat 3 oz. butter with the oil in the bottom of a thick stewpan. Put in the pigeons and brown them well on all sides. Remove, then place in the pan the rest of the butter and make it hot, then add two-thirds of the apples peeled and cored and cut into thick slices. Season very well and allow them to soften in the butter until they become transparent looking. Put the pigeons on top of the apples. Butter a piece of greaseproof paper and tuck down round the sides of the pigeons and cover with a lid. Put in a fairly hot oven, 350°. Gas 6 for 20 minutes. At the end of this time, remove the lid and the paper and cover the pigeons with the rest of the apples cut in the same way. Cook for a further 20 minutes.

Remove the contents of the pan carefully and place on a

[73]

hot dish. Warm the cream and pour it over. Pile croûtons (see recipe on page 152), cut in crescents and fried in butter, at each end of the dish. Serve very hot.

Malayan Fried Honey Pigeons

1–2 pigeons.	Honey.
½ pint sesame oil.	Salt and pepper.
1 tablespoonful aniseed.	

This recipe is certainly different! The result is splendid; but seriously, how does one force-feed pigeons with alcohol? Especially wild ones. Never mind, leave that part out!

Intoxicate the pigeons before killing with a little of any kind of spirit; this improves the flesh and it is kinder. Kill one or two intoxicated pigeons and dress. Rub well inside with salt and aniseed and outside with honey. Heat the oil until very hot and fry the pigeons until tender and rich brown. Drain thoroughly, break apart to serve, and sprinkle well with pepper.

"FOOD IN ENGLAND" DOROTHY HARTLEY

Pigeon Pâté

8 pigeon breasts.	Bayleaf.
Mixed herbs (opt.).	4–8 oz. butter.
Salt.	Brandy.
Freshly ground black pepper.	

Put pigeons' breasts into casserole dish with seasonings. Add 4 oz. butter on top and close lid. Heat in oven until cooking temperature is reached then transfer to slow oven. Bottom oven of Aga over night or Reg. 1 4–6 hrs. (approx.).

Liquidize adding brandy and extra butter if required. N.B. Pigeon breasts can be skinned and removed with knife to save having to pluck.

SUSAN BROWNLOW

Rook

There is no close season for rooks and only young rooks are fit to eat. Rook shoots are held to thin out the young birds about the second week in May. Only the breasts and sometimes the upper parts of the legs are used. The skin of a rook must always be removed with the feathers.

"A rook pie is not worth making unless some large rookery has to be thinned, when it is a pity to waste the bag of young birds brought in by the countrymen. Rooks mate in November, and live paired till the spring, when they nest together. Notice the pattern of paired birds in the winter flights and subsequent 'sets' of two adults and five to eight young birds grouped in the summer flights. Rookeries are well-organised communities."

"FOOD IN ENGLAND" DOROTHY HARTLEY

[75]

Rook Pie

6 young rooks.	$\frac{1}{2}$ pint stock.
$\frac{3}{4}$ lb. rump steak.	Salt and pepper.
$\frac{1}{4}$ lb. butter.	Pastry—$\frac{1}{2}$ lb. pie crust.

Skin the birds without plucking them by cutting the skin near the thighs, and drawing it over the body and head. Draw the birds in the usual manner, remove the necks and backs, and split the birds down the breast. Arrange them in a deep pie-dish, cover each breast with a thin strip of steak, season well with salt and pepper, intersperse small pieces of butter and add as much stock as will three parts fill the dish. Cover with pastry and bake for $1\frac{1}{2}$–2 hours; for the first $\frac{1}{2}$ hour in a hot oven to make the pastry rise, and afterwards more slowly to allow the birds to become thoroughly cooked. When the pie is about three-parts baked, brush it over with yolk of egg to glaze the crust, and, before serving, pour in, through the hole in the top, the remainder of the stock.

Rook Stew

Young rooks. Milk. Root vegetables.

Skin the birds (young rooks, of course) as soon as possible after they have been shot, and lift the meat from the breast; soak it in milk overnight and stew it gently in a casserole with a number of available root vegetables, finely sliced; season with pepper and salt and serve hot.

CHAPTER THREE

WILD DUCK
WILD GOOSE

Wild Duck

Of the many species of wild duck which are resident in or visit this country, Pintail, Teal, Mallard, and Wigeon are the ones usually shot for eating. Mallard and Wigeon are the most plentiful. Opinions differ as to which duck makes the best eating. The recipes in this section may be used to cook any wild duck, but where they suit a specific bird this is noted. Of course if any of the other breeds of duck—Pochard, etc., arrive in your larder, they can be cooked according to these receipes. Duck should be eaten fresh or hung at the most for two days. Duck shot on the foreshore may have a fishy taste or a cowey smell, according to its diet. In the chapter on the preparation of game for cooking there are full details of various ways to get rid of these characteristics.

If wild duck is overcooked it toughens it, on the other hand undercooking doesn't do the birds justice, so try to strike a happy medium; time the cooking according to size.

Young ducks should be plump with bright-coloured feet, soft breast bones, and brittle beaks. The duck Mallard is better eating than the drake, and is similar to the domestic duck though a little smaller.

Wigeon is a very beautiful bird but unless shot on fresh water can have a very cowey smell which comes from the marsh grass on which it grazes in the saltings.

Pintail has a delicate flavour and is excellent eating.

Teal is a small duck, best eaten in frosty weather; some think teal to be the tastiest of all.

Pochard has a delicate flavour if killed on fresh water.

Orange goes with wild duck as mint sauce goes with lamb.

"WINE AND FOOD" MRS. JESSOP HULTON

Roast Duck (*Standard recipe*)

1 duck.	Orange jelly.
1 glass port wine	Orange salad (see
or claret.	page 150).

Espagnole sauce (see page 298).

Standard roast duck recipe, quite rich, which exploits the affinity of duck and orange.

Draw, truss and roast as for a domestic duck, basting frequently and serving with orange jelly, or add a glassful of port wine or claret to the gravy when nearly done, using to baste the bird. An Espagnole sauce (see recipe on page 298), enriched by the addition of the strained duck gravy, may be handed separately. Orange salad is delicious with this dish (see recipe on page 150).

[79]

Duck (*with sharp sauce*)

1 Duck.   Orange or Bigarade
Fat bacon.   sauce (see page 303).
3 tablespoonsful   Seasoning.
   white wine.   3 tablespoonsful stock.

A combination between a roast and a casserole, this produces duck in a sharp sauce.

Cover the breast of the bird with fat bacon and coat it with orange or Bigarade sauce. Roast for 10 minutes. Remove the bacon rasher, baste the bird and leave it in the oven for a little longer till it is brown. Meanwhile heat the stock and wine in a stewpan. Put in the bird and juices, cover, and simmer for five minutes. Remove the bird to a safe place, pour the sauce over it and serve.

Duck with Gin and Orange

2 wild ducks.   Orange juice.
1½ tablespoon minced   1½ tablespoons minced
   celery tops.   basil.
Brandy.   1 cup uncooked wild rice.
1 teaspoon gin.   1 cup chicken stock.
Salt and black pepper.   4 tablespoons unsalted butter.
Duck giblets.   2 cups dry red wine.
1½ tablespoons parsley.   1½ tablespoons minced
Pinch nutmeg.   chives.
3 tablespoons Curaçao.   1½ tablespoons minced
1 teaspoon grated   little green onions.
   orange rind.   2 teaspoons lemon juice.

Whole roast duck, stuffed with rice and herbs in a very alcoholic sauce. The rice takes a little extra care to prepare, the rest is easy and the result delicious.

Rub the cleaned and drawn wild ducks with equal portions of orange juice and brandy, inside and out.

[80]

Wash 1 cup of wild rice. Put 4 cups of boiling water with one teaspoonful salt in the top of a double boiler, and add the rice slowly, so it does not go off the boil. Cook for 5 minutes. Then put it over boiling water in the under part of the double boiler, add 1 cup of boiling chicken stock to the rice, cover tightly, and steam until the rice is tender, about $\frac{1}{2}$ to $\frac{3}{4}$ of an hour.

While this is cooking, cream the unsalted butter with $1\frac{1}{2}$ tablespoons each of minced chives, parsley, green onions, green celery tops and basil. Then season with salt and pepper, 1 teaspoonful of gin, and a pinch of nutmeg. Put this all in a saucepan, and add the rice and the chopped giblets of the ducks. Cook, stirring thoroughly until it is all well mixed, and then stuff the ducks with this mixture of rice and giblets.

Put the ducks in a roasting dish, pouring over them 1 cup of orange juice, 1 teaspoon of grated orange rind, 2 teaspoons of lemon juice and 1 cup of dry red wine. Put the dish in the oven at 400°F. and roast from 15 to 25 minutes, depending on the age and size of the ducks. Baste frequently.

Add another cup of red wine to the juices in the pan and also 3 tablespoons of Curaçao. Bring to the boil on the top of the stove, scraping the dish well to free the sticky bits. Then pour the sauce over the ducks and serve.

Salmis of Duck in Marsala *(Mallard or Wigeon)*

4 wild ducks.

2 large onions.

4 tablespoons currant jelly.

1 tablespoon Worcester sauce.

juice from 2 pressed ducks.

Salt and pepper.

2 large carrots.

¼ lb. butter.

1 clove garlic.

Rind of 1 orange.

1 tablespoon chopped parsley.

4 oz. Marsala.

Green salad.

Bananas fried in bread crumbs.

This recipe is complicated, wasteful and delicious. The end result is breast of wild duck in Marsala sauce. A duck press is necessary to extract the juices. The remaining meat can be used up for terrines or patés.

Stuff each wild duck with half a carrot and half an onion, and put them in the oven in a roasting dish at 400 degrees for 12 minutes. Carve off the breasts from the ducks and put them on one side, having removed the skins. Take the carcasses of just 2 of the ducks, put them in a duck press and extract the juices, and put on one side for a while. In a thick pan put ¼ lb. butter with the crushed clove of garlic, and when very hot add the duck breasts and sauté them for one minute on each side. Put the breasts in a warm dish, take the garlic from the butter, add to this butter the pressed duck juices, the finely chopped pith-free rind from the orange, 1 tablespoonful of parsley, 4 tablespoons of currant jelly, 1 tablespoonful of Worcester sauce, salt and pepper to taste, and the 4 oz. of Marsala. Blend all these together, put the breasts back into it and cook for ½ a minute on each side. Put the breasts on a hot dish, pour the sauce over them, and serve with wild rice, bananas fried in bread crumbs, and green salad.

Roast Marinade Wild Duck (*old birds*)

½ cup wine vinegar.   1 bay leaf.
6 juniper berries.   1 garlic clove crushed,
Black pepper.   or one sliced onion.
1 lemon.   3 bruised cloves.

Butter.

One way to use old birds as the marinade reduces the strong flavour and helps to break down the fibres.

Lay a wild duck for two or three days in a marinade of vinegar, herbs and spices.   Lard it for roasting.   Baste frequently with butter.   Put the marinade in the baking-dish, with a little water for sauce.   Add salt, skim off the fat, and garnish with lemon slices.

Wild Duck in Brandy

2 wild ducks.   2 large onions.
4 oz. brandy.   1 cup dry red wine.
½ lb. mushrooms.   1 tablespoon chopped
Salt and pepper.   parsley.
3 oz. olive oil.   1 tablespoon butter.
1 bay leaf.   1 clove garlic.
½ teaspoon marjoram.   ¼ teaspoon allspice.

½ teaspoon thyme.

Duck pieces in brandy and mushroom sauce in a casserole. It can be made ahead of time and heated up.

Joint 2 ducks and put the pieces in a large earthenware bowl.   Marinate for 5 hours with the following; Salt and pepper, 4 oz. of brandy, 1 cup of dry red wine, 2 chopped onions, 1 tablespoon parsley, ½ teaspoon each of marjoram and thyme, ¼ teaspoon of allspice, and 1 bay leaf.

Put 1 tablespoon of butter and 3 oz. of olive oil with 1 crushed clove of garlic in a heavy pan, and when hot add the pieces of duck. Brown well on all sides for about 15 to 20 minutes, then add ½ lb. of mushrooms, sliced, and also the strained marinade. Cover and simmer until the duck is tender, about 1½ hours.

To serve, remove the pieces of duck to a hot dish, thicken the sauce slightly by fast boiling, and then pour it over the meat.

Casseroled Duck with Sweet Peppers

1 duck.	1 wineglass of white
2 carrots.	wine.
1 onion.	1 tablespoonful Madeira.
1 red pepper (sweet	Mixed herbs.
not chili).	¼ lb. gammon.
Olive oil.	1 small wine glass of
	brandy.

Very rich, casseroled duck. The alcohol makes it a little expensive, but adds that certain something.

First make stock with the duck giblets, one carrot, the onion, half the pepper, the white wine and Madeira and enough water to make ½ pint of stock when strained. Then reduce the stock to $\frac{1}{3}$ pint.

Chop the shallots, carrot and the rest of the pepper (without core and seeds), dice the gammon, and then sauté all this in olive oil. When the shallots have become golden, add the duck and continue to sauté until the meat is brown. Warm the brandy in a ladle and light it and pour it immediately over the duck. When the flames have gone add the reduced stock, put a close lid on the fireproof dish to which you have transferred all this and cook it in a medium oven for about half an hour, until the meat is tender. Take care not to dry up the sauce.

[84]

Braised Wild Duck (*Mallard, Wigeon, Teal*)

Bacon rashers.　　　　　Bouquet garni.
Butter.　　　　　　　　½ pint brown sauce.
¼ pint stock or　　　　 1 wineglass white
　giblet gravy.　　　　　 wine.

To be served in the dish in which it is cooked, the bird comes to table in a lot of gravy and will not be overcooked.

Season the duck with ground pepper from a pepper mill, and salt; place it in a braising pan lined with rashers of bacon, add a bouquet garni and ½ oz. butter, let it part cook in a hot oven till coloured. Remove, disjoint, etc., and place pieces in a stewpan. Chop up the carcase, put it back in the braising pan, and fry it in the existing fat. Make half a pint of brown sauce, to which add the gravy but not the fat from the carcase and a quarter of a pint of good stock or giblet gravy. Cook for 10 minutes, then add the whole to the meat in the stewpan and let stew for 20 minutes. Five minutes before it is ready, add a glass of white wine.

"THE SPORTSMAN'S COOKERY BOOK" MAJOR HUGH POLLARD

Canard Sauvage aux Bigarades (*young birds*)

Duck.　　　　　　　　Butter.
Flour.　　　　　　　　 1 glass port wine.
Castor sugar.　　　　　 1 glass veal (or white)
1 liqueur glass　　　　　 stock.
　Curaçao.　　　　　　　Lemon juice.
　　　　　 Seville oranges.

A good roast in orange and red wine sauce.

Take some wild ducks, allowing one for two or at most three people, as only the breast is really good and tender; it should be carved in thin slices.

[85]

Put a piece of butter in a shallow saucepan and roast the ducks in it; baste often, allowing about 20 minutes in a fairly quick oven.

Remove the ducks and keep them hot; put very little flour in the saucepan and make a little roux; add a glass of port wine, and one of veal stock; stir well and finish cooking the ducks in that for 10 minutes.

Meanwhile put in a small saucepan a little castor sugar and melt it. When it turns yellow, put in a liqueur glassful of Curaçao. Add the sauce from the ducks, the skin of one orange (pith carefully removed), cut thin and small, like matches, and a little lemon juice. Bring to the boil and cook a minute or two.

Skin the birds and pour this sauce all over; serve with it quarters of Seville orange, carefully peeled with a very sharp knife, made hot in a small saucepan.

The only possible vegetable with this dish is potatoes in some form, soufflés, sautées, Anna or Macaire.

"GUIDE TO GOOD FOOD AND WINES" ANDRÉ SIMON

Wild Duck Casserole

2 mallard.	1–2 glasses of red wine
¼ lb. butter.	according to taste.
2 heads of celery.	1 large onion.

For the Sauce

4 tablespoons oil.	2 level tablespoons flour.
3–4 tablespoons diced	1 teaspoon tomato purée.
vegetables (carrots,	1–2 glasses red wine.
onion, celery).	1 pint good stock.

An excellent casserole recipe, ideal for a dinner party. Pieces of duck in a rich sauce containing vegetables.

[86]

Ideal for a dinner party as you don't have to worry about anything spoiling—if the guests are late you just turn the oven down lower and the duck tastes even better. It's important, however, that the ducks only roast for $\frac{3}{4}$ of their normal roasting time as the blood should still be oozing from the birds when you carve them up to put the meat in the dish with the sauce.

Heat the oil and put in the vegetables and allow them barely to colour. Then stir in the flour and continue to cook to a russet colour. Add the purée, the wine and two-thirds of the stock. Bring to the boil and simmer gently for about 35 minutes. Add remainder of stock and slowly bring sauce to boil. Then strain the sauce and return to the pan.

Meanwhile spread the duck with butter and roast with the wine in a hot oven (400°F., Gas 8–9) for about 25–30 minutes. Cut the celery into small pieces, melt butter in a shallow pan and add onions (very finely sliced) and celery. Carve the duck and place on top of joints and slices of breast the celery and onion, and then spoon over the sauce. Cover the dish (silver foil will do) and cook in a slow oven (250°F., Gas 3–4) for 15–20 minutes.

Serve this with game chips (see recipe on page 149) and a green salad.

MRS. COLIN WILLOCK

Salmis de Canard Sauvage

2 wild duck.	Salt.
2 oz. butter.	Black pepper, nutmeg,
6 finely hashed	allspice.
shallots.	$\frac{1}{2}$ wine-glassful red wine.

Duck pieces in a rich sauce. Takes a little more time and trouble, but produces an excellent dinner dish.

Roast the ducks as fast as possible for 10 minutes. After

cooling, remove legs and wings. Pound the allspice with a little salt and grated nutmeg, and powder the legs and wings with this. Then grill the legs, fast at first, then more slowly until tender. Place in a fireproof dish in a low oven to keep warm, grill the wings in the same way, but they will not take so long, and put them in the same dish.

Carve the rest of the duck into long thin fillets, and lay in shallow fireproof dish which has been buttered and sprinkled with finely hashed shallots. Sprinkle some powdered spice over the fillets and put in the oven. Break up the carcases of the birds and pound in a mortar to release any juices, sprinkle the wine on to the fragments, and strain the resultant juice over the fillets. Place two legs and two wings at each end of the serving dish, and put the rest of the butter over the fillets in the centre. Grill quickly to glaze the top, withdraw the moment the fillets show signs of curling, and serve at once with orange salad garnished with black olives.

"PLATS DU JOUR" PATIENCE GRAY

Braised Wild Duck from New Zealand

3 wild ducks.	1 pint stock.
6 shallots.	Juice of half a lemon.
2 oz. butter.	Salt and pepper, and
1 oz. flour.	cayenne pepper.
	1 wine-glass red wine.

Whole braised birds in a rich sauce. A simple recipe.

Truss the ducks and then partially roast in a moderate oven. Put the giblets into a saucepan with the shallots, salt and pepper. Simmer for an hour, and then strain. Heat the butter, stir in the flour to make a white roux, add the giblet stock and, stirring all the while, bring the sauce to the boil. Add the wine, lemon juice and cayenne. Cut each duck up neatly, place in saucepan, and gently simmer until tender.

"COOKING FROM THE COMMONWEALTH" ROBIN HOWE

[88]

Roast Teal (Standard recipe)

Teal.   Melted butter.
                    Plain flour.

Brush trussed teal lavishly with hot melted butter. Place
on a rack in a baking tin. Roast in a hot oven, 450°F., for
about 20 minutes, basting frequently with drippings. If liked
under-done, roast only for $\frac{1}{4}$ hour. Before serving, dredge
lightly with flour and baste again. Garnish with cut lemon
and watercress. Serve with thin brown gravy and orange
salad.

Roast Teal (in orange sauce)

Teal.   Oranges or tangerines.
Wineglass red wine.   2 teaspoonsful Grand
Lemon juice.   Marnier or Cointreau.

The teal are roasted whole with a split orange inside them,
and then garnished with orange and watercress, and served

with a gravy made by mixing a little red wine into the dish gravy. Tangerines can be used, and sweet oranges should have a little lemon juice and, if possible, two teaspoonfuls of Cointreau or Grand Marnier poured over them.

Teal in Wyvern's Way

Teal.	2 tablespoonsful olive oil.
3 oz. onion.	1 teaspoonful wine vinegar.
3 oz. carrot.	$\frac{1}{2}$ oz. minced shallot.
Parsley.	1 teaspoonful dried herbs.
1 wineglass red wine.	Peel and juice of an orange.
Juice of 1 lemon.	Juice of 1 orange.

Breast of teal in a beautiful wine and orange sauce, very special indeed.

Three teal will be enough for this dish. After plucking, drawing and cleaning, lay them on a board and by passing a knife all round the ribs of each bird remove the whole of the breasts with the breast bones left in them. Put these breasts on a dish, pour over them a marinade consisting of two tablespoonfuls of olive oil, a teaspoon of good vinegar, $\frac{1}{2}$ oz. minced shallot, a teaspoon of dried herbs, and the peel and juice of an orange (Seville preferably). Turn and baste them with this during the day. With the bits of the teal— back, legs, wing bones and giblets (well chopped)—make a strong broth by simmering them very slowly with 3 oz. each of onion and carrot and a bouquet (bunch of parsley and seasoning) for about $1\frac{1}{2}$ hours. Strain, skim off any fat, add a claret glass of burgundy or claret, the juice of 1 lemon and the juice of 1 orange; let this just reach boiling point and then leave this sauce to keep warm in a bowl placed in a saucepan of hot water (don't let it boil) on a very low heat.

When required, take the breasts from the marinade, wipe them carefully, then brush them over with butter and grill them. Divide each breast in half by a clean cut along the centre, lay the six pieces on six rounds of fried bread, and hand the sauce you have been keeping warm, separately. Orange salad (see page 150) is delicious with this dish.

"ENCYCLOPEDIA OF GASTRONOMY" ANDRÉ SIMON

Roast Wigeon

2–3 birds.   Butter.   Little flour.
1 oz. butter.   Squeeze orange juice.

For the Sauce

1 oz. flour.   Squeeze lemon juice.
Wine-glass port   Pinch sugar.
wine.   Salt and pepper.
Truss the birds for roasting.   Baste well with hot butter,

and roast for about 20 minutes in a moderately hot oven or longer, according to the size and age of the birds. Keep them well basted with the hot butter as they have no fat of their own, and shortly before serving sprinkle lightly with flour, to give the birds a nice appearance. Meanwhile, make a brown sauce, add to it port wine, orange and lemon juice, a pinch of sugar, and pepper and salt to taste, simmer for 15 minutes, then strain, skim and serve with the birds on a hot dish, garnished with watercress and quarters of lemon, and hand the sauce separately.

Wild Goose

From the wildfowler's point of view, wild geese are fine birds, but they present the cook with problems. Wild goose is not as succulent or tasty as domestic goose. It can be extremely fishy if it has been feeding exclusively on salt marshes, although birds which have been feeding on stubbles will not be too bad. Wild goose does not get anything like so fat as the domestic goose, which is deliberately fed up for the table, and it will not render up the enormous amount of "goose-grease" when cooked that comes from the farmyard bird. It will, in fact, need added fat and plenty of basting to prevent it getting very dry.

If the bird is fishy, it can be sweetened by plunging it in boiling water containing a few pinches of bicarbonate of soda.

Only young birds are fit to eat, and geese can live to a ripe old age, so check that the bird has bright legs, soft upper-leg feathers, and pliable underbill.

Goose should be eaten fresh or only hung for one or two days, and it is best roasted. The recipes used for domestic goose will do for wild goose, but only with added fat.

Roast Wild Goose (1)

1 goose.	3 onions.
Spring of sage.	2 cloves.
Rasher of fat bacon.	Butter.

First way to roast goose. With variations of stuffing, this is the simplest way to cope with the bird. Good family meal, but not really for the special dinner party.

Prepare, stuff and truss like a domestic goose, except that it is not necessary to prick them to extract their fat. If preferred, stuff only with 2 or 3 onions, 2 cloves, a sprig of sage and a rasher of fat bacon. Place goose on a rack in a baking tin. Dredge with seasoned flour. Brush with melted fat, or lard with slices of fat bacon. Roast in a slow oven, 300°F., allowing 20 minutes per pound, basting occasionally with equal quantity of melted butter or margarine and stock. Serve with thick brown gravy, orange salad and red-currant or rowan jelly. For 6 to 10 persons.

"FAMILY COOKERY" ELIZABETH CRAIG

Roast Wild Goose (2)

1 goose.	Handful of sage.
Salt and pepper.	1 large onion.
Apple sauce.	4 oz. breadcrumbs.
Flour.	2 oz. suet.
Butter.	1 egg.

Traditional English roast goose recipe, flavoured like pork, with sage, onions, and apple. Allow 15 minutes roasting per lb. weight, and baste frequently. Vary the stuffing according to taste.

Make a stuffing with finely chopped sage, onion, breadcrumbs, suet, the chopped goose liver, salt and pepper, and beaten egg, all well mixed together. Fill the body of the bird with this. Smear the breast with butter and roast slowly, basting frequently. For the last half hour of cooking, dredge some flour over the bird to help it to brown. Make a good gravy with the stock from the boiled-up giblets, and the pan juices, and thicken with a roux if necessary. Serve the goose with apple sauce.

Roast Goose Special

1 large goose.	1 teaspoon lemon juice.
Strong cider.	1 bay leaf.
Salt and pepper.	$\frac{1}{4}$ teaspoon fennel leaves.
2 medium onions.	$\frac{1}{4}$ teaspoon ground nutmeg.
4 oz. chopped celery.	$\frac{1}{2}$ teaspoon dried tarragon.
3 cups brown bread crumbs.	1 tablespoon chopped parsley.
$\frac{1}{2}$ lb. dried or 1 tin prunes.	$\frac{1}{4}$ lb. diced cooked ham.
White wine.	1 tablespoon ground almonds.
3 pears.	Pinch of ginger.
3 apples.	1 tablespoon blackcurrant jelly.
1 pinch caraway seeds.	4 oz. butter.

A rather complicated recipe for roast goose, but it does flavour it up a bit and the sauce is sharp and savoury.

Add salt and pepper to a little cider and rub the prepared bird inside and out.

Soak the dried prunes overnight and then cook until tender in white wine. If tinned prunes are used, drain them and cook them for a few minutes in enough white wine just to cover them. Remove the stones, and keep the juice for the gravy.

[95]

Melt the butter in a heavy pan and add the chopped apples, pears, onions, and celery, and the lemon juice. After 5 minutes add all the spices except the ginger and a cup of cider. Cook until tender and then put through a sieve or an electric blender. Add the breadcrumbs, ham ground almonds, and prunes to this mixture, and add enough cider to make the stuffing fluffy but not soggy. Stuff the goose with this mixture.

Melt some butter and add a little ginger to it and paint it all over the breast of the goose.

Cook the bird in a covered tin, or in a tin covered with foil for about 1 hour. Then take off the lid, drain off any fat, and pour the prune juice and wine over the bird. Cover again and cook for 1½ hours. Remove the cover and cook for one ½ hour more uncovered till the bird is nicely browned.

Put the goose on a big serving dish and keep it hot.

Skim off fat on the dish gravy and add enough wine to make 3 cups. Add a tablespoonful of cider and some blackcurrant or redcurrant jelly if liked. Thicken with a roux.

Minced Goose Loaf

The best of the raw meat from one goose.
3 slices bread, soaked in milk.

1 goose liver.
1 tablespoon chopped onion.
Flour.

Salt and pepper.

This makes a meat loaf served hot with gravy, or cold with salad. Good family dish for a toughish bird.

Put the slices of bread to soak in milk. Mince the raw goose meat and the liver together, putting it through the mincer at least twice. Squeeze out the bread, sauté the onion in butter till golden, and mix all the ingredients well together, including enough flour to bind the mixture. Shape the whole lot into a loaf and put it on a greased baking sheet or fireproof dish. Baste it well with oil or dripping and roast in a medium oven for about 1 hour.

Goose Pâté

Goose meat.	Salt and pepper.
½ lb. belly pork.	Nutmeg.
½ lb. veal.	4 tablespoons cider.
2 tablespoons brandy.	Bacon rashers.
1 clove garlic.	6 juniper berries.

A good way to use up odds and ends of goose meat, or even the breasts of older tougher birds. Good eaten with a green salad and grated apple. Makes a soft pâté which can be sliced.

Mince together all the meats. If the goose meat has already been cooked all the better, but it can be used raw. Put the meat through the mincer two or three times if necessary until it is really broken down. Add to it the crushed garlic, juniper berries, and the brandy, and moisten with enough cider to make a soft, but not sloppy mixture. Line a big earthenware terrine, or a casserole, or a fire-proof dish with bacon rashers, and fill up with the pâté mixture. Put the dish in a bain marie, or stand in a pan of water, and cook in a slow oven until the pâté comes away from the sides of the terrine (at least 1½ hours). Remove from the oven, and put a weighted plate on top of the pâté, and leave to cool till next day, before turning out on to a plate, ready for slicing and eating.

[97]

Giblets of one goose,   Salt and pepper.
  neck, gizzard, wings,   6 oz. rice or barley or
  feet, and heart.   2 lb. potatoes.
Onion.   1 meat stock cube.
Leek.   Tablespoon chopped
Carrot.   parsley.
Celeriac (if available).

If you care to use up the real odds and ends in this way, this German recipe for giblet soup may appeal to you!

Clean the giblets thoroughly, removing the beak and eyes and skinning the feet. Put the giblets into $4\frac{1}{2}$ pints of boiling salted water with the onion and the cleaned vegetables and boil fairly fast until the meat is tender. Remove the giblets and strain off the stock. Put the stock back into a saucepan and add either the rice, barley or diced potatoes. Cook until done and then add the stock cube, salt and pepper to taste, and the edible parts of giblet meat, cut into small pieces.

"GUIDE TO GOOD FOOD AND WINES" ANDRÉ SIMON

CHAPTER FOUR

WOODCOCK
SNIPE

Some or other of these smaller game birds will be bound to come your way, the chief trouble being that they'll probably always come in ones or twos and you'll be faced with making a meal out of them, say one woodcock and two very small snipe.

Nothing you can do will really alter this situation but you will see from the recipes that the basic methods are very much the same. It is traditional that snipe, and woodcock, should be plucked, trussed and roasted without being drawn, also that the heads should be left on and the long beaks turned back to act as a skewer. There is no need to do this if you dislike the look of it, and if you also dislike the idea of trussing and cooking these small birds unempted, draw them in the usual way and use the method we give in the Stuffed Woodcock recipe. All these small game birds should feel firm to the touch and thick and hard in the vent if in good eating condition.

Woodcock

Woodcock are best two or three weeks after they have arrived in this country, when they have had time to rest up and feed. A fat bird feels thick and firm and is thick and hard in the vent, and has a vein of fat beside the breast. When fresh killed the feet are flexible and the heads and throat clean.

Roast Woodcock

Bread.   Parsley.
1 woodcock per person.   Melted butter.

Simple recipe for roast woodcock.

Brush over each bird with warm butter, place on a slice of bread to catch the succulent juices, and roast in a hot oven (450°F. or Regulo 8) for 15 minutes.

Serve on the toast with a garnish of parsley and fried breadcrumbs.

PAMELA TARLTON

[101]

Casseroled whole birds. A simple way to cook older birds.

Combine the giblets, bacon, onion, soaked bread, parsley and salt and pepper to taste, and use this mixture to stuff the birds which may then be roasted or cooked in a casserole. A small quantity of lemon juice may be added to the gravy, after straining, and the yolk of an egg may be added to the stuffing if wished.

For the Forcemeat

The giblets.	Chopped onion.
Chopped bacon.	Salt and pepper.
Chopped parsley.	A little soaked bread.

Creamed Woodcock *(a French recipe—Bécasse à Crême)*

1 woodcock per person.	Olive oil.
French mustard.	Lemon juice.
Brandy.	Game stock.

Woodcock in a succulent sauce. This is a little more complicated to cook and must be brought straight to the table, as the bird is deliberately underdone, and to keep it waiting in hot sauce would be to keep it cooking.

Take a woodcock that is fairly high, and roast it for no more than 9 minutes, so as to keep it markedly underdone, sprinkling at the outset and at least once again with olive oil, a few drops at a time. Cut it in two lengthways, and divide each half of the breast into two slices. Having ready almost a teaspoon of French mustard diluted with a little fresh lemon juice, roll the slices in this quickly, cover and keep them very warm but not positively hot. With the chopped-up carcase of the bird and the invaluable "trail" (innards), having added and somewhat reduced a tablespoon of previously burnt brandy, and a tablespoon of game stock, prepare a sauce by about 6 minutes of cooking. Pass this through a strainer, under pressure with the back of a kitchen spoon, on to slices of the best part of the woodcock. Turn these slices in the sauce, so that they may be thoroughly covered with it; put the dish on the table or side-table over a spirit-lamp or electric heater for a minute or so and serve.

"ENCYCLOPEDIA OF GASTRONOMY" ANDRÉ SIMON

Woodcock Consommé

1 quart consommé.	1 woodcock.
Lentil purée.	Game stock.
¼ pint cream.	3 eggs.

A superb dish which will take time and trouble to produce. Will establish anyone's reputation as a cook. The recipe below assumes that you know how to make consommé.

Prepare a quart of consommé (or use good tinned consommé). Roast the woodcock for seven minutes, remove the best of the meat and the trail (intestines). Put the carcase into the consommé while it is being clarified. Pound or blend together the meat, the entrails, and then add lentil purée which has previously been prepared. Only a little is needed; just about half as much in quantity as the blended meat. Add a little game stock and the cream and a pinch of cayenne, working the mixture together gradually till you have a smooth paste. Add one whole egg and the yolks of two more, and mix very well. Put the mixture into little cases, and stand these in very hot water and let them cook for about 18–20 minutes until they are set. The water must never actually boil or the mixture will curdle. Let the "royales", as they are called, cool in their cases and then slice them thinly. Add them to the clarified and strained consommé.

Woodcock Flambée

1 woodcock per person. Brandy.
Game stock. Lemon juice.
Cayenne pepper.

Woodcock pieces in a rich sauce made of the bird's intestines.

Roast your undrawn woodcock slightly underdone, then cut it into six pieces, the wings, the legs and the breast cut in half, and keep them warm. Take out the intestines and chop them finely, and press the rest of the carcase on to a pan to squeeze out as much blood as possible. Remove the carcase, mix the blood and the intestines together, pour over a glass of good brandy and set it alight. Let this mixture reduce a little, then add a tablespoonful of game fumet, or rich stock, a squeeze of lemon juice and a suspicion of cayenne pepper. Dish the pieces of woodcock and pour this sauce over them to serve very hot.

"GUIDE TO GOOD FOOD AND WINES" ANDRÉ SIMON

Beccacce al Salmi (Braised Woodcock the Italian way)

1 woodcock per person. Olive oil.
Salt. Butter.
Onion.

Slightly less rich sauce, and the birds kept in halves.

Pluck very carefully, leaving head on bird, and do not draw. Partly cook in a stewpan with a little oil seasoned with salt. Cut in two, and remove the inside. Throw away stomach and gall, but keep remainder to enrich the sauce.

[104]

Remove the birds from the pan, heat a little butter, and in it brown some onion chopped small and the insides of the birds, also cut small. Replace the birds, adding enough stock to keep moist, cover and cook till tender. Serve garnished with pieces of toast spread with the sauce.

Roast Woodcock in White Wine

| 1 woodcock per person. | Rasher of fat bacon. |
| White wine. | Toast. |

Nutmeg.

Half-birds, well roasted, in a medium rich pâté. Remove the gizzards but do not otherwise clean the birds. Bring the heads round and spear through the legs. Wrap each bird in rashers of fat bacon. Put each bird on a slice of toast and roast in a fairly hot oven for 15 minutes. Remove the bacon from the birds, cut them in half. Take out the entrails and chop them up with the bacon. Add a little white wine, salt, pepper, and nutmeg, to make a kind of pâté which is spread thickly on the toast. Place the halved birds on the toast and serve at once.

Snipe

Snipe is prepared and treated in the same way as Woodcock, and can be cooked by Woodcock recipes.

Austrian way with Roast Snipe

Season, cover with fat bacon and roast in a quick oven, 450°F., basting frequently with equal quantity of melted butter and white stock. Wash and chop liver and heart, 3 peeled shallots and 1 sprig parsley. Mix together with 1 tablespoonful finely mixed lemon peel, 1 heaped table-spoonful breadcrumbs, and salt and pepper. Stir in ½ gill red wine, and a few drops of sour cream. Melt ½ oz. butter, and cook mixture till liver and heart are tender. To serve snipe, dish up. Coat with heated sour cream. Garnish with small croûtons of bread, fried in butter and topped with liver and heart mixture. Sometimes diced pineapple or thin slices

of pineapples cooked in butter till clear is passed round with
this dish.   In season August 12th to January 31st.

"FAMILY COOKERY" ELIZABETH CRAIG

Snipe Pudding

6 snipe.   1 onion.
Cayenne pepper.   Truffles.
Lemon juice.   4 oz. chopped mushrooms.
1 dessertspoonful chopped $\frac{1}{2}$ garlic clove crushed.
   parsley.   Pinch of dried herbs as
Pinch of nutmeg.   liked.
$\frac{1}{4}$ pint red wine.   Suet crust.

Succulent snipe suet pudding.   Can be made ahead of time.
Halve the birds and remove the gizzard and trail, put the
trail on one side.   Chop the onion and sauté it in butter till
it is golden, then add the mushrooms, herbs and seasonings
and the wine and cook all together for ten minutes.   Add the
trail and rub the lot through a sieve or put it through an
electric blender.

Season the snipe with lemon juice and cayenne.   Line a
pudding basin with thin suet crust and put in the birds, with
truffles if available.   Pour all the sauce in and put on a pastry
lid.

Steam for 1$\frac{1}{2}$ hours.

"FAMILY COOKERY" ELIZABETH CRAIG

W.DICKES

CHAPTER FIVE

HARE
RABBIT

Hare

It is not difficult to tell a young from an old hare. The main guide is the teeth, white and pointed in a young animal, cracked and brown in an old one, but the general state of the body is also an indication to age; in an old hare the feel will be hard and the pelt scruffy looking. The ears of a young animal tear easily.

Young hares can be cooked by any of the methods here but the old ones are useful for pâtés or terrines. Whatever dish you choose, old hares improve with an overnight soaking in a marinade.

By country custom, a hare should be hung a week without skinning or paunching but the dressing of it after this period of time is a gruesome task, so paunch it at once and then hang it in its skin for about a week according to weather.

Potted hare freezes excellently and a few pots in the deep freeze are wonderfully useful.

Roast Hare (*young*)

1 hare.	Butter.
Thin rashers of bacon.	1 glass port wine.
$\frac{3}{4}$ pint good stock.	Flour.
$\frac{1}{2}$ teaspoonful chopped shallot.	1 small chopped onion.
Forcemeat (optional).	$\frac{1}{2}$ teaspoonful chopped parsley.
Pinch dried thyme.	Salt and pepper.

Milk for basting.

Stuffed roast hare, which takes some time and trouble to cook but makes a splendid main course.

A young hare should be selected for this excellent dish and it may or may not be stuffed with forcemeat, as preferred. It should be hung for a week, weather permitting, before cooking. After trussing brush all over with melted butter. Cover the back with the rashers of bacon, tied or skewered on. Place in a baking tin with about two cupfuls of milk, sprinkle with salt and pepper. Roast for $1\frac{1}{2}$–2 hours, basting frequently with the milk. A little additional butter will enrich the milk. The liver should have been set aside, and the gall-bladder most carefully removed. While the hare is cooking, boil the liver gently for 5 minutes, then drain, and chop finely. Melt a couple of tablespoonfuls of butter in a small saucepan, add the chopped liver, the parsley, the shallot, the onion and the thyme. Fry all this gently, seasoning well, for about 10 minutes, then, if possible, pound the mixture, reheat it, add a good tablespoonful of flour and cook together until it is a light brown, then add either stock or some of the milk used in basting the hare, stirring until the sauce boils. Add the liver mixture, simmer 10 minutes longer, then add the port wine. When the hare is nearly done, remove rashers of bacon, to brown the back, dredging it lightly with flour and basting frequently while it finishes browning. Remove strings, serve with the liver sauce and red-currant jelly, handed separately.

"GUIDE TO GOOD FOOD AND WINES" ANDRÉ SIMON

Saddle of Hare

This is how we used to cook it in Scotland for those who did not like the blood and wine ambience of the traditional jugged hare.

Cut out the middle part of the hare in one section, reserving the four legs, etc. for Jugged Hare. Wipe the saddle of hare carefully with a damp cloth to remove any small hairs that may be adhering to it. Trim away any loose skin and flatten it by cutting off the ends of the rib bones.

Now make a stock in which to cook it, with the following ingredients:—

½ lb. shin of beef cut in pieces, together with the skin trimmings, neck and liver and 2 pints of water. When it comes to the boil add:—

 1 small turnip—sliced up.
 1 small carrot—sliced up.
 Stick of celery with foliage—sliced up.
 1 onion stuck with 3 cloves.
 8 black peppercorns.
 1 Bouquet garni.

Let all these simmer gently for about three hours, then strain, rubbing the vegetables through a fine sieve. Add salt to taste and a dessertspoon of mushroom ketchup. Place the saddle in a thick casserole, if it is too large it can be cut across in two pieces. Brown the saddle lightly with a little butter. Pour over about a third of the stock which should

[112]

have reduced to about one pint in cooking. Cover the casserole closely and cook in a very gentle oven for 1½ hours, basting occasionally. When cooked, lift out the saddle and mix the left-over stock with the juices in the casserole. Thicken with a little arrowroot.

Serve gravy separately with mashed turnips, boiled potatoes and redcurrant jelly. Serves six.

If desired a little blood and port wine may be added to the gravy and then reheated, but it must not boil or it will curdle.

MRS. CHETWYND GROSVENOR

Saddle of Hare in Cream Sauce (*Hasenbraten mit Rahmsauce*)

1 saddle of hare.	1 clove garlic.
1 cup red wine.	Bacon fat.
Sour cream.	Strips of fat bacon.
4 peppercorns.	1 onion.
2 bay leaves.	1 carrot.
Salt.	Frying fat.

Root ginger, thyme, marjoram.

A German recipe for cooking the saddle, the best part of a hare. This is another dish which must be started well before serving as the hare must be marinaded for half a day. Finally it is roasted and served in its own sauce.

Skin, trim, and lard the meat. Slice the onion and carrot and put in a saucepan with all the herbs and flavouring, and add a clove of crushed garlic. Cover with half a cup of water and simmer for 5 minutes. Add wine and heat. Pour all over the hare and leave for half a day. Then remove hare and lard neatly with strips of bacon fat. Melt fat in baking dish and then place hare in dish, cover with lid and roast at Regulo 5, adding the marinade by the spoonful as the hare cooks. When the meat is tender, slake sour cream with teaspoonful of flour and add to sauce. Cook for another 10 minutes, and then strain sauce over hare before serving.   Add red-currant jelly to sauce just before straining.

Marinated Roast Saddle of Hare (*young hare*)

Ingredients for marinade:

   2 small wineglasses red wine.   1 sliced onion.

   1 small wineglass vinegar.   1 clove garlic.

             Parsley, thyme, bayleaf.

Ingredients for roasting:

   1 saddle of young hare.   3 oz. butter for basting.

   Some thin rashers of fat   Black pepper.

      bacon or salt pork.

Yet another long-term marinade recipe using different herbs.   The hare is roasted, but could be spitted if you have the equipment.

Let the hare marinate overnight, and dry well, sprinkle with black pepper, and cover with rashers before roasting.   The oven should be preheated to medium hot, and the hare put directly on the grid with the roasting pan underneath for the basting butter.   Roast for about 15–20 minutes per pound, basting frequently.   For the gravy to be served with it, reduce half the strained marinade by fast boiling and stir it into the butter and juices in the roasting pan and reheat.   Red-currant jelly goes well with roast hare.

Jugged Hare

A richer recipe than the next, which will cost more.   If you serve this as a main course at a dinner party, keep the other courses light.   It is a casserole dish which can be made well beforehand, except for adding the blood.

[114]

1 hare.	15 small onions.
½ lb. fat bacon.	Bouquet garni.
2 tablespoonsful butter.	Salt and pepper.
2 tablespoonsful olive oil.	1 tablespoonful tomato paste.
2 tablespoonsful plain flour.	¼ lb. mushrooms.
3 cloves.	Vinegar.

½ bottle Burgundy.

Joint the hare and save the blood, and keep the saddle to serve roasted, using the other parts for jugging. Cut the bacon into small thick pieces and sauté it with the onions in the butter and oil till golden. Put aside and brown the pieces of hare in the same fat. Sprinkle in the flour and let that brown, stirring the mixture. Add the wine, the bouquet garni, the cloves, the tomato paste, and pepper and salt, put the mixture in a casserole or fireproof or heavy enamel pan with a lid, add enough water to cover the contents and simmer slowly for at least 3 hours. The hare should be tender. Remove the bouquet garni and add the onions and bacon, and the mushrooms and simmer for as long as it takes to make the vegetables tender. Mix the blood with some of the gravy and a little vinegar, then add it to the contents of the casserole, bring the lot just to the boil and serve. Don't allow the dish to boil or the blood will curdle.

To Jug Hare (any age)

1 hare and (optional) its blood.	½ teaspoonful black pepper.
Bunch of sweet herbs	Little lemon peel.
—chervil, thyme,	2 tablespoonfuls ketchup.
tarragon.	Wine glass of port wine.
6 allspice.	1 oz. butter.
	1 oz. flour.

2 onions, each stuck with a few cloves.

This makes a rich casserole, highly herb-flavoured, but only requires a little port wine. Less rich than the foregoing recipe.

Wash the hare and cut it into joints, flour each piece with seasoned flour. Put into a pan with the herbs, the onions, cloves, allspice, salt, pepper and lemon peel. Cover with cold water and bring to simmering point. Simmer until tender; this will take about 2 hours. If you wish to add blood, do it now. Remove pan from heat and add blood very gradually, stirring all the time. Don't let it boil as it will curdle. Take out the joints of hare and lay them neatly in the dish in which you intend to serve them. Heat the butter, add the flour and cook for 2–3 minutes, add the liquid in which you have cooked the hare and allow to thicken. Then add the ketchup and wine. Pour the gravy over the joints of meat and let it stand where it may keep hot but not continue cooking, for 10 minutes. Serve with forcemeat and red-currant jelly.

Hare Soup (*Scots style*) BAWD BREE

1 hare, fresh killed. Sweet herbs and peppercorns.
Onion, carrot, turnip. Oatmeal and water.
Port wine.

An incredibly filling country-style soup/stew, so serve it to the very hungry on a cold day.

Skin hare and clean thoroughly, holding it over large basin to catch all the blood, which contains much of the flavour. Joint the hare and put into pot with water, carrot, onion, turnip, peppercorns, herbs, salt and pepper, and simmer for 3 hours. Strain soup. Cut the meat into small pieces and return to pot with stock; add a handful of oatmeal. Strain the blood and gradually add to the soup, stirring all the time, and bring to the boil. Then add a glass of port wine and serve. A boiled potato should be served separately for each person.

[116]

Hare Soup *(old animal)*

1 hare.	1 lb. lean ham.
3 onions.	3 blades of mace.
Thyme.	3 quarts beef stock.
Marjoram.	2 French rolls.
Parsley.	$\frac{1}{2}$ pint port wine.
Salt.	Cayenne.

Thick rich soup, more of a purée, really. Use your blender or liquidiser to reduce it all down. A meal by itself.

Cut down a hare into joints, and put it into a soup pot, or a large stewpan, with about 1 lb. lean ham, in thick slices, 3 moderate-sized mild onions, 3 blades of mace, a faggot of thyme, sweet marjoram, and parsley, and about 3 quarts of good beef stock. Let it stew very gently for full 2 hours from the time of its first beginning to boil, and more if the hare be old. Strain the soup and pound together very fine the slices of ham and all the flesh from the back, legs and shoulder of the hare, and put this meat into a stewpan with the liquor in which it was boiled, the crumbs of 2 French rolls, and $\frac{1}{2}$ pint of port wine. Set it on the stove to simmer 20 minutes, then rub it through a sieve, place it again on the stove till very hot, but do not let it boil. Season it with salt and cayenne and send it to table directly.

"MODERN COOKERY IN ALL ITS BRANCHES" ELIZABETH ACTON

HARE CHASE.

[117]

Hare in Sweet Sour Sauce (*Lepre Agrodolce*)

1 jointed hare.   1 onion.

Vinegar.   1 slice of ham in cubes.

Plain flour.   Stock.

Salt.   2 tablespoonsful sugar.

½ wineglassful vinegar.

1 heaped tablespoonful grated bitter chocolate.

1 tablespoonful of fennel.   Seedless raisins.

Tablespoonful shredded almonds.

Skin and clean a hare and cut in pieces and wash in a weak solution of vinegar and water. Flour lightly. Fry in butter in which you have browned a chopped onion and a slice of ham cut into small squares. Cover with stock, salt to taste and simmer for 1½ hours. Make a sauce of 2 tablespoonfuls of sugar, half a wine glassful of vinegar, a heaped tablespoonful of grated bitter chocolate, a tablespoonful of chopped fennel, and a few seedless raisins. Mix well and add to hare 20 minutes before serving. A handful of shredded almonds can be added, if liked, at the same time.

Hare à la Provençal (*young*)

1 young hare.   Salt and pepper.

Good pinch mixed spices.   2 cloves garlic.

1 large onion.   1 sprig dried thyme.

1 bay leaf.   ½ bottle white wine.

1 slice streaky salt pork.   1 or 2 smallish onions.

2 cups hot bouillon or water.

This dish must be begun the day before it is to be eaten. It is jointed, marinaded hare, stewed with a little pork to enrich it, or whole hare cooked till very tender.

Cut the hare into suitable pieces. Place these in an earthen-ware terrine or deep round pot, add salt, pepper, spices, large onion cut into pieces, thyme, bay leaf and garlic minced finely. Cover the whole with the wine. Cover with a lid, set in a cool place for 12 hours, turning the pieces of meat once in a while to mix with the seasonings.

Next day, fry the cut-up pork gently in a heavy iron pan, removing pieces of meat left from this operation. Add the other onions, finely cut up, and, if wished, a few more dices of salt pork or bacon. Brown all this gently, then add the drained pieces of hare, browning them until the liquid in the pan has almost entirely evaporated. Now add to this the marinade, with its seasonings. (It is advisable to tie the thyme and bay leaf together for easier removal later.) Add the hot bouillon or water, cover pan closely and cook gently until the hare is very tender. Serve "as is", covering with the sauce.

This dish, by the way, is excellent cold. If wished, the hare may be entirely boned and left whole, to be sliced neatly when cold. Good aspic jelly as a garnish is an advantage.

"GUIDE TO GOOD FOOD AND WINES" ANDRÉ SIMON

Hare à la Bouquette

1 hare with all the blood.	1 oz. beef suet.
¼ lb. mushrooms.	1 oz. ground rice.
1½ oz. butter.	Tablespoonful Bovril.
Port or claret.	6 slices of fat bacon.
Flour and water paste.	3 tablespoonfuls of brandy.
1 onion.	Bay leaf, thyme, parsley.
Basil, marjoram.	Salt and black pepper.

This is slightly more complicated, but not difficult to make and produces very rich herb-and wine-flavoured hare in a dish. Flour and water paste used as a lid is the finest way to seal in the flavours, if more time consuming to make than just using foil. Flame the dish at table for effect, provided it arrives sizzling hot.

Skin, clean, bone a young hare without washing it, preserve the blood, and cut the meat into pieces about one inch square. Put the pieces in a dish and sprinkle with finely chopped bayleaf, thyme, parsley, fresh mushrooms, basil, marjoram, and onion. Roll each bit in the finely chopped beef suet and ground rice and season with salt and black pepper. Arrange all the pieces in a fireproof dish. Mix the hare's blood with the Bovril and pour this over the hare, and fill up the dish to within an inch of the top with port or claret. Put the bacon slices on top of the hare and cover the lot with a flour water paste about 1 inch thick. Put the dish in a bain marie in the oven at a moderate setting for one and a half hours. When cooked remove the water paste and bacon, and just before serving pour the brandy very gently over the hare and set it alight.

Hare Pâté (1)

Jointed hare (except saddle).	3 onions.
Bay leaf.	2 lb. fat bacon.
Marjoram.	Stock.
$\frac{1}{2}$ bottle red wine.	Grated lemon peel.
Pepper and salt.	Bacon rashers.

Melted butter.

A good tasty, coarse-textured pâté, can be sliced to eat with salad.

Put all the joints but the saddle into a casserole with onions, herbs and bacon, cut into cubes. Add enough stock to cover all ingredients, or stock and half a bottle of wine. Cover closely and cook in a slow oven, 45 minutes. Let it cool, then put all the meat, including the bacon, through the fine plate of the mincer.

Season well with ground black pepper, salt if needed, more herbs and a little grated lemon peel.

Grease a mould. This should be a 2-pint terrine, that is a straight-sided china mould, but if you do not have such a thing, use a basin or a straight-sided fireproof dish. Do not use a metal mould.

Put the meat into the mould, do not press it down. Put a few rashers of bacon on the top and moisten with some of the stock in which you have cooked the joints. Put grease-proof paper on the top and stand the mould in a pan of hot water. Put this pan into a low oven and cook for $1\frac{1}{2}$–2 hours. When you take the pan out of the oven press evenly down on the greaseproof paper so that all the meat is consolidated, leave the paper on top while the terrine cools. It can then be stored in a cold larder until required.

If wanted to be kept for 2–3 weeks, run melted butter over the top of the meat; when cold, cover with tinfoil. It can be safely kept for 2–3 weeks.

Hare Pâté (2)

Joints of hare.	1 lb. fat bacon, cut into
2 onions.	cubes.
Bay leaf.	3–4 rashers bacon.
Mixed herbs.	$\frac{1}{2}$ pint red wine.
Lemon juice.	

Delicious hare pâté, not at all difficult to make.

Put the hare, fat bacon, onions, bay leaf and herbs into a pan and cook very slowly until the meat will just leave the bones. Take out and remove meat from bones, put hare and bacon through the mincer, add more seasoning and lemon juice. Lay some rashers of bacon on the bottom of a fireproof dish, press the minced meat into the dish, add the red wine and some more rashers of bacon on the top. Put the dish, standing in a baking tin containing water, into a moderate oven, 300°F., Gas 6, for 2–3 hours. Take out and apply light pressure until the terrine is cold.

Hare Pâté (3) *(with pre-cooked joints)*

2 lb. hare.	1 lb. fat bacon.
2 lb. pork.	1 wineglass brandy.
2 onions.	Parsley and thyme.
Salt and black pepper.	Bacon rashers.

A richer pâté.

Blend or mince all the ingredients except the bacon rashers. When well mixed, fill either one large or several small terrines with the mixture, put on top bay leaves and some bacon rashers cut into thin strips, and cover the dishes with waxed paper or foil. Stand them in bain maries, and cook in a slow oven from 1 to 2 hours depending on the size of the containers. If covered with a thick layer of lard and waxed paper, the paté will keep for months in a cool place or in a freezer.

Rabbit

Rabbits, both wild and "cultivated", undesirable as food in the years following the myxomatosis epidemic which swept the country, are now popular again. Although "myxo" is still endemic in some places, there are plenty of clean rabbits about and it is easy enough to tell at a glance whether or not they have the disease. A rabbit with "myxo" has all the symptoms of a streaming cold. It isn't worth cooking old rabbits or milky does, but young ones can be cooked in any number of ways. A young rabbit should be plump with small teeth, sharp smooth claws and ears that can be easily torn. Rabbit, like chicken, needs good sauces and good cooking to make it into anything out of the ordinary, and there are literally hundreds of recipes. Rabbit does not need to be hung, and females are tenderer than males.

To give the rabbit a gamey taste, marinade it overnight before cooking it by any of the recipes.

Sautéd Rabbit à la Carlton

1 rabbit.	3 onions.
2 oz. butter.	2 oz. bacon.
Bouquet garni.	1 tablespoonful plain flour.
1 dessertspoonful	1 oz. chopped ham.
tarragon vinegar.	1 tablespoonful parsley.
1 chicken stock cube.	

Rabbit pieces in a medium rich sauce. Looks good when served and is a definite improvement on rabbit stew.

Joint the rabbit, cut up the onions into small pieces, and fry together with the chopped bacon in the butter for about 15 minutes. Then stir in the flour and vinegar and a pint of stock. Simmer gently for an hour. Remove the herbs. Place the rabbit pieces on a serving dish, and pour the sauce over it, then sprinkle with chopped ham and parsley.

Rabbit in Marsala

1 rabbit.	1 oz. butter.
1 rasher bacon.	1 blade of chopped celery.
Salt and pepper.	1 clove garlic.
4 tomatoes or 1 small tin.	Marjoram.
Small wineglassful Marsala.	1 aubergine.
½ chicken stock cube.	1 green pepper.

This is rich and sweet and Mediterranean, and much improves the rabbit, making it fit to serve as a main dinner dish, in its own casserole or pan.

Cut the aubergine into half-inch slices and sprinkle it with salt and leave it for at least half an hour before using.

Joint the rabbit and cut up the bacon and, together with the celery, sauté the lot in the butter. When it is just brown, add the tomatoes, crushed garlic, marjoram, salt, and pepper, breaking the tomatoes with a spoon. Add the Marsala and stock to cover the contents of the pan and let it all simmer for half an hour. Then add the aubergine pieces and the chopped green pepper and let it continue to simmer until the meat and vegetables are tender. The gravy should be reduced if necessary, until it is fairly thick. If tinned tomatoes have been used this may mean a little extra boiling, but do not let the aubergines and pepper get too mushy; remove them if necessary, and replace just before serving.

Mustard Rabbit

1 rabbit.	2 tablespoonsful olive oil.
4 tablespoonsful Continental mustard.	Salt and pepper.
	Plain flour.
1 onion.	$\frac{1}{2}$ pint thin cream.
1 clove garlic.	A little stock.
2 oz. smoked bacon or salt pork.	

A long-term recipe. Rabbit pieces in mustard and garlic sauce. An unusual flavour so don't try it on those whose tastes you don't know.

This dish should be prepared the day before you want to eat it, to give the meat time to absorb the mustard flavour. Joint the rabbit, and wash and dry the joints well. Cover them all over with mustard.

Next day cook the bacon and onion, diced, and the crushed garlic in the oil. Set aside. Sprinkle the rabbit joints with flour and brown them in the same fat. Put back the onions and bacon and add a little stock and cook very gently for about $\frac{1}{2}$ hour in a covered pan. Then add cream and simmer till the meat is tender. Reduce sauce till fairly thick. Serve with mashed potato.

Rabbit Marinade

1 carrot.	1 shallot.
1 onion.	¼ pint oil.
1½ pints dry white wine.	1 clove.
2 sprigs thyme.	1 bay leaf.
1 clove.	Salt.

Peel and chop the carrot, onion and shallot. Heat the oil gently and add the vegetables, herbs and spices. Stir it frequently, browning the vegetables lightly. Add the wine and vinegar. Simmer for 45 minutes. It must be quite cool before using.

Lapin aux Pruneaux

1 young rabbit.	½ pint red wine.
¼ pint stock.	2 tablespoons wine vinegar.
½ lb. previously soaked prunes.	4 carrots.
	Teaspoon redcurrant jelly.
1 large onion.	Peppercorns.
1 teaspoon plain flour.	Seasoning.
2–3 cloves.	2–3 oz. butter.

Bouquet garni.

This is a French country recipe and prunes go well with rabbit. It is a rich and splendid stew.

Joint the rabbit and marinate it in the red wine, vinegar, spices, slices of onion, carrot and bouquet garni. Leave it overnight. Then remove the rabbit and dry with a cloth. Heat the butter in a heavy pan, and brown the rabbit in it. Sprinkle in the flour, strain on the stock and marinade, add the prunes and season. Bring to the boil and skim, simmer gently for about ¾ hour or until the rabbit is tender.

Put the rabbit on a hot dish surrounded by the prunes. Stir the redcurrant jelly into the pan the rabbit has been cooking in, and season if necessary. Pour this sauce over the meat, and serve with fried croûtons.

Lapin au Caramel

1 jointed rabbit.	1 medium onion.
4 oz. bacon cut in strips.	4 oz. castor sugar.
12 stoned black and green olives.	2 tablespoons plain flour.
3 oz. butter.	3 tablespoons Madeira.
2 tablespoons thin cream.	1 clove garlic.
2 teaspoons tomato purée.	Bouquet garni.
Seasoning.	A strip of orange peel.

2 pints stock.

Roll each rabbit in castor sugar. Heat 2 oz. of the butter and fry the rabbit in this until the sugar is slightly caramelised. Take the rabbit out and pour in a little stock and season. Put the rabbit joints back in this and leave it all on one side.

Heat the rest of the butter in another pan and fry the bacon and onions in this until brown. Stir the flour in and add the rest of the stock carefully, stirring all the time. Add the tomato purée and the crushed clove of garlic, the bouquet garni and the orange peel. Season to taste. Put in the rabbit and the liquid from the other pan, cover with grease-proof paper or foil and the lid and cook gently for about 1½ hours.

Put the rabbit pieces in a hot dish. Take the orange peel and bouquet garni from the pan. Stir in the Madeira and cream. Pour this over the rabbit. Braise the olives in some hot oil and put them round the meat. Garnish with fried croûtons, and serve it all piping hot.

[127]

1 jointed rabbit.	A small tin anchovy fillets.
Red pepper.	2 glasses sherry.
2 tablespoonful olive oil.	Salt.
1 pint brown sauce.	3 sliced onions.
Olives.	Thyme, parsley.

Bay, tarragon, chervil.

Rabbit pieces in rich and herb-flavoured gravy. Garnished with olives and herbs. A bit complicated to cook, but worth serving as a special dish.

Joint the rabbit, season with red pepper and salt, and put in a heavy pan with the olive oil, onions, thyme, parsley, bay leaf, tarragon, and chervil. Fry together for about 10 to 15 minutes till a nice golden colour, then add the anchovies and sherry. Reduce this to half the quantity, add the brown sauce, and boil it all for ¾ hour, keeping it well skimmed while cooking. Remove the joints, sieve or blend the sauce, and reboil the rabbit in it, then dish up on a border of potatoes and fried croûtons of bread and garnish with braised olives. Sprinkle chopped tarragon and chervil all over the joints.

Rabbit Pie

1 jointed rabbit.	½ lb. green bacon.
½ lb. beefsteak.	½ pint beef stock.
Salt and pepper.	Short crust or puff paste.
Forcemeat balls.	Hard-boiled eggs.

Traditional recipe for rabbit pie. If it is made to be eaten cold, add forcemeat balls and hard-boiled eggs. A good family dish.

Joint the rabbit, slice the beef and dice the pork. Put the meat in a pie dish in layers, seasoning each layer. Then three-quarter fill the dish with stock, put on the pastry lid and bake for an hour and a half until the pastry has risen and set, then turn down the heat and let the pie continue to cook slowly. Heat up the rest of the stock and add it to the pie through a small hole just before serving, but don't make the pie too wet. If the pie is to be eaten cold, put in some small forcemeat balls (see page 149) and hard-boiled eggs, cut into halves.

Terrine of Rabbit

2 rabbits plus their livers and kidneys.	1 lb. green bacon sliced.
Stock.	3 eggs.
½ oz. gelatine.	Parsley.
Mixed chopped herbs.	Salt and pepper.
	Breadcrumbs.

This makes a very good terrine containing various in-gredients which remain separate in the jelly. Excellent for cold meals or picnics. However it does take quite a bit of time to make and is a little fiddly.

Cut off the heads and necks of the rabbits and soak them for a couple of hours in salted water. Put the carcases in a casserole with half of the bacon, cover it with stock and put on a close-fitting lid. Stew or simmer gently for at least an hour, until the meat comes easily from the bones. Take the best of the meat off in big pieces.

Chop together all the smaller pieces of meat, with the cooked bacon, the herbs, one raw egg, and half the weight of this mixture in breadcrumbs. Cut the rest of the bacon into strips. Fry the livers and kidneys of the rabbit in hot butter, let them cool, and slice them very thinly. Hard boil the other two eggs.

Make the breadcrumb mixture into little balls and boil them gently in stock for ten minutes. Make up the gelatine with stock (about a pint) and pour a little into the bottom

[129]

of a mould.

Then put all the ingredients in mixed layers; sliced eggs, forcemeat balls, rabbit pieces and strips of bacon, filling up with gelatine stock as you go. Put the terrine in the fridge to set, and unmould it next day.

Harvest Rabbit

1 small rabbit to every 2 persons.	1 large onion.
1 slice of bacon to each rabbit.	Dripping.
3 prunes to each rabbit.	Seasoned flour
A bunch of fresh herbs to each rabbit.	stock.

Forcemeat balls:

Chopped bacon (or suet).	Chives (or young
Breadcrumbs.	onion tops).
Marjoram, parsley.	1 or 2 eggs.

Seasoning.

Rabbit baked whole—rich and herbal. It's fine if the look of the carcases when cooked doesn't put you off!

Skin, draw and cut off the heads, scuts, and feet of the rabbits. Wash well and leave to soak in salt water for 15 minutes. Dry well, and then fry whole in the dripping until light golden. Drain, and stuff under the ribs of each 3 well-soaked prunes and a bunch of fresh herbs. Coat with the seasoned flour. Cover the bottom of the deep baking dish with thinly sliced onion and put the floured rabbits on top with a slice of fat bacon over each, and just cover with stock. Cover and bake slowly for 1 hour. Remove the lid and bake for 1 hour longer.

Make the forcemeat balls from the ingredients above bound with the egg, or 2 eggs if as many as 3 rabbits are cooked. Fry them in very hot fat till they are deep brown on the outside, and be sure that plenty of fresh herbs are used, and they must cut a bright green. Serve on a hot dish, garnished with the onions and forcemeat balls. Strain the gravy and serve it separately.

Savoury Rabbit Giblets

Head, split in half lengthways.	
Neck.	liver.
Ribs.	lungs.
Heart.	kidneys.
2 oz. fat bacon.	1 onion.
2 oz. plain flour.	1 pint water.
Salt and pepper.	Lemon juice or red
Sugar.	wine.

For those who like to finish up all the odds and ends, this is a good way to make a savoury supper dish. Sweet and sour.

Wash the giblets and cut into small pieces, fry with the diced onion and the chopped bacon, dredge in the flour, stirring all the while and fry until brown. Then add the water and season well. Simmer gently until the meat is tender. Just before serving, season the gravy to taste with lemon juice or red wine and sugar, remove bones and serve with lots of mashed potato.

Rabbit Paprika

1 young rabbit.	Salt and pepper.
Flour.	2 oz. butter or frying oil.
2 large onions.	3 dessertspoonsful paprika.
2 fresh tomatoes.	1 chicken stock cube.
1 clove garlic.	Wineglassful dry sherry.
	1 cup sour cream.

Rabbit pieces in a bright red sharp sauce—Hungarian style.

Cut the rabbit into serving pieces and rub well with salt and pepper, and dredge with flour. Heat the butter or oil in a heavy pan and cook the chopped onions in this for 30 minutes. Don't let them burn. Add the paprika and cook for 15 minutes longer stirring all the time. Add the rabbit pieces and the tomatoes, and the stock cube dissolved in a cupful of water. Cover and let this simmer for an hour until the meat is tender. Just before serving thicken the gravy with a bit more flour if necessary. Add the garlic, if liked, with the onion and add the sherry with the stock. Add the sour cream to the gravy just before serving, which will probably thicken it enough so that no more flour will be needed.

Rabbit Rijsttafel

2 young rabbits.	1 red pepper chopped.
2 tablespoons curry powder.	Giblets from rabbits.
	4 onions.
3 tablespoons oil.	1 tablespoon root
½ teaspoonful ground turmeric.	ginger, soaked and cut into slivers.
2 cloves of crushed garlic.	2 tablespoons currants.
	1 tablespoonful flour.
2 chopped green peppers.	3 tablespoons milk.
3 cucumbers.	Stock.
Salt and pepper.	1 teaspoonful lemon juice.

A complicated Indonesian curry, but well worth making this way if you have the spices. Almost unrecognisable as rabbit!

Joint the rabbits. Heat oil in large pan and stir in the curry powder. Brown the rabbit pieces in hot oil then add finely chopped onions, ginger, garlic, peppers and turmeric.

Chop giblets finely, add to the pan with the currants; add sufficient stock to cover, simmer until the meat starts to fall off the bones.

Take the rabbit pieces out and put on one side having taken the bones out. Cut the scrubbed unpeeled cucumbers into 1-inch pieces and add to the sauce with the lemon juice. Simmer gently until the cucumbers are tender. Strain the liquid into a small pan, add flour combined with milk and cook, stirring until thickened.

Pour it back into the large pan together with the rabbit pieces and cucumber. Simmer gently for a further 5 minutes, adding a little more milk if the sauce is too thick. Serve with long grained rice.

Fried Rabbit with Tartare Sauce

1 young rabbit.	$\frac{1}{4}$ pint olive oil.
2 tablespoonsful wine vinegar.	1 chopped shallot.
	1 bay leaf.
2 cloves.	Salt and pepper.
Mace.	1 tablespoonful chopped
$\frac{1}{4}$ pint mayonnaise.	pickled gherkins.
1 beaten egg.	Breadcrumbs.

This makes a good supper dish. Rabbit cutlets with a sharp mayonnaise sauce, crisp and savoury.

Bone the legs, and remove the best of the flesh from the carcase in big pieces, and put them into a marinade made with the oil, vinegar, herbs and seasoning. After an hour, drain the rabbit pieces but don't dry them, dip them into the egg and breadcrumbs and fry in very hot oil until well browned.

Add the chopped gherkins to the mayonnaise and serve separately.

CHAPTER SIX
VENISON

Venison

"*He did give us the meanest dinner of beef*
shoulders and umbles of venison."

"UMBLES OF THE DEER" PEPYS

"The word 'umbles' has been given many meanings in
different dictionaries, and the original cookery books and
hunting books, from which the dictionaries derive, are equally
confusing. I believe that umbles were the stones, sweet-
breads, and what (in a modern pig) we should call the 'best
parts of the "fry" ', and as much a delicacy as the 'lamb
stones' of the old sheep-farming days. Later the word seems
to be used for a much coarser selection of 'fry', including
liver and lights—and in 1725 we get a reference to 'the
umbles or dowsets' in a contemptuous term. Yet, curiously,
dowsets is also the name of a white soft hasty pudding.
Speaking as a cook, and a historian, I believe that the choicer
parts of the usual 'fry' might be considered umbles. And
note that they would be used fresh—the hunter's first dish—
and served at once. (Which accounts for the number of
times the returned hero is regaled with this dish upon a
sudden and dramatic arrival.)

The chief recommendation for this unprepossessing dish is
that there was only one of it!"

"FOOD IN ENGLAND" DOROTHY HARTLEY

From the gastronome's point of view, the best deer is the
Roe Deer, followed by the Fallow Deer, then the Red Deer.
The flesh of the buck (male) is better than that of the doe

(female) and the best meat comes from animals between eighteen months and two and a half years old. Most venison tends to be dry and tough, so it must be hung, marinaded, and kept well basted or covered whilst cooking, and not be allowed to dry out. Add fat bacon to stews and casseroles.

If you have a whole beast cut the joints out from the carcase as required, otherwise hang joints in an air current and cover them with a damp cloth.

Liver should be eaten fresh and is the stalker's "perk". The first cuts ready to eat are the tenderloin fillets with kidney attached. See page 165 for identification of the different cuts.

Red-currant, rowan, and cranberry jellies are served with venison.

Roast Venison

Joint of venison.   Dripping.
A little flour.

Traditional way to cook venison in a water paste to retain all the juices and keep the meat from drying out.

Rub the meat all over with clarified fat or dripping and wrap in greaseproof paper. Make a stiff paste of flour and water and completely enclose the joint. Then wrap again in greaseproof paper and tie with string. Roast by the "slow roast" method in a moderate oven, 350°F., Mark 5, for 3–4 hours according to the size of the joint (40 minutes to the pound), basting often. Half an hour before serving, take off all coverings, dredge with flour, raise the heat of the oven and baste well. Serve with brown gravy and red-currant jelly.

1 haunch.   Salt and pepper.
Lard.   Rashers of fat bacon.

The modern way to roast venison, in foil instead of flour paste. Allow plenty of time for roasting before serving.

Rub the meat all over with salt and pepper and smear it thoroughly with lard. Take a piece of foil large enough to wrap up the whole joint and lay it flat. Place the joint upon it and cover the meat with bacon rashers. Then wrap the whole lot up so that cooking juices will be kept in and put it into a roasting tin. Cook in a medium-hot oven for 25 minutes for each pound of weight. Half an hour before serving open up the foil and baste the meat thoroughly, put it back in the oven uncovered and let it cook till nicely browned, basting again if necessary.

Serve with cranberry sauce and a good gravy made from the juices.

Marinaded Roast Venison

2½ pints good red   3 sage leaves.
   wine.   Dried rosemary.
3 lumps sugar.   Thyme.
1 tablespoonful   Nutmeg.
   peppercorns.   1 leg of venison.
3 cloves.   4 rashers thick belly
6 bay leaves.   pork.
1 tablespoonful curry   Salt and pepper.
   powder.   4 oz. butter.

Spicy roast venison. It needs advance planning to serve this at a dinner party. This marinade can be used for any cut of venison before cooking it, and will help to tenderise the meat.

[138]

Boil together all the wine herbs, sugar and spices. Pour the marinade over the venison joint and turn it twice every day for ten days, making sure the meat is well soaked in the liquor.

Remove the meat and wipe it dry after ten days. Cut the pork into strips and lard the meat with a larding needle, against the grain of the meat. Smear butter all over the joint, and put it in a roasting tin with a lid. Roast it in a medium to hot oven, and as soon as the meat is hot, baste it with the marinade, and continue basting at intervals throughout the roasting, which will take about an hour and a half.

Tenderloin Steaks

1 tenderloin cut into round steaks or escallops (6).

6 rashers of bacon.	2 bay leaves.
Butter.	Thyme.
1 medium-sized onion.	Caraway seeds.
2 oz. mushrooms.	Wineglassful dry white
1½ cups of cream.	wine.
Salt and pepper.	½ pint sour cream.
Juice of ½ a lemon.	Worcestershire sauce.

Slightly underdone steaks of the tenderest part of the beast in a marvellous rich sharp sauce. Very special indeed for a very special dinner. Not at all difficult to prepare.

Wrap each piece of meat in a rasher of bacon, and put a little butter in a heavy frying pan, or skillet, with a lid. Cook the pieces for about 6 minutes on each side, and then put them on a serving dish and keep warm while you make the sauce. Put a quarter of a pound of butter in the pan with the sliced onions and mushrooms, the bay leaves and a pinch of thyme and caraway. Let this cook for 5 minutes or until the onions are golden, then add the wine, simmer for a little longer until the vegetables are cooked and add the fresh cream, and allow to cook for another 15 minutes. Remove the pan from the heat and add the sour cream, salt, pepper, and Worcestershire sauce to taste, and the lemon juice. Heat but do not boil. Pour the sauce over the meat and serve immediately.

Leg and Loin of Venison in Cream Sauce (*Rehbraten mit Rahmsauce*)

Leg and loin of venison.	Salt and pepper.
	Nutmeg.
Crushed juniper berries.	2 carrots.
	Dripping.
Onion.	Bay leaf.
Celeriac.	2 cloves.
1 teaspoonful French mustard.	1 beef stock cube.
	Capers.
Thyme.	Grated lemon rind.

¼ pint sour cream.

Broiled venison in a fairly sharp sauce, cooked in a big casserole or fireproof dish.

Skin the meat and lard neatly. Rub with salt, pepper, crushed juniper berries and a little nutmeg. Slice an onion, 2 carrots and a celeriac. Melt a tablespoonful of fat in a saucepan and brown these. Add the meat, brown slightly and then transfer all to a casserole. Add a teaspoonful of French mustard and a bay leaf, a little thyme, 2 cloves, some grated lemon rind, and a cupful of water or preferably good stock. Cover with a lid and simmer in oven 250–300°F., Gas 3–4, until meat is tender, adding more water, if necessary. Take out meat and keep hot. Add a quarter of a pint of sour cream, mix well, heat and strain over the meat. Capers may also be added to the sauce. Serve with buttered noodles, or rice and cranberries.

Venison Stewed in Beer

Venison—to stew.   2 tablespoonfuls black
½ lb. demerara sugar.   treacle.
                1 pint beer.

A simple way to cook venison in a sweet brown gravy, what is known in France as a "Carbonade". This dish should be served with plenty of vegetables.

Dissolve the sugar and treacle in the beer. Put the well-hung meat into the stewpan or casserole, cover with the liquid, put on the lid and bring to the boil. Simmer gently until tender, the time of cooking being approximately 30 minutes to the pound and 30 minutes over.

Venison Pie (Cold)

2 lb. venison freed from all skin and sinew.
1 lb. deer liver.   1 teaspoonful finely
Pepper and salt.   chopped onion.
                The tongue.

A rather complicated recipe, especially if you include the other game as suggested. It will be a very large pie indeed.

Pass the venison and liver through a mincing machine and add the chopped onion, pepper and salt. Having a frying-pan ready with some hot bacon fat, fry together lightly, and put in a dish to cool a little. Add thin slices of deer's tongue, which has been cooked in a saucepan, and a little vegetable. The tongue will want cooking for 1½–2 hours, so that the skin will come off fairly easily. Put some thin slices of bacon in the bottom of the pie-dish, then a layer of venison and liver. Sprinkle with chopped parsley and a little crushed peppercorn between each layer, then a layer of tongue, then venison and liver, and continue the layers until the pie-dish is full. Add a breakfastcupful of stock, stand the pie-dish in a tin of water in a moderate oven, the pie-dish being covered with a closely-fitting cover. Cook for 2½–3 hours and when cooking, fill up with good venison stock. The pie is improved by the addition of a hare, grouse or duck, and a glass of port wine.

"GUIDE TO GOOD FOOD AND WINES" ANDRÉ SIMON

Spiced Venison

5 lb. boned haunch of venison.	½ oz. saltpetre. (from chemist).
½ oz. bay salt.	½ oz. black pepper.
¼ oz. powdered allspice.	1 teaspoonful ground mace.
1 teaspoonful ground ginger.	1 teaspoonful ground cloves.
3 oz. brown sugar.	3 oz. salt.
1 carrot.	Horseradish sauce.
1 turnip.	1 onion.

This produces a cold rolled joint of meat not unlike silver-side of beef but spicier. It is a most useful thing to make for a large family party—at Christmastime perhaps, as something different for the cold table.

Mix the bay salt and the saltpetre together and rub it into the boned meat. Put the joint into a covered earthenware container. The next day mix the spices together and rub this into the meat as well. Put the venison back into its container and sprinkle it with the sugar and salt mixed together. Turn it every day for five days. A liquid will form as the meat pickles, and baste the meat every day with this. After five days, wash the meat well in cold water and roll it and tie it securely. Cover it with cold water and bring it slowly to the boil. Put the vegetables in and continue boiling

[142]

for at least 2½ hours until the meat is tender. Let the meat cool in its liquid, then remove it and press it firmly by weighting a board on top of it. Horseradish sauce goes well with the meat.

Venison Meat Loaf

1 lb. venison.	Onion.
Heart.	Two tomatoes.
Liver.	½ lb. bacon or ham diced.
Grated lemon rind.	Two tablespoonsful
1 egg.	breadcrumbs.
Salt and pepper.	

A meat loaf to eat hot or cold. A good way to use up the offal and odd pieces of meat.

Mince the venison with the onion and tomatoes, heart and liver. Put this mixture with all the other ingredients and mix it well. Grease a bread tin and press the mixture into it. Cover with foil and cook in a medium oven for about 2 hours. Allow to cool before turning out, then serve cold with salad.

Venison Liver Pâté

Liver.	1 clove garlic.
Tongue.	Salt and pepper.
Heart.	Nutmeg.
4 oz. fat pork.	Tablespoonful brandy.
6 oz. streaky bacon.	2 eggs.
2 slices of bread soaked in milk.	

A good rich, spreading pâté, excellent on toast, can be served as a first dinner course, or just enjoyed for any meal.

Braise together in butter, half the liver, the tongue, heart, fat pork and crushed garlic. When this is tender mince it with the rest of the raw liver. Put it through the mincer twice at its finest setting till the meat is really well broken down. Then mix it with the bread, from which the milk has been drained, and all the remaining ingredients except the streaky bacon. Line a terrine or fireproof dish with the bacon rashers and put the paté mixture into it. Place the dish in another dish containing water (bain marie) and place it in a low oven, and cook it very gently for 1½ hours or until the paté leaves the sides of the terrine, whichever takes longest.

Put aside to cool with a weighted dish on top of the paté. Next day turn it out and eat it on hot buttered toast.

Venison Chops with Purée of Chestnuts

6 venison chops.	Salt and pepper.
Melted butter.	Purée of chestnuts
3 tablespoonsful	(see page 153).
redcurrant jelly.	¼ pint tomato sauce.

Chops in tomato and chestnut sauce; quick and easy to make.

Neatly trim and flatten 6 venison chops, season all over with a teaspoon of salt and ½ ditto of pepper.

Thoroughly heat a tablespoon of melted butter in a pan and add chops one beside another, cook for 5 minutes on each side, dress a purée of chestnuts on a hot dish (use recipe on page 153 for braised chestnuts and purée them by mashing with butter and hot milk) in a pyramid and arrange chops around. Remove fat from pan, add 3 tablespoons red-currant jelly and mix until thoroughly melted; pour in a gill (¼ pint) of tomato sauce, mix well, boil for 2 minutes, pour sauce over chops and serve.

"ENCYCLOPEDIA OF GASTRONOMY" ANDRÉ SIMON

[144]

Venison Goulash

1 lb. venison.	Stock.
Salt and pepper.	1 tablespoon paprika.
Root vegetables.	Celery.
1 small tin tomato	Thyme.
purée.	Bay leaf.

Hungarian-type venison stew. Good for using up pieces of meat.

Cube the meat and roll it in flour and brown it in hot fat. Put the meat in a saucepan with enough stock to cover, and simmer it for 1 hour. Meanwhile slice up the vegetables and sauté them in the same fat until tender. Add the vegetables to the meat and stock; with the seasonings and tomato purée put the lot in a casserole and let it cook in a slow oven for a further half hour. Serve with pickled vegetables such as gherkins.

Deer Haggis

Deer's heart, liver	Teacupful coarse
and suet.	oatmeal.
3 onions.	Salt, black
Flour.	pepper.

This is a simple type of haggis, cooked in a pudding basin, rather than the traditional sheep's paunch. A useful way of using up offal.

Boil the heart and a piece of liver for $\frac{1}{2}$ hour. When cold, mince them both very fine. Toast the oatmeal in the oven and then add this to the minced meat with the chopped onions, a tablespoon of salt and a good sprinkling of black pepper. Mix well, and put it all in a pudding basin. Make a suet crust and cover the basin with it. Boil for 4 hours, and serve it very hot.

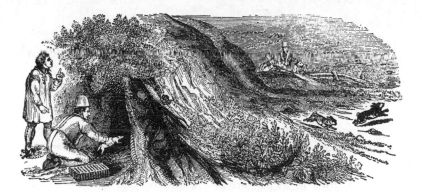

CHAPTER SEVEN
GAME MISCELLANEA

Game Soup

Carcases and trimmings of 2 partridges *or*
equivalent amount of any game.

1 oz. lean bacon.	1 oz. flour.
1 oz. butter.	1 quart stock.
1 onion.	A bunch of herbs.
1 carrot.	1 clove.
½ parsnip.	Some neat pieces of
1 stick of celery.	breast of bird.

Salt and pepper.

Put the pieces of carcase, the trimmings, and the bacon, with the fat, in a saucepan and fry them till brown. Remove the game and fry the sliced vegetables till brown. Add the flour and fry it till golden brown. Stir in the stock, bring to the boil, add the herbs and clove, return the game to the pan and simmer for 1½–2 hours. Meanwhile cut the pieces of breast meat into ¼-inch dice. Strain the soup, in it reheat the diced game, season carefully and serve.

Game Pie (Cold—no crust)

Take meat off raw bird (put aside) and boil carcase for about 5 hours to make a good jelly.

Put layers of chicken (or game meat) into a casserole with a layer of hard-boiled egg slices, and raw sausage meat and a little fat bacon or streaky pork cut into strips (if chicken, add the liver), sprinkle a little finely chopped parsley, pepper and salt and continue until the dish is three-quarters full. Pour strained stock in to just cover (retain the rest till later), and simmer slowly in the oven for an hour. When cold, remove fat from the top and pour in the remaining stock to fill with a lot of very finely chopped parsley and herbs (chervil especially) in it. Leave for top to set. Serve cold with separate salad. Jelly should be just wobbly when cut.

Game Pie Crust

1 lb. flour.   6 oz. lard.

1 teaspoonful salt. $\frac{1}{4}$ pint milk and water.

Sieve the flour and 1 teaspoonful salt. Melt the lard, add the milk and water and bring to the boil, then pour this mixture into the flour and mix with a wooden spoon into a soft dough. Leave until it is cool enough to handle before using.

Game Forcemeat

2 oz. suet.	¼ teaspoonful mixed
1–2 oz. ham or	herbs.
bacon (optional).	Grated rind of
4 oz. breadcrumbs.	½ lemon.
2 teaspoonfuls	Salt and pepper.
chopped parsley.	Beaten egg.

Chop the suet and ham (if used) and mix with the breadcrumbs. Add the parsley, herbs and lemon rind, season well and add enough beaten egg to bind. Use to stuff game, make forcemeat balls, etc.

Game Gravy

Bones, giblets *or*	1 clove.
trimmings of game.	6 peppercorns and 1
Cold water to cover.	piece of onion to
1 bay leaf.	each pint of water.
Thyme.	Salt.

Make stock from the above ingredients. Drain all fat from the roasting tin and rinse the tin with game stock, using no flour. Boil the gravy and skim it.

Game Chips

6 medium-sized	Deep fat.
potatoes.	Salt.

Scrub and rinse the potatoes. Peel them thinly and cut them into strips the size of a wooden match. Drop them into cold water as they are cut. Rise and drain and dry in a clean cloth. Put them into the frying basket and lower them gently into hot deep fat at 360°F. (Keep the heat fairly high, as the potatoes will have cooled the fat.) When the potatoes are soft but now brown, about 1 minute, lift out of the fat and heat the fat to 375°F. Put back the basket and leave in the fat until the potatoes are crisp and golden brown —about 2 minutes. Drain on absorbent paper, sprinkle with salt and serve immediately.

Red-currant Jelly

To 1 pint of juice allow 1 lb. of sugar.

Pick and wash some red currants, drain them, but leave them rather wet. Put them into a large jar or crock, stand this in a saucepan of water, and steam over the fire until all the juice is extracted from the fruit. Or the jar containing the fruit may be placed in a somewhat cool oven and left for several hours or even overnight. Then pour the currants with their juice into a jelly bag, and let them drain until the juice has ceased to drip. Do not use pressure if you want the best-quality jelly. Measure the juice and for each pint allow 1 lb. of sugar. Put both together in a preserving pan, and boil 5 minutes, or until the jelly will set. A large quantity may require rather longer, but it is much better to boil only a little at a time. Pot in small glass jars. This recipe can also be used for rowan or cranberry jelly.

Orange Salad

4 sweet oranges.	1 tablespoonful French
½ teaspoonful castor sugar.	dressing.

Chopped tarragon and chervil *or* chopped mint.

Peel the oranges thickly with a saw-edged knife, so that all the pith is removed. Cut out the natural orange sections. Place in a salad bowl, sprinkle with sugar. Pour the dressing over and sprinkle with tarragon and chervil or with chopped mint.

6 oz. cooked game
   (pheasant, hare, etc.).
2 oz. cooked ham.
Beetroot.

Potatoes.
White of 1 hard-boiled
   egg.
Stuffed olives.
Watercress.

For the dressing—
Yolk of 1 hard-boiled egg.
Black pepper and salt.
½ teaspoon made mustard.

2 tablespoons olive oil.
1 tablespoon white
   vinegar.

To make the dressing, remove the yolk from the hard-boiled egg, beat in a basin with the seasonings, stir in the oil and the vinegar. Mince the game and ham, moisten with 1 tablespoonful of dressing, turn into small moulds or patty tins and press down. Dice the beetroot, potatoes and egg white. Toss in the dressing and arrange on individual dishes. Turn the game moulds carefully on to the bed of vegetables. Garnish each with a slice of olive and arrange watercress round the edge.

Marinade

Marinading meat or game means to cover it with a mixture of wine, herbs, spices, onions and vinegar for any period up to 14 days. The effect of putting tough meat into this mixture is to break down the tissues and shorten the cooking time.

½ cup vinegar.
Grating of nutmeg.
Salt and pepper.
4 finely chopped
   onions.

1 cup red wine.
Bay leaf.
Small teaspoonful grated
   thyme.

Make a marinade of the seasonings, herbs, wine and vinegar, add the chopped onion and pour over the game meat.

[151]

1 quart jellied game   2 sticks of celery.
   stock.   2 egg whites and shells.
1 oz. gelatine.   1 glass sherry
Bouquet garni (parsley,   (optional).
   thyme, bay leaf). $\frac{1}{4}$ pint vinegar.

Let the stock become quite cold, and remove every particle of fat. Put it into a stewpan with the gelatine, herbs, celery cut into large pieces, the egg whites previously slightly beaten and the shells previously washed and dried. Whisk over heat until nearly boiling, then add the wine and vinegar. Continue the whisking until quite boiling, then reduce the heat and simmer for about 10 minutes, strain till clear, and use as required.

Croûtons

Take some rather stale and close-grained white bread, and cut it into $\frac{1}{4}$-inch slices; remove crusts and either cut slices into plain dice or stamp into fancy shapes with special cutters. Heat some butter until smoking but not brown, fry croûtons in this, tossing to colour on all sides.

Breadcrumbs

Fresh breadcrumbs: Remove crusts from slices of stale bread, then rub bread through a fine sieve with the palm of the hand.

Dried breadcrumbs: Put pieces of stale bread or crusts in a moderate oven, 350°F., and bake till crisp and pale brown. Crush on a pastry board with a rolling pin, then rub through a wire sieve. Store all prepared crumbs in an airtight tin.

Braised Chestnuts

Split the skins at the pointed ends and put the chestnuts into a saucepan; cover them over with cold water and bring to the boil. Take them out of the water and skin them. Put them back in a pan with just enough stock to cover, and simmer for 45 minutes or an hour.

Maître d'Hôtel Butter

Cream 3 oz. of butter. Then mix 1 tablespoonful of minced parsley (first dipped in boiling water) into butter. Beat in 1 tablespoonful of lemon juice drop by drop. Season with salt and cayenne pepper to taste. Spread this mixture about $\frac{1}{2}$ inch thick on a flat tin or board. Put in cool larder or fridge to harden and then cut into squares.

CHAPTER EIGHT

HANGING, HANDLING
AND PREPARATION
OF GAME

Hanging

The real purpose of hanging game is to enable the fibres of the flesh to break down and decompose so that the meat will be more tender. It is very difficult to give exact times as it depends entirely on personal taste. Some prefer slightly tougher meat with a fresh taste, while others enjoy very tender meat with decidedly 'high' smell and flavour. These times therefore are only very approximate, and are for average seasonable temperatures. If the weather is hotter than average, hang for the shortest length of time given, and if colder than usual, for the longest. The older the game, the longer it must hang. Birds are ready for cooking when the tail, inside leg, or breast feathers can be plucked out easily. Game birds are always hung by the neck (although some say you should hang a peasant by its feet, until the body drops!) Overhung flesh will have blueish patches on it. Game should always be hung in a shaded place in a current of air, well out of the reach of cats, dogs or foxes.

Partridge:	5-12 days.
Pheasant:	3 days to 2 weeks.
Grouse:	3–10 days.
Blackcock:	3–4 days.
Ptarmigan:	3–4 days.
Capercaillie:	Bury it in the ground for a few days, or hang it until it is really tender.
Pigeon:	2–3 days.
Quail:	Can be eaten straight away, or hung for up to 2 days.
Woodcock and Snipe:	Can be eaten straight away, or kept for up to 6 days, but remember that both woodcock and snipe are often cooked with the entrails left in them, so they shouldn't be left too long.

Wild Duck (Mallard, Teal, Widgeon, etc.):	Can be eaten straight away, or hung up to 2 days. If left any longer the flesh is liable to turn rank.
Wild Goose:	1–2 days.
Hare:	About 1 week without paunching, a little longer in cold weather. Suspend it by the hind feet with a bucket under the nose to catch the blood, which makes good gravy.
Rabbit:	Eat straight away with no hanging.
Venison:	3 days to 2 weeks. There is a great deal of difference between these times, but apart from taste, it depends on many factors. A young roe deer in perfect condition will only need about 3 days, while a tough old fallow or red deer could need a good two weeks to make it tender. For the average taste, test the hung meat every day by running a skewer into the haunch. So long as the skewer has no unpleasant smell when withdrawn the meat is in good condition, but if it does get rather too "high", wash it in warm water and dry it well before cooking. If there is no fly-free larder available, rub the carcase with a mixture of flour, powdered ginger, and pepper. The furrow of the backbone should be well dressed with pepper. Wrap the carcase in muslin before hanging in the larder, but inspect it every day and give it a fresh coating of flour and ginger when necessary. Wipe with a cloth to remove any moisture which may have formed.

Good game birds should be firm with plump flesh and weigh heavy for their size. Spurs short and round, flight feathers pointed, and the feathers under the wing downy. As the birds age, the flight feathers become rounded and the spurs more pointed. Another way of telling if the bird is young is by the feet, legs and beak which should be bright in colour and supple to the touch. Simple recipes can be used for young birds in good condition, but if they were battered in the shooting or are of doubtful age, it is far wiser to cook them for longer, to disguise some of these blemishes.

Young wild ducks and geese have bright bills and feet, and the feet of ducks are reddish in colour. The foot webbing in young birds can be torn quite easily.

The flesh of wild duck has a fishy flavour, but there are various ways of getting rid of this. 1, Simmer the duck for five minutes in salted water with an onion or carrot. 2, Put an onion and a tablespoonful of salt in the cavity and place the duck in a dish of boiling water $\frac{1}{4}$ inch deep. Bake for ten minutes in the oven, basting frequently. Then drain. 3, Simmer the duck for five minutes with any of the following in the cavity: a potato, an orange, apples, onions, or a lemon.

The fishy flavour in wild goose can be lessened by plunging it in boiling salt water with a pinch of bicarbonate of soda.

Preparation of Game Birds

Plucking   When the birds have been hung for the appropriate time they must be plucked. There are two ways it can be done, either by plucking the feathers in the direction in which they grow, or against the grain. It does not matter a great deal, just choose whichever is easiest for you. It is important not to tear the skin, especially the tender part over the breast. One perfects one's own method of plucking. Over the breast, hold down the flesh with the fingers of one hand outspread, while the other flicks out the feathers. It needs a light but firm touch, especially if the bird is over-hung, when it may tear easily, even though the feathers are looser. The large feathers on the wings should be plucked singly, and if they are tough to get out, use a pair of pliers. Start plucking at the top with the neck and wings, then the body and tail. When all the main feathers are out, remove little bits of down and fluff by burning very carefully over an open flame, swinging the bird gently over it until all the bits are burnt off. These downy feathers can also be removed by the more elaborate method of pouring melted paraffin wax over the bird, and when it is quite cool, peeling it off and all the feathers with it.

Drawing Slit the skin from the breast towards the head, making a slit just large enough to remove the crop and wind-pipe. Take these out carefully. Make another incision from the vent to the abdomen, and pull out the entrails, taking care not to break the gall bladder, which is attached to the liver. When all the entrails are out, wipe the inside of the bird, and also inside the neck with a damp cloth. If the gall bladder does break, wash the inside thoroughly, and dry afterwards with a cloth.

Trussing Lay the bird on its back and turn the wings under; bring the legs close to the body and put in a metal or wooden skewer, first through the flesh of the wing, middle of the leg, and the body, then out of the other side through the other leg and wing. Put a piece of string over each end of the skewer, pass it round the vent, fasten the legs tightly, and tie up firmly.

This is the basic method of trussing to keep the bird compact, but it varies slightly according to the type of bird. PHEASANT, PARTRIDGE, AND QUAIL: The legs should be pressed in under the breast, between it and the side bones, in order to plump up the breast. Pass a skewer through the pinions on the wings, and the legs, to keep them in place, and tie the legs together, but do not cross them.

GROUSE, BLACKCOCK, AND PTARMIGAN : Cut off the first two joints of the wings, leaving only one joint each. Press the legs down firmly to the sides between the side bone and the breast, and pass a skewer through the wings, legs and body in the same way as for basic trussing. Tie a piece of string round each end of the skewer, cross it over the back of the grouse round the body, and tie the legs together with it.

PIGEONS: Cut the head and neck off close to the body, and chop off the toes at the first joint. Cross the legs by cutting a slit in the skin of one and passing the other through it. Skewer and tie in the usual way.

SNIPE: Skin the neck and head. Twist the legs right round, so that the feet come close in to the body. Bring the head round and tuck the beak under a wing. Skewer the wings, and if a number of birds are being prepared, have the heads all on the same side. If the entrails are not removed from the bird before cooking, be very sure to remove the crop which could contain a lot of grit and spoil the whole dish.

WOODCOCK: These are trussed in the same way as snipe, although the beaks are put right through the thighs and body to act as skewers.

GOOSE: Chop off the neck close to the body leaving a large piece of skin to fold under. Chop off the two end pinions of the wings, so there is only one joint left on each. Cut the legs off at the first joint. Put a skewer through one wing, the body and then the other wing. Pass a second skewer through the end of the wing joint, the thick part of the leg, and out of the other side in the same way. Secure the legs with a skewer through a piece of the loose flap of skin, then under the first joint of the leg, through the body, under the other leg, through the flap of skin of the other side. Cut off the end of the vent and make a hole in the skin large enough for the tail to be pushed through, and fasten it there. Don't forget to put the stuffing inside the bird before this is secured. Tie with string where necessary.

DUCK: Truss in exactly the same way as Geese described above, but cut two joints off the wings.

CAPERCAILLIE: Truss as the basic recipe described on p.159.

To Bone Game Birds

Cut the neck off close to the body leaving a flap of skin to turn over. Lay the bird, breast down on a table, and make a cut through the skin right down the middle of the back. Then with the point of a sharp knife, work down one side, cutting as close to the bone as possible. Lift the flesh as you work, so you can see what you are doing, and take care not to cut through the skin. Disjoint the legs and wings from the body and keep scraping the flesh away from the carcase right round to the top of the breastbone. Do the same on the other side, and lift the carcase out. Bone the leg starting from where it was disjointed from the body, and scrape the meat away from this bone until the next joint is reached. Break the cleaned bone away from this and start on the next bone, gradually turning the leg inside out as you go. Bone the second leg, and then scrape off as much flesh from the wingbones as possible. Cut off the lower joints completely.

When all the bones are removed, spread the bird out, skin side down, and tidy it up by removing any pieces of sinew, or gristle, and any discoloured bits at the back or tail.

To Bard Game Birds

Game birds have little natural fat and are liable to dry out while being cooked unless they are protected in some way. Wrap either slices of fat bacon or thin pieces of salt pork round the birds and tie firmly in place with string. Bacon is usually used, but it does impart far more of its flavour to the bird than the rather milder salt pork.

Preparation of Hares

One hare serves 6–8 people.

Paunching: With a pair of scissors or a sharp-pointed knife, snip the skin at the fork and cut it up to the breast, being careful to cut the skin only. Pull the pelt gently away from the stomach, and open the paunch by cutting the inside skin in the same way as the pelt was cut. Draw out the entrails and dispose of them. Remove the kidneys and put on one side; also take out the liver. Be careful not to tear the gall-bladder, but keep it intact as it is cut away from the liver, and throw it away. Draw out the lungs and heart, and threw away the former.

Skinning: Cut the feet off at the first joint. Loosen the skin round the back legs with a sharp knife. Then holding the end of the leg, bend it at the joint. The flesh can then be grasped and the skin pulled off. Do the same to the front legs. Next, pull the skin off the head, cutting it through at the ears and mouth. The eyes should be cut out with a knife. Wipe over the whole animal, both inside and out, with a damp cloth.

Jointing: First remove the legs, cutting through the joints with a sharp knife. The hindlegs can be cut in two pieces each if the hare is a good size. Next cut the back into several pieces by inserting the sharp knife between the vertebrae.

Many people use a meat cleaver for jointing hares, but the bones splinter badly and these sharp bits can entirely ruin a well-flavoured dish. It is far better to find the junction between any of the bones with a heavy knife, and if it does not separate very easily, tap the back of the knife gently with a hammer. Cut the ribs in two lengthwise, and remove the head. Trim all the pieces of meat. Trimmings and any bits of skin and head can be used for flavouring in stews or soups.

Boning: Cut off the head and the forelegs and lay the hare on its back. Begin boning at the neck by cutting through the thin layer of flesh over the breastbone. Press the knife as close as possible, working away in little strokes, and lifting the freed flesh with the other hand, so that you can see what you are doing. In this way cut the flesh down to and along the backbone, being careful not to cut through the meat on the back of the hare. Disjoint the hindlegs carefully from the body and draw out the backbone. Now cut through the flesh of the legs and take out the bones cleanly using the point of the knife. Do the same with the forelegs, which were previously detached from the rest of the body. When all the bones have been removed spread the hare out and cut away all the sinews and trimmings. It will probably look rather ragged, but so long as there is a good straight piece of flesh from the back, the leg meat can be put inside this and the whole rolled together to form an oblong.

Trussing: Cut the sinews of the hind legs and bring the forelegs towards the back, flat against the sides, and skewer them. Now bring the hind legs forward flat against the front ones and skewer them. Press the head well back between the shoulders and run a skewer down the mouth and into the back to keep the head in position. Curl the tail up onto the back of the hare and fasten it there with a small skewer. Pass a piece of string round the end of each skewer, and tie on top of the back, so as to keep the legs well pressed to the body. Put a piece of foil over the head to stop it burning, particularly the ears, if you can bear to leave them on! If you are going to stuff the hare, don't forget to do this before it is tied up in all these knots.

Carving: Slices are cut out of the back from the neck downwards, rather like carving the breast of a turkey. When all the meat has been cut away from both sides of the spine, the legs are removed in the same way that you take a wing off a chicken. Then deal with the shoulders, by a semicircular cut round the joint.

Rabbits

One rabbit serves 3 to 4 people.

Rabbits are paunched in the same way as hares, but this should be done as soon as they are shot. Before rabbits are cooked, they should be soaked and washed in salt water for a time to make the flavour less strong.

Skinning, jointing, boning, and trussing are all exactly the same as for hares, but carving is a little different.

Carving: Separate the legs and shoulders on either side then divide the back crossways into equal parts. Use this method of carving for a small rabbit, but a very large one can be sliced in the same way as a hare.

Venison

Any animal with antlers is venison and although this can include a moose or a reindeer, in this country it is Red, Roe or Fallow deer. The flesh of venison should be dark and very finely grained with clear white firm fat. The meat of the Roe Deer is the finest, then the Fallow and last the Red Deer; the buck is superior to the doe in all types.

[164]

The haunch of venison is the hind leg and half the rump. These can be jointed separately, which makes it easier to cook. Between the rump and ribs is the saddle, which many people think is the best cut of all. Next come the shoulders. If these have been damaged by shot, they can be boned and used for stews etc., but undamaged ones are good for simple roasting dishes. The breast is always used for casseroles, soups etc.

The best cuts of venison, steaks, chops, roasts, and saddle have very little fat indeed, so they may need to be larded (see this page). This can be done either before or after marinating, but if it is done before, the meat will need slightly less time in the marinade.

If you have a whole venison, the joints are cut out as needed. The first cuts ready on the hung deer are the tender loin fillets with the kidneys attached, as the liver is taken out straight away when the deer is shot.

To Lard Game

This is a process whereby long strips of fat salt pork or bacon are threaded through the flesh with a special larding needle to provide extra moisture inside as well as on the skin.

PART TWO
FISH

The Angler

"He at the least hath his wholesome walk and merry at his ease, a sweet air of the sweet savour of the mead flowers; that maketh him hungry. He heareth the melodious harmony of fowls. He seeth the young swans, herons, ducks, coots, and many other fowl with their broods; which me seemeth better than all the noise of hounds, the blasts of horns, and the cry of fowls; than hunters, falconers, and fowlers can make. And if the angler take fish, surely then there is no man merrier than he in his spirit. Also, whoso will use the game of Angling, he must rise early, which thing is profitable to man in this wise, that is to wit, most to the heal of his soul. For it shall cause him to be holy; and to the heal of his body for it shall cause him to be whole. Also to the increase of his goods, for it shall make him rich."

CHAPTER NINE

SALMON
SEA TROUT
TROUT
CHAR

"This dish of meat is too good for any but anglers or very honest men."

IZAAK WALTON

Salmon

This superb fish which lives and feeds in the North Atlantic and ascends many of our rivers from January to November is, if cooked correctly, the ultimate in fish dishes.

Salmon range in size from 5 lbs upwards to as much as 30 lbs, but around 8 to 10 lbs is average. It can be cooked in a number of different ways as you will see from the recipes in this section, but poaching or baking in foil is, in most people's opinion the best method for retaining its perfect flavour.

Poached Salmon (*whole fish*)

Place the cleaned fish in a fish kettle and just cover with cold court bouillon (p. 285). Bring slowly to simmering point and cook very gently – the water must only tremble – allowing 8 mins per lb for fish weighing over 5 lbs. Drain and serve hot or if to be eaten cold, allow to cool in the bouillon to retain moisture of flesh. Hot poached salmon may be served with Sauce Bearnaise (p. 306) or Hollandaise (p. 304). Cold salmon with Sauce Mayonnaise (p. 305).

Poached Salmon (*steaks and cuts*)

Wrap steak or piece of fish in foil and cover with cold salted water in a pan which leaves no more than 2 or 3 inches space round and above the fish. Bring very slowly to simmering point, then cook very gently for 12–15 mins according to thickness of piece. Drain and serve hot or if to be eaten cold leave to cool in the foil in the water. Serve with sauces as recommended for whole fish.

Baked Salmon (*whole fish or cuts*)

Wrap fish in foil folding over the edges tightly. Butter or oil can be smeared over the fish if liked but not necessary. Bake in moderate oven (350° F. Gas 4) for approx. 15 mins to the lb. Leave to cool in foil if it is to be eaten cold.

Salmon Pâté

Cooked salmon.	Cream or mayonnaise.
Worcester or tomato	Black pepper.
sauce to taste.	(Butter).

Put salmon in liquidiser. Add enough cream or mayonnaise and sauce so that when blended, mixture is consistency of a meat pâté. (Put in small pots and pour over clarified butter.) An excellent use for odd bits of left-over salmon.

[171]

This mousse sets well without gelatine, and you serve it straight from a soufflé dish.

¾ lb. cold cooked salmon

White sauce made with 1 oz. butter, 1 oz. flour, ¾ pint milk.

| 2 oz. butter. | 1 – 2 tbs cream. |
| 1 – 2 tablespoons sherry. | salt and pepper to taste. |

Pound up flaked salmon in a bowl with a wooden spoon adding cold white sauce gradually. Add seasoning. Cream butter until soft, and half whip cream. Then gently stir this in with the sherry (vigorous stirring will curdle it). Add a few drops of cochineal if salmon is not a good pink. Turn into a soufflé dish and put in a cool place. When firm (about 15 minutes) pour over a thin layer of aspic. See page 152. Garnish this, when cool, with thinly sliced cucumber and finish with another layer of aspic.

Hot Salmon Soufflé

3½ oz. butter.	3 oz. plain flour.
1½ tablespoonsful anchovy essence.	4 egg yolks.
	1 pint cold milk.
Red pepper and salt.	10 oz. finely chopped
1 tablespoonful lemon juice.	raw salmon.
	3 boned anchovies.
6 egg whites, whipped stiff.	1 oz. butter.
	Chopped parsley.
Browned bread crumbs.	

Excellent soufflé for soufflé experts. Must be served immediately, with any good salmon sauce.

Put in a saucepan the butter, flour, anchovies, and anchovy

essence, egg yolks, salt and pepper, and just less than a pint of milk. Stir this all well together while it comes not quite to the boil. Then add two more tablespoonsful cold milk, lemon juice, salmon and egg whites.

Butter and paper a soufflé tin so that the paper stands about 4 inches above the tin, pour in the prepared mixture, sprinkle it with breadcrumbs, break ½ oz. butter in little pieces all over it, and bake in a moderate oven for three quarters of an hour. Meanwhile keep your fingers crossed. Remove from the oven, take off the paper band and replace with a folded napkin. Sprinkle with chopped parsley and bear triumphantly to the table. Go to town on the sauce as well.

Grilled Salmon Vermouth

2 fresh salmon steaks	Butter.
1 inch thick.	½ teaspoonful dried
Lime juice,	tarragon.
unsweetened.	Salt and black pepper.
4 oz. dry vermouth.	

A quick easy way to cook salmon. The fish will be moist and tender with an unusual flavour from the lime juice, vermouth and tarragon. If fresh limes are unobtainable, use bottled juice, unsweetened if possible.

Put the salmon steaks in a shallow fireproof dish and squeeze lime juice over them, dot generously with butter, and add salt and pepper and dried tarragon. Pour the vermouth round the steaks but not over them. Put the dish under the grill about 4 inches from the flame. Cook for about 10 minutes, basting once or twice after 5 minutes. Be careful not to wash the tarragon off the steaks. Turn the fish, season again, and grill for a further 5 or 6 minutes, basting towards the end of the cooking time. A little more vermouth can be added during the cooking if it gets too dry.

Salmon Steak Cussy

1 slice salmon steak	Salt.
2 inches thick.	1 chopped shallot.
Salad oil.	Cussy sauce.
Red pepper.	Prawns (optional).

Poached salmon steaks with mushroom and caper sauce. If you wish, a few prawns, heated in the bain marie, can be sprinkled over the steak when it is served.

Season the salmon steak with olive oil, salt and shallot, and red pepper. Put it in a baking tin or fireproof dish which can be stood in a bain marie or another tin or dish containing boiling water. Cover the salmon dish with aluminium foil. Cook in a moderate oven in the bain marie for 15 to 20 minutes.

Place the salmon on a very hot dish, pour some Cussy sauce over it (see page 315) and serve at once.

Slices of Salmon Suedoise

¼ inch thick salmon slice per person.	
Pepper, salt, and mustard.	Suedoise Sauce (see page 309.)
Raw egg.	1 oz. butter to each egg.
White breadcrumbs.	Deep oil or clarified butter.

Salmon slices in egg and breadcrumbs with a cold mayonnaise and horseradish sauce. Easy to cook, but it takes a little care to fry the slices without spoiling the look of the covering.

Season the salmon slices with salt, pepper and dry mustard. Beat up the egg and add warm butter. Dip the slices into this and then into breadcrumbs. Fry in deep oil or butter for six to eight minutes. Serve with Suedoise Sauce.

Salmon Cutlets à la Bergen

½ lb. cooked salmon.
2 tablespoonful liquid aspic jelly.
1 dessertspoonsful lemon juice.
French bread.
Clotted cream.
Cucumber salad.

1 tablespoonful thick Tartare Sauce.
¼ pint stiffly whipped cream.
Fresh butter.
Aspic jelly.
Red pepper.
Chopped parsley or tarragon or chervil.

Rich sharp salmon pâté on French bread.

A much more complicated recipe but one well worth doing for a special meal. It can be made ahead of time and looks so nice. Will also use up odds and ends of cooked fish.

Rub the salmon through a sieve or put through an electric blender and then mix it with the tartare sauce, the liquid aspic, the whipped cream and the lemon juice. Cut the French bread into quarter-inch slices and fry these in butter. When they are cool, mask them with clotted cream, and put on a good layer of the salmon mixture. Smooth it over with a wet warm knife so that it looks well, sprinkle the cutlets with finely chopped aspic jelly and with whichever herb you prefer. Dust with red pepper and serve with cucumber salad.

Kippered Salmon

Herring salt.
Rum or whisky.

Olive oil.
Demerara sugar.

Salmon.

Delicious smoked salmon, only possible if you can manage to do some home smoking (see page 286).

Cut the fish in half lengthways, remove the backbone and

[175]

wipe the fish clean with a dry cloth. Lay the halves in a big deep dish and cover all over with herring salt. Leave thus for 24 hours, then wipe off the salt and hang the fish up in a cold still place to drip for 6 hours. Put them back on a clean tray and cover them with olive oil and leave for another six hours. Drain away the oil and wipe the fish clean of it with a cloth soaked in spirit. Lay the fish in a clean dish yet again and cover with Demerara sugar, and leave them for another 24 hours. Wipe off the sugar and hang the fish to drain again, for six hours. Put back in the dish and cover with olive oil once more. Wait another 24 hours, drain and wipe clean with a cloth soaked in spirits and then the fish is ready to smoke.

The fire should be set with peat, oak chips, and oak saw-dust, and lit on two successive evenings. Leave the fish hanging over the fire even when it has gone out, during the first day. Then it is ready to eat.

A little juniper added to the fuel imparts a different flavour.

Baked Salmon New Orleans

2 lb. salmon.	½ cup olive oil.
1 teaspoonful sugar.	1 tablespoonful
Pinch of salt and	Worcestershire sauce.
pepper.	1 tablespoonful vinegar.
1 clove of garlic.	2 cupfuls uncooked
1 red chillie pod	diced potatoes.
(or less if not	3 oz. mushrooms.
liked too hot).	2½ cups cooked tomatoes.
1 onion.	

American-style recipe in which the strong taste of the sauce rather masks the delicate flavour of the salmon.

Sprinkle the cleaned salmon with salt and pepper, and put the garlic and chillie inside it. Mince the onion. Brown

the sugar in a pan and lay the salmon in it with the onions.
Cover with the tomatoes and all ingredients except the mushrooms. Bake in a hot oven for 15 minutes, then add the
mushrooms and bake again until the fish is tender.

CULINARY ARTS INSTITUTE ENCYCLOPEDIC COOK BOOK

Salmon Roe
(as a garnish)

Wash the roes thoroughly to clear them of all fibre, in
clean water and then drain them and set them on an oven tray
or tin plate and place them in a cool oven until quite dry.
Beat with a fork to separate the 'seeds', and place in a bottle,
corked, and store in a cool, dry place, where they will keep
for several weeks. They are used in spoonfuls, sprinkled over
white fish or other fish dishes as a garnish.

(As a Substitute for Caviare)

Wash the roes thoroughly in milk and water, and then in
clear water, removing all fibre scrupulously, and drain
thoroughly. Sprinkle 4 oz. of salt over each $1\frac{1}{2}$ lb. of the
spawn or roes and allow to remain in this for 48 hours,
turning occasionally in the brine. Then lay them on a board
in a warm place, such as the back of the stove or in front of
the fire, until quite dry (about 8 to 12 hours) . Crush with a
weight, press into a jar or jars, adding to each $1\frac{1}{2}$ lb. 12 drops
of the spirit of nitre and as much saltpetre as can be heaped
on a sixpence.

AN OLD RECIPE

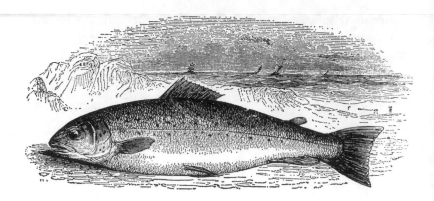

Sea Trout

For me, a sea trout at Christmas is something of a ritual. To admire the fish once more; to read the details on the label and look them up in my fishing diary, adds another dimension to angling. A winter wind whines outside the kitchen door as I go back in memory to a dusk-shadowed pool and the enchantment of a summer night long past . . . The gnats are dancing. There is the scent of bog-myrtle; the sound of water from the weir. Owls are hooting in the darkening woods. I feel the slow draw of the fish as it takes the fly; the nerve-tingling excitement as we fight it out in the darkness . . .

HUGH FALKUS from his book *Sea Trout Fishing*

Sea trout can be cooked by any of the recipes suitable for salmon. Fishmongers often call sea trout "salmon trout".

Jellied Sea Trout

Trout.   Aspic jelly (see
Cucumbers.   page 316).
Tomatoes.   Gherkins.

Jellied fish surrounded with bright vegetables. Looks pretty. Can be made well before you eat it.

The fish is cleaned and boiled in a fish kettle in salted water. Remove the fish from the kettle very gently as it must be kept whole. When drained lay it in a deep dish and surround it with peeled tomatoes, diced cucumber, and chopped gherkins. Cover the whole with aspic jelly and decorate with cucumber peel. Allow to set.

Sea Trout Cussy

1 sea trout.	4 oz. butter.
1 tablespoonful	Pinch of nutmeg.
chopped parsley.	Cussy sauce (see
2 chopped shallots.	page 315).

Pepper and salt.

Baked fish in Caper sauce.

Butter a big fireproof dish and put the whole cleaned fish into it. Put plenty of butter knobs on the fish, and sprinkle it with a mixture of the herbs and seasonings. Wrap the whole dish in foil, and bake in a moderate oven for 35 minutes. Remove the foil and allow to cook a little longer until the juices have nearly evaporated.

Pour Cussy Sauce over the fish and serve at once.

Sea Trout poached in Red Wine

1 3-lb. trout.	$\frac{1}{2}$ pint red wine.
Bunch of herbs.	1 bay leaf.
Pepper and salt.	6 peppercorns.
$\frac{1}{4}$ oz. flour.	$\frac{1}{2}$ oz. butter.

$\frac{1}{4}$ pint cream.

Salmon trout poached in red wine, served in the thickened cooking juices.

Place the whole cleaned fish in a buttered fireproof dish, and add the herbs, seasonings and wine. Put it in a slow oven and poach gently for 45 minutes, basting several times. When the fish is cooked, strain off the juices, make a roux with the butter and flour and add the juices gradually, stirring all the time. Then add the cream and reheat, adjust the seasoning, and serve separately.

A Cragg Cottage Breakfast

Clean and dry a small sea trout (1–1½ lb).
Wrap the fish in a slice of bacon.
Place fish on a rack inside a roasting tin.
Cook in a hot oven for about twenty minutes.
Serve hot with extra slices of bacon, slices of fried bread and slices of cold tomato.

KATHLEEN FALKUS

WD

Trout

"*Restorative Broth of trouts learn to make;*
Some fry and some stew, and some also bake.
First broyl and then bake is a rule of good skill;
And when thou dost a fortune a great trout to kill
then rost him and bast first with good claret wine:
But the calvor'd boyl'd trout will make thee to dine,
With dainty contentment both the hot and the cold;
And the marrionate trout I dare to be bold,
For a quarter of a year will keep to thy mind,
If covered close and preserved from the wind;
But mark well, good brother, what now I doe say,
Sauce made of anchovies is an excellent way,
With oysters and lemmon, clove nutmeg and mace,
When the brave spotted trout has been boyled apace,
With many sweet herbs; for forty years I,
in Ambassadours kitchins learned my cooker-y
The French and Italian no better can doe;
Observe well my rules and you'll say so too."

BARKER'S DELIGHT, 1657

Always spotted, but varying in colour according to locale, trout makes wonderful eating. There are many recipes, but the fish is so good that the simple ones take a lot of beating.

Very Small Trout Fried

Clean and dry the fish, season inside with salt and pepper, and fry in butter until crisp.

Large Reservoir Trout

Larger fish can be cleaned, fried gently in butter or split, the backbone removed and the fish dipped in oatmeal, fried in fat, and served with melted butter, or Maître d'Hôtel sauce (see page 153). Or wrapped in foil, and cooked as for baked salmon (see page 171).

Trout (or any muddy-tasting river fish)

Cut, clean, wash and dry your fish. Fillet if necessary. For each pound of fish take a piece of garlic the size of your little finger nail, half a teaspoonful of powdered turmeric, juice of half a lemon, salt and freshly ground pepper. Make these into a paste with a tablespoonful of olive or corn oil. Coat all the surfaces of the fish carefully with the mixture and leave to marinate for at least two hours. Grill.

BRIGID WITHERBY

The Irish Ghillies' Way of Baking Trout

All you do is land on a suitable island in an Irish lough—or anywhere else of course—gut and clean your fish quickly in the lake. Meanwhile build a largish wood fire in a hollow scooped in the ground. Make this fire in true pioneer's style so that the best possible draught blows along the trench.

[182]

Now all you need is a newspaper or two. Wet them in the lake also. When your fire has died down and you have a fair pile of hot ash, wrap your trout individually in wet newspaper having first stuck a knob of butter and some salt inside them. Screw them up tight and bury them in the ashes. When the paper at last begins to smoulder, they should be done.

Delicious. It is rather like tinfoil cooking, all the flavour is trapped inside.

COLIN WILLOCK

Otak-Otak

2 trout.	$\frac{1}{2}$ cup milk.
Cabbage leaves.	Butter.
$\frac{1}{4}$ teaspoonful coriander.	Frying oil.
Pepper and salt.	Chopped onion and garlic.
1 egg.	Red pepper.
Tomatoes.	Lettuce.

Indonesian recipe for stuffed trout. Takes a little time and trouble, but makes a change.

Beat the fish gently with a wooden meat mallet to loosen the skin; then carefully remove the flesh without damaging the skin. Remove all the bones from the flesh and chop the meat. Mix the meat with ground coriander, seasoning, onion, garlic, egg and milk, and fry it in the butter. Don't let the mixture get too dry. Fill the fish skins with this stuffing so that they look like whole fish again, wrap each fish in cabbage leaves, tie round with nylon thread if necessary, and steam for about 20 minutes.

Remove the cabbage leaves and put each fish in very hot frying oil to brown before serving.

Garnish with tomatoes, lettuce and chopped red pepper.

Trout.	Seasoning.
1 rasher back bacon.	½ slice of ham per fish. .
for each fish.	Sliced lemon.
Butter.	Parsley.

Rolled trout in bacon, fried, with ham and butter.

Clean and scale the trout. Season and wrap each fish in a rasher of bacon, tying with thread. Put sufficient butter in the pan to fry the fish and place the trout in the hot butter. Cut the ham into strips and put over the fish. Fry on both sides, and serve hot, pouring the juices, the ham and butter from the pan over the fish. Garnish with parsley and lemon slices.

Boiled Trout

Trout	Meat stock (beef
White wine.	stock cube).
Salt.	Cloves.
White bread crusts.	Cinnamon.
Thyme.	Marjoram.
Rosemary.	Parsley.
Butter.	Wine vinegar.

Another old but still excellent recipe for boiling fish. The gravy is as good as the fish.

Put the fish in a saucepan with enough white wine to cover them one inch deep. Add three tablespoonsful of meat stock and the salt. But first, stick a few cloves into the fish and rub them with some powdered cinnamon. Boil fast and when the fish is half cooked put in a handful of white breadcrusts, and turn down the flame. Add chopped herbs and let the mixture go on cooking till the fish is done and the gravy and breadcrumbs have blended together and are nice and thick. Melt a little butter in a pan with a tablespoonful of vinegar and add it to the gravy. Serve immediately.

Truite au Bleu

Trout.	Wine vinegar.
Court bouillon.	Sauce Hollandaise (see page 304).

Classic recipe for "blueing" trout.

Clean but do not scale the fish. Place in a dish, and pour enough vinegar over it to coat the whole surface. Have enough herb-flavoured court bouillon boiling to cover the fish. Put in the fish, bring the bouillon to the boil, and remove the saucepan. Cover it tightly and let it stand for five minutes before removing the fish carefully and serving it with good sauce.

Hell-fire Trout

Trout.	Butter.
Parsley.	Chives.
Garlic.	Shallots.
Basil.	Salt and pepper.
Carrot.	Leek.
Onion.	Cloves.
Red wine.	White wine.
Mushrooms.	

This is a very old recipe, but produces a tasty fish in wine gravy, and is well worth trying.

Clean and prepare the fish. Work together the herbs and seasonings and mushrooms with enough butter to make a filling for the fish. Put the fish, stuffed with this mixture, into a fireproof dish just bit enough to hold them and pack round a carrot, a leek, and an onion stuck with three cloves. Pour over a mixture of wines in the proportion of two-thirds white to one-third red, enough to cover the trout by about an inch. Cook over a fast flame and when the liquor is boiling fast, set light to the vapour. Go on cooking until the liquid has thickened almost to the consistency of sauce, remove the vegetables, adjust the seasoning and serve.

Recipe from *The Compleat Angler*

Take your Trout, wash, and dry him with a clean napkin; then open him, and having taken out his guts, and all the blood, wipe him very clean within, but wash him not; and give him three scotches with a knife to the bone, on one side only. After which take a clean kettle, and put in it as much hard stale beer, (but it must not be dead), vinegar, and a little white wine and water, as will cover the fish you intend to boil: then throw into the liquor a good quantity of salt, the rind of a lemon, a handful of sliced horse-radish root, with a handsome little faggot of rosemary, thyme, and winter savory. Then set your kettle upon a quick fire of wood, and let your liquor boil up to thy height before you put in your fish; and then, if there be many put them in one by one, that they may not so cool the liquor as to make it fall. And whilst your fish is boiling, beat up the butter for your sauce with a ladleful or two of the liquor it is boiling in. And being boiled enough, immediately pour the liquor from the fish: and being laid in a dish, pour your butter upon it; and strewing it plentifully over with shaved horse-radish, and a little pounded ginger, garnish the sides of your dish, and the fish itself, with a sliced lemon or two, and serve it up.

A Grayling is also to be dressed exactly after the same manner, saving that he is to be scaled, which a Trout never is; and that must be done either with one's nails, or very lightly and carefully with a knife, for fear of bruising the fish. And note, that these kinds of fish, a Trout especially, if he is not eaten within four or five hours after he be taken, is worth nothing.

[186]

Char

The flesh is flaky and orange coloured.   Any recipe for trout can also be used for char.

Char à la Creme

The fish.	Cup of fresh cream.
Milk.	1 clove of garlic.
Flour.	Chopped parsley.
Butter.	Slices of lemon.

Salt and pepper.

Butter-fried fish in garlic cream sauce.

Clean the fish and remove head and fins.   Dip in milk and flour, and fry in butter.   Put on a plate and season with salt and pepper.   Add to the remaining butter in the pan a cup of fresh cream, the crushed garlic and the parsley, beat all well together and heat.   Pour the sauce over the fish and serve with slices of lemon.

"LA PÊCHE ET LES POISSONS DE RIVIÈRE" MICHEL DUBORGEL

Potted Char

Cook in the oven with the head on and when the eyes go white, then it is ready. Flake fish off the bones, mix into a paste with cream or white sauce, adding seasoning as required. Put into a pot and press down tight, then pour melted butter over the top and allow to set.

LOCAL WINDERMERE RECIPE

Butter the interior of an earthenware crock with a well fitting lid. Place in it pieces of fresh char with a few peppercorns, pinch of mace and small quantity of allspice. Add good quality fish stock (bones and heads made up with white wine) to almost cover, and cook for 1 hour in moderate (325°—350°) oven with lid weighed down. Cool, drain, remove skin and bones, pound flesh in mortar with clarified butter. Press through fine sieve and pot, covering with fine layer of clarified butter.

BRIGID WITHERBY

CHAPTER TEN

PIKE BREAM
RUFFE TENCH
CARP BARBEL
PERCH GUDGEON
ROACH LOACH
RUDD BLEAK
EELS GRAYLING

Pike

"There was a Pike taken at Hailbrun, in Swabia, in 1497 with a brazen ring attached to it, on which was inscribed in Greek characters 'I am the fish which was first of all put into the lake by the hands of the governor of the universe, Frederick the Second, the 5th October 1230'. This fish must have been at least two hundred and sixty seven years old, and it is said to have weighed three hundred and fifty pounds."

"A slim young pike with smart fins
And grey striped suit, a young cub of a pike
Slouching along away below, half out of sight,
Like a lout on an obscure pavement."

FROM ''FISH'' BY D. H. LAWRENCE

Pike with Horseradish Sauce

The fish. 2 oz. butter. Flour. Horseradish. Boiled fish with hot horseradish sauce to lift the flavour.

Clean the Pike but do not scale or remove head. Place the fish in enough lightly salted water to cover it. The fish can be rolled if he is too big for the saucepan. Simmer for 20 minutes. Drain fish, but keep liquor.

Melt the butter in a pan and add a tablespoonful of plain flour, blend, and then add sufficient of the fish liquor to make a sauce the consistency of thin cream, heating gently and stirring all the time. Just before serving, add grated horse-radish to the sauce, but do not cook further. Serve the fish and sauce separately.

MRS. SPENCER'S SWEDISH RECIPE

Pike with White Wine

The fish. $\frac{1}{2}$ glass white wine.
Chopped onions.   Yolk of one egg.
                3 oz. butter.

Fish poached in wine, with egg sauce.

Clean the fish and put it in a fireproof dish with the butter and surround with the onions. Pour half a glass of white wine over the fish and cover the dish with aluminium foil. Bake for half an hour in a medium oven. Strain off the liquid and thicken it with the beaten yolk of egg and a little melted butter, and pour over the fish before serving.

Baked Pike

The fish.   Cream or top of the
Breadcrumbs.   milk.
                Beaten egg.

Pike baked in egg and breadcrumbs, with cream to enrich it. Serve with sauce Tartare or any good fish sauce (see sauce section).

Clean the fish, remove head and scales, and cut into pieces. Roll the pieces in beaten egg and dip in breadcrumbs. Place in a buttered fireproof dish and bake in the oven. Ten minutes before serving, pour over the cream and put back in the oven. The breadcrumbs will take up the cream, and the dish can then be placed under the grill for a minute or two to brown off the top.

MRS. SPENCER'S SWEDISH RECIPE

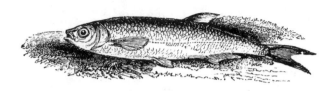

Bleak, Loach, and Gudgeon

Three little fishes hardly worth cooking, but if you must, look up the recipes for smelt and cook them likewise.

Roach and Rudd

These two fish of the carp family make good eating just cleaned, dipped in milk, rolled in seasoned flour, and fried in butter. Serve with melted butter and slices of lemon.

Carp

Blue Carp

| The fish. | Mixed herbs. |
| Sliced onions. | Peppercorns. |

Wine vinegar.

Classic recipe for blueing carp, served with a piquant sauce. The fish is gently boiled.

Clean the fish but do not scale. Tie the fish head to tail in a circle and put into a pan, covered with vinegar. Bring to the boil and add other ingredients. Simmer very gently until the fish is tender, but still firm. Lift out carefully, and wash in hot water. Serve on a hot dish with whipped fresh cream, horseradish cream, or browned butter containing chopped capers and parsley.

"500 RECIPES FROM ABROAD" MARGUERITE PATTEN

When preparing carp for cooking it is best to give them a good soak to remove the muddy flavour. Two soaks in salted water, followed by one soak in salted water with a little vinegar added. This is done after scaling and cleaning. Be very careful when removing the head to take away the gall stone which is just behind it, or the fish will taste bitter.

Handful chopped	Butter.
sorrel.	Chopped chives.
Bread.	Parsley.
Shallots.	3 eggs, hardboiled.
Cream.	3 raw yolks.
Salt and pepper.	Thyme.
Garlic.	Mushrooms.
Bayleaf.	Capers.
Plain flour.	Fish stock.
Chopped anchovies.	Lemon juice.

Rather a lot of ingredients to produce grilled stuffed carp in a rich sauce. All very tasty, but more of the other ingredients than of the carp.

Put a handful of prepared, washed and chopped sorrel, a piece of butter, a piece of bread, chopped chives, parsley, and shallots into a saucepan, and simmer for 10 minutes; add some cream and simmer till mixed. Hardboil three eggs, chop the yolks and add to the mixture with three raw yolks, salt and black pepper. Stuff the cleaned carp with this mixture and sew it up, put the whole to marinate in oil seasoned with salt, pepper, chives, garlic, thyme, and bayleaf. When ready, grill, basting with the marinade.

Put chopped mushrooms in a saucepan and simmer in a little butter, let them cool and add a pinch of flour, capers, chopped anchovies, parsley, chives, shallots, butter, stock.

salt and pepper. Cook gently and finish with a little lemon juice or a dash of vinegar.

Serve the carp on a hot dish with this sauce.

MANUEL DE LA FRIANDAISE, 1796

Gingerbread Carp

1 2-lb. carp.	¼ pint wine vinegar.
1 oz. each currants	1 onion.
and seedless raisins.	3 cloves.
1 lemon, sliced.	2 oz. gingerbread.
1 bay leaf.	1 level tablespoonful flour.
2 tablespoonsful demerara sugar.	

Sweet gingery, fruity sauce over lightly boiled fish, try it on yourself before making it for a dinner party.

Put ¼ pint of water into a saucepan and add to it the vinegar, fruit, lemon and onion, and herbs, and bring to the boil. Put the scaled and cleaned fish into the saucepan and simmer it gently for 30 minutes. Remove the fish to a warmed dish. Put the gingerbread, sugar, and flour into a bowl and moisten it with water, and then blend it with the cooking liquor. Stir till it boils, add seasoning to taste, simmer until the sauce is reduced to a reasonable thickness, remove the bay leaf and clove, pour over the fish and serve hot.

Compleat Angler recipe

Take a Carp, alive if possible, scour him, and rub him clean with water and salt, but scale him not; then open him; and put him, with his blood and his liver, which you must save when you open him, into a small pot or kettle; then take sweet marjoram, thyme, and parsley, of each half a handful, a sprig of rosemary, and another of savoury; bind

them into two or three small bundles and put them in your
Carp, with four or five whole onions, twenty pickled oysters,
and three anchovies. Then pour upon your Carp as much
claret wine as will only cover him; and season your claret
well with salt, cloves, and mace, and the rinds of oranges
and lemons. That done, cover your pot and set it on a quick
fire till it be sufficiently boiled. Then take out the Carp;
and lay it with the broth, into the dish; and pour upon it
a quarter of a pound of the best fresh butter, melted, and
beaten with half a dozen spoonfuls of the broth, the yolks
of two or three eggs, and some of the herbs shred. Garnish
your dish with lemons, and so serve it up. And much good
do you.

"THE COMPLEAT ANGLER"

Carp à la Russe

The fish.	Glazed onions.
Flour.	Mushrooms.
Butter.	Sour cream.
2 glasses dry white	1 tablespoonful vinegar.
wine.	2 tablespoonfuls grated
Sauerkraut.	cheese.

Carp poached in white wine and served with very sharp
vegetable sauce. Only for those who like sauerkraut.

Clean and scrape the fish and cut it into sections. Roll
the pieces in seasoned flour and place in a buttered oven
dish. Add the white wine and heat on a low flame until the
wine is almost boiling, then put the pan in a moderate oven.
Have ready some sauerkraut, and the glazed onions and mushrooms. When the fish is cooked, add some sour cream and
the vinegar to the gravy, and the cheese. Serve the fish on
a bed of the vegetables with the gravy over. Garnish with
small pickles.

"GUIDE TO GOOD FOOD AND WINES" ANDRÉ SIMON

Perch

"Perch and small boys have a good deal in common. Both species go around in gangs of anything from two to two dozen or more. Both species are rather greedy, rather ferocious and rather beautiful. In fact I would say that the perch is more beautiful than the boy, though not nearly so interesting."

"FISHING FOR BEGINNERS" MAURICE WIGGIN

Perch in White Wine

White wine.	2 oz. flour.
Salt and pepper.	Chopped parsley.
Bouquet garni.	Sliced onion.
2 oz. butter.	The fish.

Fish poached and served in its own thickened sauce.

Put the cleaned fish in a fireproof dish, and cover with the white wine. Add salt, pepper, sliced onion and bouquet garni. Cook for a quarter of an hour until the fish flakes easily in the fingers. Remove the skin, and place the perch on a serving dish. Make a roux with the butter and flour and blend in the liquor in which the fish has cooked. Add some chopped parsley which has been lightly fried in butter and pour the sauce over the fish. Serve very hot.

Perch à la Belenne

Fresh perch.	Olive oil.
Paprika.	Salt.
Shallots.	Gherkins.
Anchovy fillets.	Sherry.

Espagnole Sauce.

This recipe for baked perch takes a little time and trouble to prepare, but the result with the fish served in its own greaseproof paper wrapping is very good indeed.

Wash, scale, and cut off the fins. Dry the fish well with a cloth and season with olive oil, paprika, salt, finely chopped shallots, and gerkins, and on each fish put three anchovy fillets in a slanting position. Wrap each perch in heart-shaped pieces of greaseproof paper, turning up the edges of the paper so the liquid will not drain away. Into each fish pour 1 tablespoonful of sherry and Espagnole sauce, fold the top of the paper over, lift each piece carefully into a baking tin and cook in a moderate oven for about 15 minutes. When the paper is brown, the fish will be cooked, and they should be lifted in this on to the individual plate for serving.

Beignets de Perche de Tante Maria Duborgel

The fish.	White of egg.
Flour.	Brandy.
Olive oil.	Lemon quarters.
	Salt.

Fish cooked in batter.

Take any sized perch, clean, skin, and fillet it. Make a batter as follows: Put into a bowl a quarter of a pint of water, add a pinch of salt and stir in just before the mixture

[198]

is completely blended. Stirring all the time add a spoonful of olive oil and a spoonful of brandy. Leave the batter until just before you use it, then fold in a white of egg beaten stiff. Cover the fillets with this mixture, and put them into a very hot frying oil. Serve with lemon quarters.

"LA PÊCHE ET LES POISSONS DE RIVIÈRE" MICHEL DUBORGEL

Perch Souché

Perch.
Lemon juice.
½ oz. glaze if
   available.
Bunch of mixed
   herbs.
12 peppercorns.
Salt.
3 raw egg whites.
Lettuce.

Butter.
1 wineglassful white
   wine.
3 medium onions, sliced.
Strip of celery.
4 cloves.
1 dessertspoonful Bovril.
Fresh parsley, tarragon,
   chervil.
½ beef stock cube.

Herb soup and fish combined—very pleasant and filling.

Clean and fillet the fish and put to marinate in a well-buttered fireproof dish with white wine and a little lemon juice. Meanwhile, put all the fish trimmings in a saucepan with the sliced onions, glaze, Bovril, ½ pint beef stock, peppercorns, salt, celery, and cloves, and simmer for about ½ hour. Strain it and skim off the fat, add the marinade from the fish, add three raw egg whites to each quart of liquor, and whisk very well, bring just to the boil and simmer for 10 minutes. Strain again, and then add the fish fillets, and the fresh parsley, tarragon, and chervil chopped small and the lettuce cut into strips and shreds, simmer for about 8 minutes, and then serve in deep bowls with Grissini or very crisp dry toast.

"LA PÊCHE ET LES POISSONS DE RIVIÈRE" MICHEL DUBORGEL

Bream

Stuffed Bream

1 bream weighing	Flour.
1½–2 lb.	1 tablespoonful lemon
1 oz. butter.	juice.
Salt and pepper.	Forcemeat.

For the Forcemeat

½ small onion, chopped.	1 dessertspoonful chopped parsley.
1 oz. grated cheese.	Grated lemon rind.
2 oz. sliced mushrooms.	Salt and pepper, nutmeg.
1 small cupful cooked rice.	Cayenne pepper.
	1 oz. butter.
1 tablespoonful chopped chives.	4 tablespoonfuls cream.
	1 beaten egg.

Baked, stuffed fish. This is a good recipe with wide uses.
Fry the onion and mushrooms in butter and mix with the
rice and cheese, add all other ingredients and blend well.

Wash and clean the fish and put nearly all the butter in the bottom of a fireproof dish. Stuff the fish with the forcemeat and place in the dish. Sprinkle it with flour and seasoning, and dot with the rest of the butter, then sprinkle with the lemon juice. Cover the dish with greased paper or foil, and bake in a moderate oven for 40–50 minutes according to the size of the fish. This recipe can also be used for fresh haddock, hake, halibut, or cod.

Breme à la Mode du Pecheur

The fish.   White wine.

Shallots.   Butter.

Breadcrumbs.

Simple recipe for baking fish in white wine.

Place the cleaned fish upon a bed of chopped shallots and breadcrumbs, in a fireproof dish, and cover the fish with the same mixture. Add the white wine and part of butter and cook in a medium oven for 25 minutes, adding wine and butter as needed to keep the fish moist.

"GUIDE TO GOOD FOOD AND WINES" ANDRÉ SIMON

Baked Bream

Baked fish with onions and garlic. Highly flavoured.

Clean the fish and remove head and fins. Score the sides. Chop the onion and garlic and place this in the bottom of a fireproof dish. Slice the lemon thinly and put one slice in each of the scores on the fish. Lay the fish in the dish and squeeze the juice from any of the lemon that is left over on to the fish. Pour two tablespoonfuls of oil over the fish and sprinkle with breadcrumbs. Cover with lid or aluminium foil and cook in a moderate oven for 30 minutes. Remove the foil and leave the fish in the oven until the breadcrumbs are browned and the fish is cooked right through. Serve very hot.

MRS. PILCHER'S RECIPE

Tench

"The tench is the physician of fishes, for the Pike especially, and that the Pike, being either sick or hurt, is cured by the touch of the Tench. And it is observed that the tyrant Pike will not be a wolf to his physician, but forbears to devour him though he be never so hungry."

IZAAK WALTON

Tench à la Poulette

The fish.   ½ litre white wine.
Salt and pepper.   1 oz. flour.
2 oz. butter.   Bouquet garni.
Fish pieces in plain white wine sauce.

Cook the cleaned fish in court bouillon, and remove the skin. Cut into small pieces. Make a roux with the butter and flour and add the wine, let this cook for 10 minutes, gently, stirring with a wooden spoon. Add the pieces of fish, the bouquet garni, and the seasoning, and let it simmer gently for 10 minutes more. Then blend into this, two beaten egg yolks. Remove the bouquet garni. Garnish with chopped parsley and serve hot.

"LA PÊCHE ET LES POISSONS DE RIVIÈRE" MICHEL DUBORGEL

Stuffed Tench

The fish.   Breadcrumbs.
Chopped parsley.   Hardboiled egg.
Chopped mushrooms.   White wine.

Baked stuffed fish cooked in white wine. Very savoury dish.

Split and clean the fish and stuff with a mixture of mushroom, egg, breadcrumbs, and parsley. Place in a fireproof dish and cook in oven for 30 minutes basting frequently with white wine.

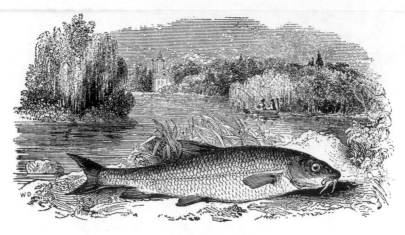

Barbel

Boiled Barbel in Court Bouillon

Court bouillon.   Butter.

Parsley.   Capers.

Boiled fish in thin caper sauce.

Clean the fish and boil in court bouillon. Serve in a sauce made by reducing two cupfuls of the court bouillon, thickened with a nut of butter, some chopped parsley and capers.   If served cold, provide Mayonnaise (p. 305) or Vinaigrette sauce (p. 303).

"LA PÊCHE ET LES POISSONS DE RIVIÈRE" MICHEL DUBORGEL

Stuffed Barbel

Mushrooms.   Hardboiled egg.

Bechamel sauce.

Baked stuffed fish in white sauce.

Clean and split the fish and stuff with chopped mushrooms and hardboiled egg.   Cook in a fireproof dish and serve covered with white sauce.

"LA PÊCHE ET LES POISSONS DE RIVIÈRE" MICHEL DUBORGEL

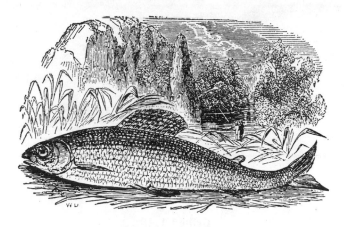

Grayling

"Umbar or grayling is an amorous fish, that loves a frolic as he loves his life, whose teeth water after every wasp, as his fins flutter after every fly. Pray, when you fish him, fish him finely, for he loves curiosity, neat and slender tackle; and ladylike, you must touch him gently, for to speak plain English, he is tender about the chaps."

FRANCK

Grayling should be eaten very fresh. It has an aroma of water thyme, and this must not be allowed to fade before the fish is cooked. Any recipe for trout will do for grayling, but the scales should be removed carefully, without bruising the fish, before cooking.

Buttered Grayling

Deep fried fish with butter.

Clean, scale and remove head and tail. Season inside with salt and pepper and drop into deep fat. Turn once and when the fish is done, remove and drain carefully. The skin should come off quite easily now, and the fish is served with plenty of melted butter.

Eels

Grilled Eel

Clean and skin the eels and cut them into chunks. Dip in flour, or breadcrumbs, and grill or fry. Serve with tomato sauce, or with lemon slices and chopped parsley.

Jellied Eels

2 lb. eels.	1 sprig of parsley.
1 large onion.	2 pints cold water.
1 bay leaf.	Whites and shells
1 tablespoonful vinegar.	of two eggs.
2 oz. leaf gelatine.	Salt and pepper.

Traditional recipe for jellied eels to eat cold.

Clean and skin the eels and put into a saucepan with the water and all ingredients except the eggs and gelatine. Simmer until the eels are tender. Take out the fish, cut into pieces and remove the bones. Strain the liquid and return to the pan, and add the crushed egg shells and lightly whisked whites of the eggs. Add the gelatine and bring to the boil. Simmer for 2 minutes and strain again. Line a mould with the pieces of eel, add the jelly and leave to set.

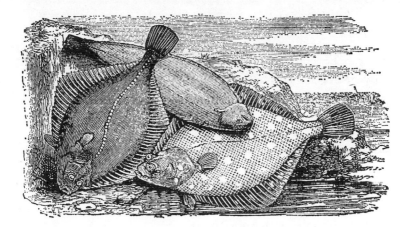

CHAPTER ELEVEN

SOLE
PLAICE
FLOUNDER
DAB
TURBOT
HALIBUT
SKATE
BRILL

Sole

Sole can be cooked in so many ways with so many sauces and vegetables. Dover sole is the best, and is quite different from Lemon sole, though both may be cooked in the same way.

Fillets of Sole Florentine

Fillets of sole.   Lemon juice.
Butter.   Leaf spinach.
Pepper and salt.   White sauce.
Fillets of sole with spinach.

Cook the fillets of sole in butter, season with pepper and salt and lemon juice. Line a fireproof dish with leaf spinach boiled and drained and tossed in butter. Place the fillets of sole on the spinach, cover with white sauce, and brown in the oven.

Fried Sole

Remove the dark skin and dip in flour, sprinkle with salt and pepper and lemon juice, and then dip into beaten egg and breadcrumbs and fry in pure oil, very hot.

Fillets de Sole Bonne Femme

8 fillets sole.   Juice of half a lemon.
$\frac{1}{2}$ pint dry white   2 tablespoons chopped
   wine.   parsley.
1 sliced carrot.   Salt and pepper.
1 sliced onion.   Bouquet garni.
4 oz. button   Sauce Hollandaise made
   mushrooms.   with four yolks.
                 $1\frac{1}{2}$ oz. butter.

Classic recipe for sole cooked in white wine and mushrooms with Hollandaise sauce.

Wash and dry the fillets. Fold the ends under and place in a lightly buttered fireproof dish. Lay the sliced vegetables round, season well, and add the bouquet garni. Pour the wine over and cover the dish with buttered greaseproof paper, and then poach the fish in a moderate oven. Meanwhile, wipe and slice the mushrooms and place them in a pan with the butter, lemon juice, and seasoning. Cover with greaseproof paper and then the lid. Shake over a gentle heat for 5–7 minutes. Keep hot.

Make the Sauce Hollandaise (see Chapter sixteen) using 2 tablespoonfuls of the fish liquor for the base. Add the mushrooms and parsley.

When the fish is cooked, remove it from the pan and place on a hot dish. Reduce the remaining liquor until only two tablespoonfuls remain, and add this to the sauce. Pour the sauce over the fish and place the dish under a very hot grill until the food is lightly browned.

"THE IRIS SYRETT COOKERY BOOK"

Sole à la Bon Homme

1 sole.	Butter.
Lemon juice.	Bon Homme sauce. (see page 317)
Stuffing.	Paprika.

Stuffed baked white fish, covered with a rich sauce. It requires many ingredients with the sauce and is a recipe to be used for special occasions as it is complicated but delicious. Can be used for all large flat fish.

Remove the skin from a sole, trim off the fins, head and tail and wash it well in salted water. Dry it carefully, then with the point of a knife split the underneath fillets straight down, breaking the bone about an inch from the tail. Break the bone also about an inch from the head, and very carefully remove the bone and fill up the space with the farce. Put the sole on a well buttered dish, farce side down, sprinkle with a little lemon juice and salt. Cover with buttered paper or foil and bake in a moderate oven for about 15 minutes. Remove from the oven, pour over the Bon Homme sauce, brown under the grill for a few minutes and sprinkle with paprika. Serve, in the same dish, as hot as possible.

FARCE. Mix all the ingredients together carefully before using as a stuffing.

Stuffing

8 raw oysters, diced.	4 mushrooms, diced.
Liquor from the oysters.	4 soft herring roes (diced) fresh or tinned.
Teaspoonful chopped parsley.	1 ounce fresh white breadcrumbs.
1 oz. warm butter.	1 raw egg yolk.
Saltspoonful curry powder.	Strained juice ½ lemon.

Sole Dugléré

1 sole.	Breadcrumbs.
2 tomatoes.	1 dessertspoonful tomato purée.
1 small onion.	
1 glass dry white wine.	1 oz. butter.
Parsley.	1 dessertspoonful flour.

Sole in white wine and tomato sauce.

Peel the tomatoes and remove the pips, and then chop them. Peel and chop the onion. Melt 1 oz. of butter and blend with the flour. Put the chopped vegetables and the parsley in a fireproof dish and lay the seasoned sole on them. Add the white wine, and cook gently in the oven. Remove the sole from the liquor and boil the liquor until it is reduced by half. Blend the flour and butter previously combined, with this liquor, add the tomato purée. Pour the sauce over the sole and cook 5 minutes more in a hot oven.

Plaice

Plaice is in season from May until Christmas, and is best eaten filleted and fried.

Fried Plaice

Either dip the filleted plaice in seasoned flour and fry in a shallow pan, or dip into seasoned flour, and coat with egg and breadcrumbs, or dip into batter, and fry in deep fat.

Serve with Sauce Tartare (see page 305).

Stuffed Plaice

1 large plaice about	Browned breadcrumbs.
1½ lb.	Stuffing.

½ pint seasoned brown stock.

Remove the dark skin only from the plaice and cut down the centre as for filleting, on that side only. Raise the fillets but do not remove them. Fill the cavity with the stuffing and place in a fireproof dish. Pour the stock over and bake for 45 minutes in a moderate oven. Sprinkle over the browned breadcrumbs just before serving.

Stuffing

4 tablespoonfuls breadcrumbs.	¼ teaspoonful dried herbs.
1 oz. chopped suet, or butter.	Grated lemon rind.
	½ teaspoonful salt.
1 teaspoonful chopped parsley.	½ teaspoonful pepper.
	Egg to bind.

Mix all the ingredients together.

Flounder

Fried Fillets of Flounder

Dip the fillets in beaten egg, and then in breadcrumbs, and fry in butter. Or dip in flour and fry in deep fat.

Swedish Rolled Fillets with Lemon Sauce

This dish can be made with any flat fish, but is especially good made with flounder.

Filleted flounder.   Court bouillon.
Shrimps.   Lemon slices.
Dill or parsley.   Lemon Sauce.

Make each fillet into a roll and skewer with a cocktail stick. Place in a saucepan and cover with court bouillon. Simmer for 10 minutes. Drain the fish and keep hot on a plate while making the sauce. Pour the sauce over the unskewered fillets, garnish with the shrimps, parsley or dill, and lemon sections.

Lemon Sauce (see page 302).

"500 FOREIGN DISHES" MARGUERITE PATTEN

Dab

Cook in the same way as flounder.

Dab with Roe Stuffing

6 dabs.   Lemon juice.
Roe stuffing.   1 oz. butter.

Cut off the heads of the fish and wash. Remove the dark
skin. Cut the fish down that side as if for filleting and lift
the flesh but do not remove. Fill with the roe stuffing.
Place the fish in a fireproof dish and sprinkle with lemon
juice. Pour melted butter over the fish and bake for 20
minutes in a moderate oven. Serve with Hollandaise Sauce
(see page 304).

Roe Stuffing

4 soft herring roes. $\frac{1}{2}$ oz. flour.
Milk.   Pinch cayenne.
Salt and pepper.   Lemon juice.
            Tablespoonful breadcrumbs.

Wash the roes and place them in a fireproof dish and just
cover with milk. Add seasoning, cover with a lid or foil,
and cook in a very slow oven for 30 minutes. Melt the
butter in a saucepan and mix in the flour. Add the milk
from the roes and cook till the sauce thickens. Add the
beaten roes to the cooled sauce. Season to taste, and add
breadcrumbs if the mixture is not thick enough.

Turbot

The best of the large flat fish, turbot can be cooked "Bonne Femme" or "Florentine" as in the recipes for Sole, or in any of the ways suitable for white fish with any of the sauces.

Baked Turbot with Shrimp Sauce

Turbot. Salt and pepper.
Squeeze of lemon. Cream.

Slice the turbot into large pieces and place in a fireproof dish. Season with salt and pepper and a squeeze of lemon, and cover with cream. About half a pint should be plenty. Stand the dish in another dish of water, and bake slowly, basting frequently. When cooked, drain and place on a serving dish, and keep hot while you make the shrimp sauce (see page 306).

Halibut

The best halibut is the smallest one, and if caught between March and October, it is especially good. Bigger halibut is usually cooked in steaks.

Chicken Halibut with Cheese Sauce

Fillet a small halibut and season with salt and lemon juice. Roll the fillets and place in a fireproof dish with a dab of butter on each. Cover the dish with foil and cook in a moderate oven until the fish is done. Serve with Cheese Sauce (see page 300).

[214]

Baked Halibut

Halibut steaks can be cooked in much the same way as the fillets in the last recipe. Remove the dark skin by dipping the fish into boiling water before cooking, and season the fish well before putting it in a fireproof dish. Put some milk in the bottom of the dish to keep the fish moist and cook very gently. Serve the fish with any sauce suitable for white fish.

Skate

Skate with Black Butter

2 lb. skate wings.	1 tablespoonful
4 oz. butter.	chopped parsley.
Court bouillon.	2 tablespoonfuls
2 tablespoonfuls capers.	wine vinegar.

Wash the skate, and cut it into slanting pieces. Place the fish in the hot court bouillon and simmer for 20 minutes. Remove the fish and scrape off the skin. The fish is then placed on a serving dish and kept hot. The butter is melted in a sauté pan and when it is deep brown is poured over the fish. Heat the vinegar and reduce by half, pour this over the skate, and then sprinkle on the capers and chopped parsley.

Skate au Gratin

Skate wings.	A little flour.
Sliced onions.	Butter.
Chopped shallot and	Breadcrumbs.
parsley.	Salt and pepper.

1 oz. sliced mushrooms.

Skin the fish and cut into pieces. Put all ingredients into a buttered dish, except for the flour and butter. Cover with a lid and cook for about an hour at 350 °F. When cooked strain off the liquor, and make a roux with the flour and butter, adding this liquor. Pour the sauce over the fish and sprinkle with breadcrumbs. Brown under the grill.

Brill

Baked Brill with Crayfish

Rather like Turbot but not quite so good, it should be cooked in the same way as Turbot or Sole.

1 brill.	2 oz. butter.
2 tablespoonfuls finely chopped shallot.	1 teaspoonful finely minced herbs.
	Breadcrumbs.
¼ lb. mushrooms.	6 crayfish cooked in
1 gill stock.	court bouillon (see
1 gill Madeira.	page 285).

Clean the fish and score it across the back. Spread the minced shallot and mushrooms in a buttered baking dish and pour in the stock, and Madeira. Lay the fish in back down. Melt an ounce of butter in a saucepan and stir in as many white breadcrumbs as will absorb it. Add pepper, salt, and the herbs and spread over the fish. Bake for half an hour, basting frequently. When cooked, lift the fish carefully on to a flat dish and pour the gravy round, serve garnished with the crayfish, some fresh parsley, and sliced cucumber.

CHAPTER TWELVE

COD	GURNARD
HAKE	JOHN DORY
HADDOCK	DOG FISH
WHITING	HERRING
POUTING	MACKEREL
LING	BASS
SHAD	SPRATS
RED MULLET	PILCHARD
CONGER EEL	WHITEBAIT

Cod

Swedish Boiled Cod

1 cod.   Butter.
Water.   Hardboiled eggs.
Coarse salt.

Clean the fish and remove head, but keep in one piece. With a sharp knife score the sides of the fish deeply. Have your fish kettle ready with enough boiling water to cover, and put in a small handful of coarse salt. Place the fish in the water, and boil gently for about 8 minutes. Remove carefully and serve with plenty of melted butter into which you have chopped the hardboiled eggs.

MRS SPENCER'S SWEDISH RECIPE

Fish Curry

1 lb. cod.   1 tablespoonful chopped
1 oz. butter.   parsley for garnish.
1 onion.   1 dessertspoonful
2 tomatoes.   curry powder.
2 teaspoonfuls lemon
   juice.

Chop the onion and fry lightly in the butter, then add all the other ingredients including the fish chopped into pieces. Add a little water and simmer for 20 minutes. Serve with boiled rice and garnish with chopped parsley.

Serve with popadams, sliced banana sprinkled with coconut, tomatoes chopped small and sprinkled with chopped chives moistened with vinegar. Many small savoury dishes go well with curry.

[218]

Danish Baked Cod with Mushroom Sauce

Cod cutlets.		Paprika.
Bacon.	Salt.	Butter.

Cut up enough bacon into small pieces to cover the bottom of the fireproof dish you are going to use. Then rub the cod cutlets with salt and paprika and place them in the dish. Cut up some more bacon and put on top and dab with butter. Bake in a moderate oven for 40 minutes. Baste while cooking, and when done, strain off the liquid to add to the sauce. Make the sauce by cooking $\frac{1}{4}$ lb. mushrooms in a little milk, mix with the stock and thicken with cream.

Cod with Sweet and Sour Sauce

1 codling.	1 turnip.
1 oz. cornflour.	Oil.
1 onion.	Sweet and sour sauce
1 carrot.	(see page 304).

Leave the head and tail on the cleaned fish, and score the sides of the fish about 1 inch apart. Make a paste of the cornflour with a little water and coat the fish with this. Cook the fish slowly in hot fat until just tender. Chop the vegetables and fry in the oil for 1 minute, add them to the sweet and sour sauce and pour over the fish.

Hake

A fish very like cod, with bones that are easy to remove. Cook hake by any recipe suitable for white fish. Recipes for fresh haddock and for cod are specially suitable for hake, but baking is probably the best way to cook this fish.

Haddock

If there is any sea fish more than another that requires good cooking, it is the one which, according to the legend, St. Peter drew out from the lake of Galilee to obtain the tribute money, leaving the mark of his finger and thumb on its shoulders.

In season from September to February, fresh haddock may be cooked according to any recipe for white fish.

Grilled Fresh Haddock with Mustard Sauce

Haddock.   Butter.
Pepper and salt.

Take a small haddock and slit it down the back by the side of the bone. Clean it and remove the bone by slipping the point of a knife underneath and gently working away the flesh. Cut off the head, tail, and fins. Season the haddock inside, brush fish and grill with melted butter, and grill the fish on both sides till done. Serve with mustard sauce, and garnish with parsley. Mustard sauce (see page 311).

Ham and Haddie

Lightly smoked   Thin slices smoked ham.
haddock.   Pepper.

Skin the fish and cut it into neat pieces. Fry the ham, and remove it from the pan and keep it hot while you fry the fish in the same pan, adding a little butter, and turning once. Season with pepper. Heap the fish on a dish and place the ham slices round it. Serve at once.

Fillets of Haddock with Lobster Cream

2 fillets of haddock.　　Paprika.

Salt.　　　　　　　　　　Butter.

Lobster cream sauce　　Parsley.

　(see page 315).　　　Oil for frying.

Croûtons.　　　　　　　Glaze (if available).

Grated Parmesan cheese.

A fairly simple recipe turned into something out of the ordinary by the Lobster sauce and croûtons.

Season the haddock with salt and paprika and put it in a well-buttered dish covered with foil. Cook for 15 to 20 minutes according to size of the fillets. Dish it up in a shallow dish, and pour round it the lobster sauce. Sprinkle the fish with chopped parsley, and down the middle of the fillets put a row of croûtons of bread, ring-shaped, about 1½ inches in diameter, and ½ inch thick. These should be deep fried to a gold brown colour, then brushed over with a little warm glaze, the glazed side dipped into grated Parmesan cheese.

French Baked Haddock 'Aux Fines Herbes'

Haddock.　　　　　　　Parsley.

Mushrooms.　　　　　　Garlic if liked.

Onions.　　　　　　　　2 wineglassfuls white wine.

Place the haddock, which has been cleaned, and the head and fins removed, in a fireproof dish. Surround the fish with the chopped mushrooms, onions, and parsley, and the crushed clove of garlic if you like it. Pour the wine over the fish and bake in a moderate oven till done, basting frequently. Serve in the baking dish.

Clean the haddock thoroughly and split them, removing the heads. Salt them thoroughly and leave them overnight. Brush off the salt and hang them in the open air to dry for 2 or 3 hours. Then smoke them (see page 286). The cask method does well for haddock, but be sure that they heat evenly as it spoils them to get alternately hot and cold. When they are a fine yellow colour they are done, which should take no longer than 12 hours.

Whiting

Whiting is tasteless but digestible, and can therefore be much improved by good cooking.

Merlans Bercy

4 large fillets or 4 whiting.	Butter.
	2 oz. mushrooms.
3 shallots.	Lemon juice.
Wineglassful of white wine.	Chopped parsley.
	Salt and pepper.

Whiting cooked in white wine and mushrooms, baked and grilled.

Place the whiting fillets, or the split and opened whole fish, in a buttered fireproof dish. Chop the shallots and put round the fish. Sauté the chopped mushrooms in butter. Season the fish and add the mushrooms, keeping back the butter they were cooked in. Pour the wine over the fish, and add the juice of a lemon.

Cook in a moderate oven, basting frequently. When cooked, put the fish in another hot dish, and reduce the liquid in which the fish cooked by half, then pour it over the fish. Sprinkle over the butter from the mushrooms, and grill till brown. Sprinkle with chopped parsley and serve.

Fried Whiting

Split the fish and clean it, and remove the backbone. Sprinkle with salt and pepper and flour. Then dip in beaten egg and breadcrumbs. Melt sufficient butter in a pan and fry the fish in this. Serve with Maître d'Hôtel butter (see p. 153).

Or: Split the fish as above, and cut into fillets. Dip in batter and fry in oil. Serve with Sauce Tartare (see page 305).

Pouting

This is the fish you catch so easily when you are after something much better. Unfortunately, it doesn't keep for more than a few hours, and doesn't cook or eat well. So don't bother to cook it, not even for the cat.

Ling
Fried Sliced Ling

Ling may be cooked by any recipe used for Cod. It fries well in slices.

2 lb. ling.	Frying oil.
1 egg.	Flour.
Breadcrumbs.	Salt and pepper.

Wash and dry the fish and cut it into slices, sprinkle with salt and pepper then roll in flour. Brush with beaten egg and dip in breadcrumbs. Fry in hot oil, drain and serve with Sauce Tartare, or any white fish sauce.

Shad

Baked Shad

The twaite shad, and the allis shad are both edible, the allis shad being the better fish. The twaite shad has teeth and has a line of dark spots along its sides. It is caught in rivers and estuaries when it migrates there.

1 fish.   Salt and pepper.   Butter.

Clean and bone the fish and season it. Soften the butter and spread all over the fish, then place it in a fireproof dish, and bake for 20 minutes. Serve with any savoury sauce.

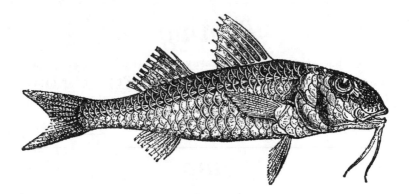

Red Mullet

"Mullets were often brought alive in glass vases to table, and a barbarous pleasure was derived from witnessing the changes of colour they underwent in expiring. Apicus invented a mode of suffocating the Mullet in a kind of pickle, and Seneca endeavoured to put an end to these practices, disgraceful to a people who stood foremost in ancient civilisation."

[224]

To Clean Mullet

Mullet, like woodcock, is usually eaten uncleaned, but if you don't like this, clean in the usual way but leave the liver behind.

Rougets à la Nicoise

4 mullets.	6 green olives.
½ lb. ripe tomatoes.	Seasoned flour.
1 clove garlic.	Oil for frying.
8 anchovy fillets.	Seasoning with a
6 black olives.	pinch of sugar.

Mullet Italian style, with lots of olives, garlic and tomatoes.

Scale and clean the fish if desired, and wash and dry well. Roll the fish in the seasoned flour and fry well on both sides in the hot oil, for about 6 minutes. Skin the tomatoes and cut them into quarters, sauté in another pan, in hot oil and garlic crushed with a little salt, the anchovy fillet, and the stoned olives. Season with pepper and mix gently. Spread this mixture over the fish; garnish with chopped parsley and slices of lemon.

"THE IRIS SYRETT COOKERY BOOK"

Rougets au Safran

4 mullets.	2 oz. butter.
1 each onion,	3 egg yolks.
tomato, shallot.	2 tablespoons thick
Pinch of saffron.	cream.
1½ gills dry white	1 oz. butter.
wine.	Seasoning.
Seasoned flour.	

Wash and scale the fish, clean if desired. Score on the sides. Spread the butter in a fireproof dish and sprinkle with chopped shallot and onion. Roll the flesh in the seasoned flour and place in the dish. Mix the saffron with wine and water enough to cover the fish and pour it over. Dice the tomato and put on the fish and leave the whole to marinate for at least half an hour. Cover with greaseproof paper and cook gently, for a quarter of an hour. When cooked, drain the fish and lay on a serving dish. Whisk the egg yolks and cream and add to the liquor in a fresh pan, thicken over a low heat without boiling. Whisk in the remaining $\frac{1}{2}$ oz. butter. Season if needed and sprinkle with parsley. This is very good served with plain boiled rice.

"THE IRIS SYRETT COOKERY BOOK"

Baked Mullet in Paper Cases

3 red mullets.	$\frac{1}{2}$ oz. flour.
1 teaspoonful lemon juice.	$\frac{1}{2}$ oz. butter.
	2 tablespoonfuls sherry.
Salad oil.	1 teaspoonful anchovy
Salt.	sauce.

Cayenne.

Baked mullet in a creamy rich saffron sauce. Looks good, tastes good.

Sprinkle each mullet with a little salt. Cut three pieces of greaseproof paper large enough to roll the fish in and oil the paper well. Roll each fish up in a piece of the paper, tie the ends firmly and twist the string round once or twice to keep the paper together. Lay in a baking tin and cook in a moderate oven, for 20 minutes or a little more if the fish are big. Keep the fish hot. Melt the butter in a pan and add the flour, the liquor from the fish, the anchovy sauce, the lemon juice, the pepper, and the sherry, in that order. Remove the string from the fish, but let them remain in the papers, lay on a hot dish, and serve with the sauce separately.

[226]

Conger Eel

Conger Eel can be cooked in any way suitable for white fish.

Stewed Conger Eel

Onions.   Cider.
Butter.   Eel.
Flour.

Eel stewed in cider.

Brown two chopped onions in two ounces of butter, and then thicken with two tablespoonfuls of plain flour. Add the sliced eel, and season with salt and pepper. Add enough cider to cover the fish and then cover the dish with a lid or with foil, and place in the oven, cooking slowly for an hour. Serve the fish in the sauce, thickening it further with flour if necessary.

"GUIDE TO GOOD FOOD AND WINES" ANDRÉ SIMON

Sennen Cove Conger Stew

1 saucepan full of   Court bouillon or water.
   potatoes.   Salt.
Milk.   Parsley.

Eel stewed in milk.

Wash the conger and cut into finger-sized strips, heaps of them. Place on the potatoes and season well, add parsley, milk and court bouillon or water to cover. Put on the lid and simmer until done.

Conger eel.	6 borage leaves.
2 shallots.	12 marigold petals.
1 cabbage.	Salt and pepper.
1 pint fresh peas.	Parsley.
½ pint milk.	Thyme.
1 dessertspoonful flour.	Butter.
1 dessertspoonful vinegar.	Lemon.

Unusual soup flavoured with marigold petals.

Wash the fish and put in a saucepan with a quart of water, add the salt and pepper, parsley and thyme. Simmer for 30 or 40 minutes. Strain the liquid and put it in another saucepan. Wash and shred the cabbage, chop the shallots and borage. Add these, with the peas, to the boiling liquid and cook till tender. Mix the flour with a little milk and thicken the soup with this and cook for 5 minutes. Add the rest of the milk and a small piece of fresh butter, and serve the soup with the marigold petals floating on it.

If preferred, the conger pieces can be eaten as a separate dish.

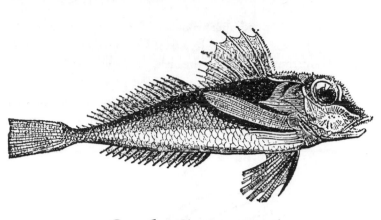

Red Gurnard

Broiled Gurnard

In season from July to April, this ugly little fish makes a noise like a cuckoo. Or possibly it is the cuckoo which makes a noise like a gurnard?

The fish must be cleaned and scraped, heads and fins removed, and then dried well. Score the sides of the fish deeply and then dip in flour, and brush over with melted dripping. Grease the grill with dripping, and cook slowly turning several times. Serve the fish hot with a sauce of melted butter.

Baked Gurnard

2 gurnards.	Lemon juice.
1 oz. butter.	3 tablespoonfuls white
2 tablespoonfuls	wine.
chopped mushrooms.	Pepper and salt.

2 tablespoonfuls browned breadcrumbs.

Clean and skin the fish and remove heads and fins. Score three times on each side. Sprinkle them with two tablespoonfuls of finely chopped mushrooms, a little pepper and salt, and lemon juice. Lay them in a well-buttered, deep fireproof dish. Pour the wine over the fish, and put the butter, in dabs, on the top. Lay a thickly buttered paper over and bake in a quick oven until they are cooked, basting frequently with the wine. About 5 minutes before they are done, sprinkle the browned breadcrumbs on top. Serve in the same dish, garnish with parsley and lemon.

John Dory

Caught mostly in the Autumn and Winter, John Dory is neglected by cooks in this country, but it is well worth cooking.

Dory Fillets Fried in Batter

Clean and bone the fish, cut into pieces; coat the fish with batter and fry till crisp. Serve with Sauce Tartare (see Chapter 16).

Boiled Dory

Clean the fish and remove head and fins. Place in a fish kettle and cover with equal parts of wine and water. Simmer till cooked. Remove the fish and strain; allow to cool and serve with a sauce of lemon juice and oil, and a sprinkling of salt and pepper. Or serve with Shrimp Sauce (see Chapter 16).

Dog Fish

Edible all the year round, this fish doesn't taste as bad as he looks.

Curried Dog Fish

1 large onion.	1 oz. sultanas.
1 large apple.	Tablespoonful dessicated
1 large carrot.	coconut.
2 tomatoes.	Tablespoonful lemon
Dessertspoonful curry	juice.
powder.	½ pint stock.
1 tablespoonful flour.	Boiled rice.
Cooking oil.	Dog fish.

Heat the oil and cook the chopped onion until soft. Then add the other vegetables cut up small, and the sultanas, and cook gently until it begins to colour. Sprinkle the curry powder into the mixture and continue to cook for 5 minutes. Make a paste of the flour with some of the stock. Heat the rest of the stock, and add slowly to the paste, stirring all the time. Add this sauce to the ingredients in the pan, and simmer till thickened. Add more stock if necessary. Place half of the curry mixture in the bottom of a fireproof dish or casserole. Cut the cleaned and skinned dog fish into pieces and lay in the dish, and pour the rest of the curry mixture over the top. Cover, and cook in a moderate oven for 45 minutes. Just before serving add the lemon juice and the coconut. Serve with boiled rice.

F. D. FINN'S FAVOURITE RECIPE

Garlic Dog Fish

Boil or poach the dog fish in salted water to which has been added as much crushed garlic as you fancy.

Herring

A fish which is equal to any in flavour and nutritional value.

Grilled Herrings

Clean the fish and scale it, and remove the head. Wipe, and season with salt and pepper after scoring the sides deeply. Rub just a little olive oil over the fish and cook under a hot grill turning once. Serve with mustard sauce (see page 311).

Herrings Fried in Oatmeal

Clean a fresh herring, cut off its head, open it out flat by splitting it up the back. Take out the backbone and as many other bones as will come with it. Dip the fish in fine oatmeal and fry in shallow fat for 3 minutes on each side.

Harengs aux Betteraves

4 herrings.	2 oz. butter.
1 large beetroot.	1 tablespoonful French
2 tablespoonfuls oil.	mustard.

Seasoning.

Herrings with hot beetroot and French mustard sauce.   A new flavour.

Clean the fish, and place them in the oil in a shallow dish. Season well and allow to stand for an hour, turning from time to time.   Then drain, and cook under a hot grill for about 3 minutes each side.   Meanwhile, dice the beetroot. Melt half the butter in a pan, add the beetroot and heat it gently in the butter.   Season.   Melt the rest of the butter in a clean pan and stir in the mustard.   Season well.   Put the herrings in a long flat dish and put the beetroot garnish round the sides, pour the sauce over the herrings.

"THE IRIS SYRETT COOKERY BOOK"

Fillets of Herring Marinaded on Brown Bread

¾ inch-thick-slices stale brown bread.	
Butter.	White wine.
Filleted herrings.	Red pepper.
Parsley.	Olive oil.
Watercress.	Tarragon vinegar.

Such a simple recipe but one which will go down well!

Put your herring fillets into a dish so that they fill it and pour over them enough white wine to cover them, and leave them for twelve hours.

Lightly toast the bread and butter it thoroughly.   Put the fillets of herring on the toast, skin side up, put the slices in a buttered tin and cover with a sheet of buttered greaseproof paper or aluminium foil.   Cook for about 5 minutes in a hot oven, remove the covering and sprinkle with a good dusting of red pepper, garnish with watercress which has a dressing of oil and tarragon vinegar and serve at once, cut into fingers if you wish. Use up the marinade to make fish sauce. If you prefer it, dispense with the watercress and make a fish sauce with the marinade according to one of the recipes in Part 3 of this book.

Soused Fillets of Herring

6 fresh herrings.	Pepper.
2 teaspoonfuls	Salt.
chopped chives.	Boiling water.
2 teaspoonfuls	Vinegar.
chopped parsley.	Salad oil.
2 bayleaves.	Watercress.
12 peppercorns.	Allspice.

Cold pickled herring, useful for hors d'oeuvres.

Fillet the fish, then wash and dry, and lay on a board with the skin side down. Sprinkle with the chives, parsley, pepper, and salt. Roll up the fillets and bind firmly with tape. Put in a fireproof dish and sprinkle the spices, bayleaves, and salt on the top. Fill the dish with vinegar and water in the proportions of three parts of vinegar to one of water, and cover. Bake slowly in a moderate oven for 1 hour. Allow to cool and then remove fish, wiping off any solids. Arrange on a dish and garnish with watercress. Season lightly with vinegar, salad oil, pepper, and salt.

Potted Herrings

"Get herrings enough to fill up your dish
And into the stomach of each little fish
a peppercorn put; this will give it a flavour;
Then layers of alternate onion thin sliced.
And herrings and bay leaves—each layer well spiced
Then over the whole some vinegar pour;
Diluted with water—a pint or still more;
Three hours in the oven, with moderate heat,
Will make it quite fit for the hungry to eat."

Mackerel

Some say that mackerel, fresh out of the sea and grilled, is the finest eating fish there is, and in the summer those who are lucky enough to be there when the mackerel are about go out with feathers or spinners and catch them, sometimes, as fast as they can be pulled in. It is only right that so handsome a fish should taste so fine, without complicated cooking or sauces. But mackerel spoils very quickly and must be cooked fresh. Never cook a mackerel that has gone limp and lost his glitter, he might be poisonous.

Grilled Mackerel

Clean the fish and cut off head and fins. Score deeply down each side several times. Grease the grill and place the fish on it, cooking until brown before turning over to do the other side.

Or, after cleaning split the fish and grill, cooking the open side first.

Season the fish with a pinch of salt and cayenne, and serve with Maître d'Hôtel butter (see page 153), garnish with lemon slices and parsley.

Or, grill as in the first method, and when cooked open the fish and remove the backbone, and sprinkle with chopped shallot, tarragon and parsley, a pinch of salt and cayenne, and little dabs of butter. Put in a fireproof dish with just a little water and a splash of wine or vinegar, and cook in a hot oven for 5 minutes.

Dry Fried Mackerel

Remove the head and clean the fish. Score deeply down each side and fry over a moderate heat in a dry pan. Serve in the same way as grilled mackerel.

Cold Mackerel with Breton Sauce

4 mackerel of even size.	2 tablespoons mild French mustard.
2 egg yolks.	1 scant dessertspoon wine,
Salt and pepper.	cider or tarragon vinegar.
3 oz. softened butter.	2 tablespoons chopped
Peeled, seeded and	fresh herbs.
diced cucumber, to garnish.	

Cook the mackerel in the way you prefer. I find a good way of cooking fish to be eaten cold is to wrap each one in a piece of well-oiled aluminium foil and to bake them in a very moderate oven, Mark 3, 325°F. This method preserves all the flavour of the fish and keeps it moist and firm; it also dispenses with the need for a fish kettle, which very few households can boast nowadays. A good-sized fish cooked on the bone will take 35 to 40 minutes this way—less long, of course, if it is boned before cooking. To do this split the cleaned and beheaded fish down the belly and spread it open. Loosen the backbone carefully with your fingers and you will be able to draw it out gently, taking most of the small bones with it.

To make the sauce, blend the mustard with the egg yolks and the vinegar, and add salt and pepper to taste. Soften the butter until it has almost but not quite melted, taking care not to let it get oily, and very gradually mix it into the egg yolks until it has the consistency of a mayonnaise. Stir in the chopped herbs—whatever herbs you can lay hands on; parsley and chives are essential and tarragon and chervil an ideal addition. The character of the sauce will also be somewhat affected, of course, by your choice of vinegar and mustard, but it is in any case certain to look pretty and to taste delicious. It is quicker and easier to make than mayonnaise and makes a pleasant change from it, not only with mackerel or herring but also with cold meat, particularly cold pork, and it is especially popular with those who find mayonnaise too rich. Serve the cold filleted mackerel, the skin gently scraped off them, masked with this sauce and garnished with small, crisp dice of peeled and seeded cucumber.

On a cold summer day serve hot grilled mackerel with new potatoes. Score the mackerel before grilling with deep diagonal slashes on each side and fill these cuts with strong yellow Dijon mustard. Oil the fish well before grilling and refresh the mustard before serving if you like.

MARGARET COSTA

Soused Mackerel

Remove the heads and clean the fish, split and remove backbone. Roll from tail upwards and put in a fireproof dish.

Cover with a half and half mixture of vinegar and water and add one peppercorn per fish. Cook for at least 2 hours in a slow oven. If liked, a bay leaf or a pinch of allspice can be added. Eat hot or cold.

Mackerel Balls

3 mackerel.   1 egg.
Teacupful of   Salt and pepper.
   breadcrumbs.

Clean and skin the fish, remove the bones. Put the fish through a mincer. Mix all the ingredients together and make into balls with the hands, not too big. Fry in hot fat. If the mixture is too moist, add more breadcrumbs.

Bass

Poached Bass

Simple poached fish with white sauce.

Put the fish into a salted court bouillon and bring it to the boil, then poach very gently till tender. Drain, and serve with Sauce Hollandaise. (See page 304)

Sprats

In season from October to March.

Savoury Sprats

Sprats.   Parsley.

Dill.   Seasoning.

Bone the sprats; with the fingers, break off the head and ease out the backbone with the thumb, bringing the gut with it, and opening the fish. Wash and drain well. Chop the dill and parsley very small and sprinkle it with salt and pepper. Press the inside of each fish into this so that it is coated with the mixture. Then press two fish face to face with the seasoning inside, and fry in a shallow pan in hot oil.

MRS. SPENCER'S SWEDISH RECIPE

Sprats Fried in Batter

1 oz. butter.   Egg white.

¼ lb. flour.   Cold water.

Parsley.   Boiling water.

Lemon.

Make a batter by melting 1 oz. of butter in a tablespoonful of boiling water; add this to ¼ pint of cold water and stir it into a ¼ lb. of flour. Beat the white of an egg until it is stiff and blend it with the flour and water. Dip each washed and dried sprat into this and drop into deep fat. Serve very hot with fried parsley and lemon quarters, and brown bread and butter.

Sprats.   Butter.
Tin of anchovies.   Breadcrumbs.
Seasoning.

Bone the sprats as above and then roll each fish with a piece of anchovy in the middle. Pack the rolled fish in a fireproof dish, sprinkle with breadcrumbs and seasoning, and a few dabs of butter, and cook in a moderate oven.

MRS. SPENCER'S SWEDISH RECIPE

Broiled Sprats

Fasten fresh sprats in rows with a skewer run through the eyes, dredge with flour. Rub your grill with butter, and lay the sprats on, cook quickly till brown, turn over and cook the other side, and serve very hot with slices of lemon and brown bread and butter.

Pilchard

Unfortunately pilchard do not travel well out of tins, so the only chance you will have to eat them fresh is if you catch them around our southwestern coasts. The Pilchard may be distinguished from the Herring by the fin, which is exactly in the middle of the back, while in the herring it is nearer to the tail.

They can be cooked in the same way as herrings.

Pilchard Hot Pot

Clean and scale the fish, split open and remove bones. Grease a fireproof dish and lay the fish in. Make a sauce with butter, flour, and milk, salt and pepper, tomato purée, to taste, and cover the fish with this. Partly boil some potatoes, slice and completely cover the fish with these. Dot with butter, grate a little cheese over, and bake for 15 minutes in a moderate oven. Brown under the grill and serve.

Smelt

The true smelt is in season from September to April, and smells of cucumber. The sand smelt is not so good a fish, but also smells faintly of cucumber and can be cooked in the same way as smelt.

Stewed Smelts

Put your smelts into a deep dish with white wine and water, a little rosemary and thyme, a piece of fresh butter and some large mace, and salt, let them stew half an hour, then take a handful of parsley and boil it, then beat it with the back of a knife, then take the yolks of three or four eggs, and beat them with some of your fish broth, then serve up your fish upon sippets, pour on your sauce, scrape on sugar, and serve it.

Smelt à la Stoeher

1 lb. smelt.	½ cup fish bouillon.
A little water.	1 beaten egg yolk.
2 tablespoonfuls butter.	Grated cheese.
	Dessertspoonful flour.
Pinch of salt.	

Boiled fish in cream sauce.

Clean the fish and simmer until tender in water, with the salt and half the butter. Melt the remaining butter and blend in flour. Combine the court bouillon and egg yolk and add to the flour mixture and cook until it begins to thicken. Pour the sauce over the fish and grate cheese on top. Brown off under the grill.

Whitebait

"The delicacy of Whitebait needs no comment. Pennant states it to be delicious, and says that epicures of the lower order resort to the taverns adjacent to the places where it is taken, for the purpose of enjoying it."

Fried Whitebait

Wash the fish well and dredge with flour. Shake in a sieve to separate each fish and to remove loose flour. Fry in deep fat for a few minutes, shaking gently to keep separated. Drain well on soft paper and serve with slices of lemon and brown bread and butter.

Don't put too many fish in the fat at once. Just a handful at a time. When all the fish are cooked, put the lot back in deep fry until they are crisp, before serving.

Devilled Whitebait

Cook as above, but divide into two piles, and sprinkle one pile with salt and cayenne pepper.

CHAPTER THIRTEEN

LOBSTER	MUSSELS
CRAB	OYSTERS
CRAYFISH	SHRIMPS AND PRAWNS
CRAWFISH	COCKLES
SCALLOPS	LAMPREYS

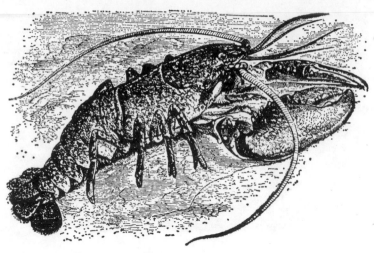

Lobster

Boiled Lobster

Standard method of boiling lobster, to dress and serve cold.
Heat enough court bouillon to cover the lobster, and when
this is boiling, holding the live lobster in the middle of the
back, put it in head first. Cover, and cook for 20 minutes
or a little more if it is a big lobster. Let him cool in the
liquid.

Pull off the small claws and pick out the meat. Crack the
big claws, removing meat if required or leaving it in if the
lobster is to be served cold in his shell. Split the tail right
down with a sharp knife, and the body, being careful not to
break the stomach, a small sac just behind the head. Remove
all traces of the intestinal canal which shows as a dark thread
down the tail. Throw away the spongy tissue which lies
between the meat and the shell. Remove the intestinal cord
from the body also, and remove the stomach if the shell is to
be used to hold the meat. Keep any bright red coral, and the
green liver for sauce or garnish.

[244]

Soufflé of Lobster à la Diable

1 lobster.
Saltspoonful each French
  and English Mustard.
Dust of red pepper.
Tarragon vinegar.
Teaspoonful anchovy
  essence.

Whites of 8 eggs.
Yolks of 6 eggs.
Salt.
Pinch of chopped tarragon.
2 tablespoonsful whipped
  cream.

An extravagant soufflé for soufflé experts. Very special but must be served immediately it is cooked.

Chop the lobster meat finely, with the creamy part of the head meat. Stir the egg yolks with the mustard, pepper and salt, tarragon and tarragon vinegar, and the anchovy essence. Add the lobster and the whipped cream. Whip the egg whites until they are very stiff, fold in. Butter the soufflé dish and put a band of well-buttered paper round it, standing three inches higher than the dish. Pour the mixture in and cook for 12–15 minutes. Remove the paper band, replace with a napkin, sprinkle with red pepper and serve.

Lobster Thermidor

Boiled lobster.
2 tablespoons butter.
A little minced onion.
A pinch of cayenne
  pepper.

1 tablespoonful tomato
  purée.
Grated cheese.
½ glass dry white wine.
1 cup white sauce.

½ lb. mushrooms, chopped.

Classic recipe for serving lobster hot in cheese sauce. Good enough for any party.

Take all the meat out of the lobster and cut small. Heat butter and put the lobster into it with the onion, the pepper and the white wine. Cook gently for 5 minutes and then add the mushrooms and the tomato purée. Cook this mixture for a few minutes and then put it into the lobster shells, on a fireproof dish. Pour the white sauce over and sprinkle with grated cheese and bake briefly in a hot oven. Brown off under the grill and serve piping hot.

Mexican Lobster

Cooked lobster.	1 oz. sugar.
Oil.	Pinch of ground
1 large onion.	cloves.
1 green pepper.	Bay leaf.
1 lb. cooked tomatoes.	¼ lb. mushrooms.
Salt.	Tabasco sauce.

A more savoury way of cooking and serving hot lobster.

Cut the lobster into small pieces. Put three tablespoonfuls of oil into a pan and add the onion, tomatoes and pepper chopped small and all the seasonings, and simmer for 15 minutes. Take out the bay leaf and add the mushrooms and the lobster, and another two tablespoonfuls of oil. Simmer until all is heated through and serve.

C.A.I. ENCYCLOPAEDIA

Crab

Boiled Crab.　Dressed

Crab meat.　　　　　Oil.
Lemon juice.　　　　Vinegar.

Standard method of boiling and dressing crab to eat cold.

Crab should be boiled by placing in cold water and bringing gradually to the boil. This method seems to inflict less pain than plunging them in boiling water. Cook for 20 minutes after it has come to the boil. Remove all the meat from the body and the claws, keeping the claw meat separate. Discard the entrails. Mix together the coral, or red meat, and the body meat and season with a few drops of oil, and lemon juice, or vinegar. Then shred the claw meat and season likewise. Arrange the meat back in the washed and dried crab shell with the body meat and coral across the middle and the claw meat each side.

Crabmeat Casserole

1 cup of cooked crabmeat.	Pinch of cayenne.
3 cups of milk.	½ pound grated cheese.
Plain flour.	1 green pepper.
Butter.	4 oz. mushrooms.
Seasoning.	Breadcrumbs or flaky pastry.

A good way of preparing crabmeat for baking in shells, or to present as a kind of casserole pie.

Make a thick white sauce by heating 2 oz. of butter in a pan, adding two tablespoonfuls of flour, and the milk stirred in very gradually. Then add the cheese, stirring until smooth over a very low flame, or in a double boiler. Then add all the ingredients except the breadcrumbs (or pastry) and mix well. Put the mixture in a shallow casserole or fireproof dish, cover with breadcrumbs (or pastry) and bake in a moderate oven till browned. If breadcrumbs are used for the cover, put on a few dabs of butter, and sprinkle with cayenne pepper. This dish can also be served baked in empty crab shells or individual dishes.

Crab Newburg

½ lb. cooked crab meat.	Salt.
	Cayenne.
1 cup of cream.	2 egg yolks.
2 oz. butter.	Tablespoonful sherry.

Crab in sherry sauce to eat on toast as an entree.

Cook the crab meat in the butter for about 5 minutes, then add the seasonings and sherry. Blend the egg yolks and cream. Remove the crab from the stove and add the egg mixture then reheat in a double saucepan till the mixture thickens, being very careful that it does not boil. Serve on rounds of hot buttered toast, or on muffins.

Crayfish

A small *Freshwater* crustacean. In America there is another species of freshwater lobster they call a Crawfish!

> "*I went to the Bayou just last night*
> *There wasn't no moon but the stars were bright*
> *Got a big long hook on a big long pole*
> *And I pulled Mr. Crawfish out of his hole.*
> *See I got 'um, see the size*
> *Strooped and cleaned before your eyes*
> *Sleek in look. Fresh and ready to cook*
> *Now take Mr. Crawfish in your hand*
> *He's gonna look good in a frying pan.*
> *Fry him crisp or boil him right*
> *He'll be sweeter than sugar with every bite.*"

Boiled Crayfish

Just boil your crayfish in white wine court bouillon for about 10 minutes, drain, and serve cold. The central portion of the fan-shaped tail should be removed, taking the black spinal cord with it.

Crayfish Risotto

Crayfish.	Butter.
Onion.	Flour.
¼ lb. rice.	Cream.

Boil the crayfish in court bouillon as above. Melt some butter and cook the chopped onion in it until just coloured, then add the rice slowly. Then pour over this enough of the court bouillon to cook the rice. Put all in a double boiler and cook slowly till the rice is done. Meanwhile shell the crayfish and drop them in melted butter and cook until coloured. Sprinkle with a little flour and add enough cream to cover the crayfish. Cook until just on the boil, stirring all the time. Serve the crayfish piled on the rice.

Crayfish à la Meunière

Butter.	Salt and pepper.
Thyme.	Bay leaf.
White wine.	Plain flour.
Butter.	Parsley.

Sautéd and poached crayfish in white wine, served in its own thickened juices.

Sauté the crayfish in very hot butter, and when well browned, season with salt and pepper, powdered thyme and bay leaf. Put in a fireproof dish and add enough dry white wine to cover the fish. Cover and bake in a hot oven for 20 minutes. Drain but retain the stock. Boil the stock down by half and thicken with a little blended flour and butter, pour over the crayfish and serve garnished with parsley.

Crayfish à la Bordelaise

Live crayfish.	White wine.
Bunch of mixed herbs.	Sherry.
Turnip.	Cloves.
Leek.	Mace, peppercorn.
Carrot.	6 onions.
Heart of a stick of	Butter.
celery.	Lemon juice.
Glaze.	Parsley.
Sugar.	1 oz. glaze.
Red pepper.	

If you have access to plenty of crayfish, this is a rather special way to serve them. It's not a bit difficult, and can be made a little beforehand and kept hot. Served in nice modern individual earthenware dishes or something of the kind, it makes a splendid first course.

Wash the crayfish several times in cold water to get rid of any grit or sand and then dry them, and put them into a stewpan with the wine, enough to cover them, and two wineglassfuls of sherry, herbs, cloves, two slices of turnip, half a leek, mace, peppercorn, one carrot, two onions and the celery all sliced fine. Boil for $\frac{1}{2}$ hour and then remove the fish, and strain off the liquor. Reserve one whole crayfish per person, and crack the shells of the rest and extract the meat. Cut the rest of the onions very small and cook in the butter for twenty minutes, without browning, add the crayfish liquor and let it go on cooking until the lot has the consistency of thick paste. Add one ounce of glaze or half a beef stock cube, lemon juice, castor sugar, parsley and a little red pepper, and whisk all well together. Put the crayfish meat in the sauce and warm without boiling. When ready to serve, have heated some suitable small dishes and put the mixture in. Put one whole crayfish which was kept back for this purpose, on top, garnish with parsley, and serve very hot.

"GUIDE TO GOOD FOOD AND WINES" ANDRÉ SIMON

Crawfish

This is a spiny lobster without claws which is caught around our southwestern coasts, is nearly as good as lobster to eat and is cooked the same way. Don't confuse it with 'crayfish' which is a little fresh-water lobster.

Crawfish Curry

1 crawfish.	1 teaspoonful curry paste.
2 onions.	1 oz. flour.
1 apple.	2 oz. butter.
½ pint milk.	Salt.
1 tablespoonful coconut.	Boiled rice.
1 teaspoonful curry powder.	

Boil the crawfish and split him open, remove the uneatable parts and pick out all the meat from the body and the claws, and the creamy parts from the head. Cut the flesh up small. Peel and chop the onions and the apple, and cook in the melted butter for 15 minutes without browning. Add the curry powder and paste and a little milk. When this is thoroughly cooked add the crawfish. Soak the grated coconut in the rest of the milk for half an hour then strain the milk and use it to mix the flour to a smooth paste. Stir this into the curry, bring to the boil and add salt to taste. Simmer very gently for half an hour and serve with plain boiled rice and garnish with cut lemon and parsley.

Scallops

The shell of St. James, the emblem of the pilgrim. Best eaten in January or February.

To Open Scallops

Place the shells on the stove top and they will open by themselves. Remove the beard, and black parts, but leave the coral.

Coquilles Saint Jacques à la Bretonne

4 scallops.	1½ oz. white breadcrumbs.
½ onion.	2 oz. butter.
1 shallot.	Salt and pepper.
Chopped parsley.	1 tablespoonful brandy.
1 gill dry white wine.	

Classic recipe for scallops cooked in wine and brandy and served in their own shells.

[253]

Chop the onion and shallot and cook in the butter until soft. Add the washed scallops, cut into quarters, and add the wine and brandy. Bring to simmering point and add breadcrumbs, parsley, pepper, and salt. Simmer for a few minutes and then put the mixture back into the scallop shells. Brown the breadcrumbs and sprinkle over the mixture in the shells. Dot with butter, and pipe a thin border of Duchesse potatoes round the edge of each. Brown under the grill.

Baked Scallops

Breadcrumbs.	Salt and pepper.
Parsley.	Lemon juice.
Shallot.	Butter.

Take the scallops right out of the shells, and scrub the shells clean. Then line the shells with breadcrumbs, the chopped parsley and shallot and the seasoning. Put the scallops back in the shells and sprinkle more of the bread-crumb mixture on the top. Moisten the tops with melted butter and lemon juice and bake in a hot oven for about 20 minutes.

Mussels

Mussels should be washed well before cooking, and the shells scraped to remove any mud and beards. Discard any with shell open. While they are being cooked the pan should be constantly shaken until the shells open, when the mussels are done.

Moules à la Marinière

2 quarts mussels.
White wine court bouillon.
Butter.

Standard recipe for Moules Marinière, but add a clove of garlic to the court bouillon if liked.

Add the butter to the boiling court bouillon, add the cleaned mussels, cover with the lid, and shake over a hot flame for about 5 minutes, or until the shells open. Remove from the heat. Take one shell from each mussel, and pile the mussels in their half shells on to a dish, strain over them the liquor they were cooked in, and sprinkle with chopped parsley. Serve at once.

Mussel Pilaff

2 quarts mussels.	½ gill oil.
½ lb. rice.	Pinch of saffron.
1 chopped onion.	Stock.
2 oz. grated cheese	Bouquet garni.
(preferably Gruyère).	Seasoning.

Mussels in saffron rice, this is a tasty and filling dish. With the addition of pieces of other fish; white fish, prawns, and perhaps some chicken and beef, and a few peas, it turns into a kind of Spanish "paella".

Cook the cleaned mussels as above, and remove from their shells. Keep the liquor they were cooked in and strain it. Heat the oil and add the chopped onion, cooking until soft. Then add all the other ingredients. Total quantity of liquid should be three times the volume of the rice. Cover the dish and put it in a moderate oven for about 25 minutes. When cooked remove the bouquet garni, pile up the mixture on a dish and sprinkle with grated cheese.

"THE IRIS SYRETT COOKERY BOOK"

Mussel Pudding

½ lb. S.R. flour.	Water.
3 oz. finely chopped	Mussels.
suet.	Pepper.
Salt.	

Make a suet crust, roll out and lay on a piece of greased greaseproof paper. Wash the mussels very well and remove the beards. Put them in a pan without liquid over a very low flame, and they will open almost immediately. Scoop them out on to the dough, turn in the edges to cover the mussels, wrap the paper round, enclose the whole in a pudding cloth and tie well and steam for 1½ hours.

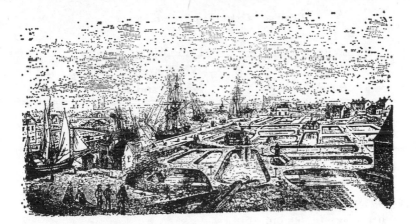

Oysters

The native, which is an oyster from Colchester or Whitstable, or other Kentish or Essex beds, should be eaten exactly as it is. Open the oyster by inserting the knife at the hinge and snapping the ligament which attaches the oyster to the flat shell. Serve in the other half of the shell in its own liquor. A squeeze of lemon, red pepper, and Tabasco Sauce are flavourings if desired.

Angels on Horseback

Use large oysters and cook them in their own liquor by simmering until the edges curl. If they are cooked too long they will be very tough. Then drain the oysters and wrap each one in a piece of bacon, tying round with thread. Grill until the bacon is crisp and serve on toast.

C.A.I. ENCYCLOPAEDIA

Oysters.   Lemon juice.
Flour.   Worcestershire sauce.
Butter.   Pepper and salt.

Open and drain the oysters, and dip each one in flour.
Heat the butter and cook the oysters until brown. Make
a roux with butter and flour and stir in the liquid from the
cooked oysters. Season with salt, pepper, lemon juice and
Worcestershire sauce to taste. Bring to the boil, and then
pour over the oysters which have been put on toast. Serve
with slices of lemon.

Fried Oysters

Just dip in egg and breadcrumbs and fry in hot fat.

Oyster Stew

3 pints oysters.   2 medium minced onions.
2½ cups milk.   4 tablespoons butter.
1 clove garlic.   2½ cups cream.
½ cup chopped celery tops.   ½ cup dry white wine.
1 bay leaf.   1 teaspoonful salt.
½ teaspoonful white pepper.   Little cayenne pepper.
Chopped parsley.   Paprika.

Put 3 tablespoons of butter in a pan and fry the onions
and crushed garlic in it, until they are golden brown. Throw
away the garlic. Heat the milk and cream in a double
saucepan over boiling water, then add the cooked onions and
butter they were cooked in, the celery tops, bay leaf, and
1 pint of chopped oysters. Stir them well together and
heat without boiling for 20 minutes, then strain through

a fine sieve, and put the strained liquid back in the top of the double boiler.

In another saucepan put the remaining 2 pints of whole oysters, with their liquid, with salt, white pepper and cayenne pepper to heat. As soon as the edges of the oysters start to curl, pour them into the contents in the top of the double saucepan with their liquid and add 1 tablespoonful of butter and the dry white wine. Cook for a minute or so longer, and then serve in heated bowls with a sprinkling of chopped parsley and paprika.

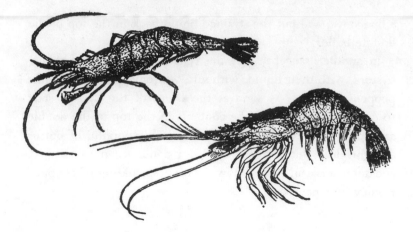

Shrimps and Prawns

Shrimp de Jonghe

1 lb. of cleaned shrimps.	1 oz. butter.
2 tablespoonfuls of white wine.	1 clove of garlic, chopped.
	2 tablespoonfuls chopped
Pepper and salt.	leek.

2 slices of dried bread, crumbled.

Baked shrimps in a thick sauce of breadcrumbs, white wine, and garlic.

Put the shrimps in a fireproof dish, add the wine and pepper, and dot with butter. Add the garlic, leek, and salt to the breadcrumbs and rub together until they are a smooth paste. Spread this over the shrimps, and bake in the oven (moderate) for 20 minutes.

Creamed Shrimps

Shrimps.	Celery salt.
White sauce.	Green pepper.

Make a smooth white sauce and flavour it with celery salt. Add the shrimps, and a tablespoonful of green pepper chopped very fine. Heat till boiling and serve on hot buttered toast.

Shrimp Rarebit

½ cup milk.	Pinch of cayenne pepper.
4 oz. cheese.	Salt.
Dessertspoonful	½ pint cleaned shrimps.
Worcestershire sauce.	1 egg.

Melt the grated cheese in the milk, and add the seasonings and Worcestershire sauce. Then add the shrimps and simmer gently till they are heated through. Remove from heat and add the beaten egg. Reheat till the mixture thickens but do not boil. Make pieces of toast and butter them, and then pour the mixture over the toast, making sure that you cover every bit. Then put under the grill till the mixture begins to bubble and the top is browned.

Prawns in Soya Sauce

8 oz. prawns.	2 tablespoonfuls sherry.
3 slices ginger.	1 dessertspoonful sugar.
3 tablespoons soya sauce.	1 dessertspoonful salt.
1 small onion (Spring	1 dessertspoonful cornflour.
onions when available).	

Crisp fried prawns Chinese style. A very savoury and rich dish.

Wash the prawns and clip the whiskers and feet, but do not remove the shells. Make the sauce by blending the cornflour with a little water, adding the sherry, sugar, salt, and soya, and bring to the boil and thicken. Heat some frying oil and drop in the prawns, the sliced ginger and the sliced onion (about three tablespoonfuls of oil will be plenty). Then add the sauce and heat all together for about 10 minutes.

"500 RECIPES FROM ABROAD" MARGUERITE PATTEN

Fried Scampi

Scampi.   Batter.

Sauce tartare.   Lemon.

Be sure that the scampi are dry. Dip them in batter and lower into hot deep fat and fry for 4 minutes only. Drain, and serve with slices of lemon and sauce tartare.

Pear and Prawn Curry

1 4-oz. tin peeled prawns or big shrimps, more if you have them.

1 oz. butter.

$\frac{1}{2}$ a green pepper diced.

1 small chopped onion.

1 small red pepper diced.

$\frac{1}{2}$ a peeled and chopped apple.

1 oz. ground rice.

2 teaspoons curry powder.*

1 pint chicken or fish stock.

1 teaspoon red jam.

1 teaspoon chutney.

Salt.

Juice of $\frac{1}{2}$ a lemon.

1 oz. sultanas.

2 pears, peeled, cored and sliced.

1 teaspoonful curry paste made by combining: 1 tablespoonful each ground coriander seed and ground caraway seed, 1 teaspoon each ground turmeric, ground black pepper. $\frac{1}{4}$ teaspoonful cayenne pepper, $\frac{1}{2}$ teaspoonful nutmeg, 2 tablespoonsful anchovy essence, 2 teaspoonsful vinegar.

Like all curries, this contains many ingredients, but it is really very good indeed. The curry paste is a standard one to use with curried fish, and the recipe generally can be adapted for different fish curries. Obviously the more prawns you can afford the better. This can be served on boiled rice with popadams as an entrée, or given the full treatment and made with lots of prawns and served with a variety of "sambals" or side dishes as a main course. If you follow the recipe carefully it will make your reputation as a curry cook!

Melt the butter and sauté the onion until it is transparent but do not let it brown. Add the apple and peppers and cook gently for 3 or 4 minutes. Stir in the ground rice and curry powder and cook for another 5 minutes. Add the stock gradually, and the rest of the ingredients. Simmer for 25 minutes.

Prawn Patties

Puff pastry patty cases.	½ green pepper sliced.
½ pt. thick white sauce.	1 blade of celery, chopped.
1 oz. butter.	½ clove of garlic.
4 oz. prawns.	Paprika.
5 oz. cooked peas.	Salt and pepper.

Heat the butter and fry the prawns and the peas gently for two minutes, then add the celery and the pepper, sliced small. Cook for a minute or two then add the garlic, crushed. Make the thick white sauce and add the salt and pepper, stir well, then add all the other ingredients except paprika, which is used to garnish the finished article. Allow to cool, then fill the pastry cases with the mixture, put a whole prawn on top of each and sprinkle with paprika.

3 teaspoons coriander.	2 teaspoonsful vinegar.
Pinch powdered	$\frac{1}{4}$ teaspoonful salt.
ginger.	$\frac{1}{2}$ teaspoonful black
2 teaspoons sugar.	pepper.
2 cloves crushed	1 lb. shelled prawns
garlic.	or shrimps.

Lovely crisp spicy shrimps. This doesn't take long to cook, and makes a good entrée, but it is the precooking and peeling of the shrimps which takes the time.

Combine all the ingredients except the prawns and then coat the prawns all over with the mixture and leave them for half a day. Deep fry them in hot oil, drain, and serve, and what a change from the eternal scampi.

Curried Prawns

1 small onion.	Salt and pepper.
2 oz. butter.	Cupful of thick
2 oz. flour.	cream.
Teaspoonful curry	1 oz. sultanas.
powder.	1 pt. prawns.

Sauté the sliced onion in butter, then add the flour and curry powder, blending well, add salt and pepper and cream. Heat the sultanas and prawns in this sauce, and serve with boiled rice.

Lamprey

Henry the First, known as Henry Beauclerk, was never known to be guilty of any other excess in eating or drinking, but he died of "a surfeit of lampreys". One would like to know his recipe in order to avoid it! Possibly his cook did not remove the two filaments in the back of the creature, which are poisonous. If you still want to eat lampreys try them this way:

Lampreys Matelote

Put a pound of lampreys in half a litre of boiling red wine. Cook for one hour and thicken with melted butter and flour.

Stuffed Lamprey

1 medium-sized lamprey.   1 egg.
Suet forcemeat (parsley and   Breadcrumbs.
   thyme stuffing).   1 lemon.
                Anchovy sauce.

Stuffed fish baked in egg and breadcrumbs.

Rub the fish with salt, wash, and remove the poisonous cartilage and strings down the back. Fill the body with the stuffing and sew it up. Butter some greaseproof paper and wrap the fish up in it. Cover with hot water and simmer for 20 minutes. Drain and dry. Melt some butter in a baking dish and put in the fish. Bake for half an hour in a moderate oven, basting frequently. Strip off the skin, brush the fish with beaten egg and coat with breadcrumbs. Bake until browned and serve garnished with lemon, with anchovy sauce.

Cockles

Cockle Soup

2 quarts fresh cockles.	Small stick of celery, chopped.
1½ oz. butter.	1 oz. flour.
2 pints cockle liquid.	Chopped parsley.
1 pint milk.	Pepper and salt.

Cockles should be eaten fresh, but in order to clean them before cooking, put them in a bucket, cover with fresh water and sprinkle in a good handful of plain flour. The cockles will eat this over the course of twelve hours and will expel any sand and grit, etc. they have in their intestines. Drain them off and wash well in two or three lots of fresh water, before cooking.

Boil the cockles in plenty of water till they open. Strain the liquid, and shell the cockles. Heat the butter and blend in the flour. Gradually add the liquid and milk, stirring all the time. Add the chopped celery, salt, and pepper. Simmer for 30 minutes. Add the shelled cockles and the parsley and simmer for a few more minutes before serving.

CHAPTER FOURTEEN

FISH AND CHIPS   FISH PIE
BOUILLABAISSE   ROES
RISOTTO AUX FRUITS DE MER
BISQUE   CHOWDER
FISHCAKES   KEDGEREE
GEFILTE FISH   TIMBALE

Fish and Chips

You can fry many fishes, either in steaks or in fillets, dipped in batter, and serve them with potato chips and call it fish and chips: but I am quite unable to give you a recipe which will reproduce the exact and magnificent flavour which is "Fish and Chips". Is it the deep frying oil used again and again until it has a flavour all its own? or is it the flavour of printer's ink from the news-wrapping-paper? or—what is it?

This most delectable English dish has replaced roast beef, or boiled beef and carrots, as our national dish. It needs no seasoning but salt and vinegar, and the drink that goes best with it is a cup of tea!

Fish Pie

1 lb. white fish cooked in court bouillon.	1 lb. mashed potatoes. Butter.
$\frac{1}{2}$ pint parsley sauce.	Seasoning.
Grated lemon rind.	Browned breadcrumbs.

Flake the fish and mix it with the sauce and seasoning. Place in a greased pie dish and cover with potatoes and dot with butter. Sprinkle crumbs over and bake for 20 minutes in a fairly fast oven.

This is a basic recipe for fish pie, but it can be improved by various additions. Hardboiled egg chopped and added to the parsley sauce. Anchovy sauce added to the white sauce instead of parsley. A tablespoonful of white wine poured over the fish before putting on the potatoes. Or flaky pastry substituted for potatoes.

Roes

Herring Roe Savoury

1 hard roe.
1 soft roe.
½ teaspoonful cayenne.
½ teaspoonful curry powder.

2 oz. butter.
½ teaspoonful salt.
½ glass white wine.
Chopped parsley.

Place all the ingredients in a saucepan and cook together for 10 minutes, slowly. Then blend thoroughly, if possible in an electric liquidiser. Allow to cool, and serve as a spread, or on biscuits, or in small pastry cases. Wonderful for cocktail parties.

Fritters of Herring Roes

Simmer either soft or hard roes in salted water for 10 minutes. Dry well, then dip in batter and fry in deep fat. Serve with fried parsley and slices of lemon.

Herring Roes à la Mode

Fresh herring roes (or tinned).
Lemon juice.
Butter.
Mushrooms.
Frying batter.

English mustard.
Red pepper.
Parsley.
Fat bacon.
Deep fry.

Battered savoury herring roes fried and served with tomato salad. Very easy and unusual. Will not hurt by being kept warm for a while before serving.

Mask the herring roes all over with the mustard and season with lemon juice and red pepper, warm butter, chopped parsley and chopped mushroom. Roll each roe in a very thinly cut piece of cooked fat bacon, dip each into frying batter, and fry in hot oil until crisp and golden. Put on a very hot dish, and garnish with parsley, and lemon slices, and serve with dressed tomato salad.

Herring Roe Puffs

Rough puff pastry.
Herring roe stuffing (see page 213).

Cut the pastry into strips about ½ inch thick, spread roe stuffing on to half the strips and cover with the other half. Place on a baking tray, brush with egg and cook for 15 minutes.

Devilled Soft Herring Roes

Butter.	Hot toast.
Made mustard.	Parsley.
Salt and pepper.	Herring roes.

Place two tablespoonfuls of butter in a small pan by the side of the stove, add half a teaspoonful of mustard and the salt and pepper. Melt the butter and add the roes. Simmer gently until the butter be absorbed by the roes. Serve on hot buttered toast, sprinkling with parsley.

Boiled Cod's Roe

4 oz. roe per person.
1 dessertspoonful vinegar.
Warm salted water.

Wash the roe and tie it in a muslin bag. Place in warm salted water and add the vinegar. Cook till tender, for about three-quarters of an hour. Drain and serve on toast with lemon parsley butter.

Fried Shad Roe

Boil the shad roe for 20 minutes in water to which has been added a dessertspoonful of salt and a tablespoonful of vinegar. Drain and plunge in cold water. Drain again and season with pepper and salt, dredge with flour and fry in deep fat until it is golden brown. Serve with fried bacon.

Dried Mullet Roe

Take out the roe whole and cover it with salt. Leave for 5 hours, then press, but not strongly, between two boards. Then wash, and dry in the sun, when it soon becomes fit for use.

As a Substitute for Caviare

Wash the roes throughly in milk and water, and then in clear water, removing all fibre scrupulously, and drain throughly. Sprinkle 4 oz. of salt over each $1\frac{1}{2}$ lbs. of the spawn or roes and allow to remain in this for 48 hours, turning occasionally in the brine. Then lay them on a board in a warm place, such as the back of the stove or in front of the fire, until quite dry (about 8 to 12 hours). Crush with a weight, press into a jar or jars, adding to each $1\frac{1}{2}$ lb. 12 drops of the spirit of nitre and as much saltpetre as can be heaped on a penny.

Salmon Roe *(To preserve them for garnishing)*

Wash the roes throughly to clear them of all fibre, in clean water and then drain them and set them on an oven tray or tin plate and place them in a cool oven until quite dry. Beat with a fork to separate the (seeds), and place in a bottle, cork, and store in a cool, dry place, where they will keep for several weeks. They are used in spoonfuls, sprinkled over white fish or other fish dishes as a garnish.

Freshwater Bouillabaisse

I think the first and most important fact about a freshwater bouillabaisse is *the more the merrier*. The more mixed the bag, the more intriguing the final flavour. Do not include bream or chub, however, unless desperately pressed: the former is mainly slime, the latter mainly bones. But most general sorts of fish may be chucked in. I rate perch and gudgeon at the top—tastier than trout—and you can also add roach, rudd, and dace. Pike are an excellent ingredient, and eels are admirable. To my mind, the perfect ingredients for this dish are perch, gudgeon, pike, and eel (but some connoisseurs dote on carp).

Clean and cut up the fish. You want about a couple of pounds for a decent meal. Cut about half this into small bits, the rest into larger chunks. For the trimmings you'll want a couple of good-sized onions, four tomatoes, as much garlic as you can stand, a bay leaf, a pinch of saffron, parsley and fennel, and olive oil.

Slice the onions, peel and pulp the tomatoes. Put the larger, firmer lumps of fish into a pan, and all the vegetable trimmings, and pour in just enough oil to cover the fish. Then pour boiling water over the whole lot and cook fast and furiously for 5 minutes. Take the pan off the heat, and when the mixture has dropped below boiling point, add a generous glass, maybe two, of white wine, and the softer, smaller pieces of fish. Boil the lot for 7 minutes more.

Pour off the liquid into soup bowls, with croûtons of fried bread, or pieces of toast. Put the fish flesh into a dish and garnish with the parsley. Serve both at once, the liquid and the flesh, and let joy be unrestrained. Should be consumed with white wine, or stout. The cook, especially, needs a drink, for, as the poet so justly observed,

A freshwater bouillabaisse
Includes Dace
Even if you can't spell it
You can smell it.

MAURICE WIGGIN'S FAVOURITE FISH RECIPE

Risotto Aux Fruits de Mer

3 or 4 scallops.	1 teaspoonful oil.
1 pint mussels.	Pinch of saffron.
2 or 3 oz. shelled	Bouquet garni.
shrimps.	2 oz. blanched almonds.
1 cup Patna rice.	1 medium-sized onion.
1 cup white stock.	1½ gills dry white wine.
2 oz. butter.	Seasoning.

Garnish 2 hardboiled eggs quartered. Green and
black olives, pinch of paprika.

Wash the scallops well, then poach them in the wine,
with the bouquet garni, seasoning, and a slice of onion.
Cook 4 or 5 minutes. Draw aside and allow to cool in the
liquor. Wash the mussels in several waters and remove
their beards. Place them in a large pan, cover well. Shake
it over a good heat until all are open. Strain off the liquor
and keep it. Remove all but half a dozen of the mussels
from their shells, leaving the remaining ones in the shells for
the garnish. Keep them hot by standing them in a colander
over hot water. Melt the butter and oil in a fairly large,
strong pan. Add to it the rest of the onion finely chopped,

[273]

and soften it without colouration. Then add the rice and stir it quickly until it is coated with butter. Heat the stock, add to it the liquor from the mussels and scallops making it up to rather less than three cupfuls. Stir in the saffron and pour this on the rice. Now add the scallops roughly chopped, and the mussels and shrimps, and almonds. Mix and season well. Cover with a piece of greaseproof paper and the lid and cook in a moderate oven until the rice is done, without disturbing the rice.

Stone the olives. When the rice is cooked place in a hot dish to which has been added a spoonful of oil (hot) and rough it up with a fork. Decorate the dish with the eggs, olives, and remaining mussels. Dust with paprika.

Other fish such as oysters, crayfish, or crabs can be added if liked.

"THE IRIS SYRETT COOKERY BOOK"

Bisque

Is a fish soup or purée made with any shellfish.

Cook the lobster, or whatever you are using, in white wine court bouillon. When cooked remove from the stove and add a wineglassful of sherry, and leave overnight with the lobster in the liquid. Add 1 lb. of fresh tomatoes and reheat, cooking until tomatoes are soft. Allow to cool again, and then remove the lobster and pound all edible parts and the shell of the body and big claws in a mortar. Then pass this through a fine sieve, and discard what will not go through, putting the sieved fish back into the court bouillon and simmer very gently for 2 hours. Then allow to cool from boiling point and add two beaten egg yolks, a little fresh cream, sherry or brandy to taste, and serve. Season with cayenne pepper and salt. Pass tomatoes through the sieve back into the liquid. The soup can be thickened with a roux made of flour and butter if wished, instead of the yolk of egg.

Fish Chowder

2 lb. cod or fresh haddock.	Dessertspoonful salt.
1 lb. potatoes, cubed.	Pepper.
1 sliced onion.	3 cups scalded milk.
Small piece of	1 tablespoonful butter.
salt pork (2 oz.).	4 dry biscuits.

Clean and skin the fish. Take the head, tail and backbone and put them in a saucepan with pepper and salt and two cups of water. Simmer for 20 minutes, then drain and keep the liquor. Cut the salt pork small and fry until the fat is all out, and cook the chopped onion in this. Then put in the potatoes and two cups of water and boil for 5 minutes, then add the pieces of fish and the liquor from the bones. Simmer for 10 minutes more and add the butter, the milk, and the biscuits, crumbled coarsely.

Fish Cakes

1 lb. cooked fish	1 teaspoonful
(any white fish).	chopped parsley.
1 oz. butter.	1 teaspoonful
1 oz. flour.	anchovy essence.
½ pint milk.	Seasoning.
2 eggs.	Oil.
White breadcrumbs.	

Flake the fish and put into a basin with the parsley, and 1 oz. of breadcrumbs. Melt the butter in a saucepan and blend in the flour and then the milk. Season and add the anchovy essence. When boiling stir in one egg yolk. Pour this on to the fish and mix well, and allow it all to get cold. Then taking a piece of the mixture the size of an egg, place on a floured board and shape into a neat cake. Dip into beaten egg and then into fine breadcrumbs, and fry in very hot oil.

The same mixture with the addition of as much cooked potatoes as you like makes the fish go further.

Kedgeree

Super Kedgeree

6 tablespoonsful butter.	3 finely chopped onions.
$\frac{1}{8}$ teaspoonful cayenne pepper.	$\frac{1}{2}$ teaspoonful finely chopped ground saffron, or turmeric.
$\frac{1}{4}$ teaspoonful ground allspice.	$\frac{3}{4}$ pint water.
4 ground peppercorns.	1 tablespoonful lime juice.
1 bay leaf.	Rice.
	Salt and pepper.

1 lb. flaked cooked fish, preferably smoked haddock, but any white fish will do.

Heat the oil and cook the onions till golden, remove and put aside. Fry the spices together in the same oil until they are dark brown, then add the water and lime juice, the bay leaf, salt and rice, and simmer it till the rice begins to soften —about fifteen minutes. Add the fish and go on simmering until the kedgeree is quite dry. It should reach this stage as the rice completes cooking, and watch out that it doesn't catch on the bottom of the pan, but don't stir too fiercely or the fish will disintegrate too much. Served with sliced

hard boiled eggs and chutney and it bears little relationship
to what usually passes for Kedgeree in this country (see previous recipe).

Classic Kedgeree

1 lb. any cold fish	2 oz. butter.
(haddock preferred).	Salt and pepper.
¼ lb. rice.	Cayenne.
	2 hardboiled eggs.

Boil and dry the rice. Divide the fish into flakes, cut up
the whites of the eggs, and rub the yolks through a sieve.
Melt the butter in a pan and add the ingredients all together.
Stir till hot and then turn on to a dish and decorate with the
sieved egg yolk which has been kept for this purpose.

Gefilte Fish

Can be made with carp, bream, haddock, or mackerel.

3 lb. fish.	Salt, and pepper.
2 large onions.	2 slices white bread
2 eggs.	soaked and squeezed.
1 large sliced carrot.	Parsley.
	2 stalks celery.

Skin and bone the fish, keeping the skin intact to use as
wrappings. Chop the fish finely, add 1 grated onion, the
eggs, salt, pepper, and soaked bread. Make this into neat
cakes and use the fish skin to support these. Dice the other
onion and the celery and place in the bottom of a saucepan
with the fish bone. Then put the fish shapes on top, cover
with water, boil quickly, then turn heat low and simmer
for 1½ to 2 hours, reducing the liquid by half. Remove

from the heat and allow to cool, put the fish shapes on to a separate plate, strain off the liquid and allow to set into a jelly which can be used as a garnish. Also use sliced carrot as a garnish.

"580 DISHES FROM ABROAD" MARGUERITE PATTEN

Fish Timbale

¾ lb. any white fish.	½ teacupful of shelled
¾ lb. flaky pastry.	shrimps or prawns.
Stale bread.	¼ lb. mushrooms,
White sauce	sliced.
thickened with	A few oysters if
cream.	available.

Roll out the pastry to ⅛ inch thick and line a well-greased deep cake tin with it. Cut a pastry lid the size of the tin. Line the pastry in the tin with greaseproof paper and put in pieces of bread to prevent sides falling in. Put on the lid lightly and bake in a hot oven for 25 minutes. Remove lid and take out bread and paper. Flake the fish and add to sauce (see page 315) with shrimps, mushrooms, and oysters. Stir all together and cook gently for 10 minutes before putting in pastry case, replacing lid, and heating all together before serving.

CHAPTER FIFTEEN

CONDITION OF FISH
HOW TO PREPARE FISH
COOKING METHODS
COURT BOUILLON
SMOKING FISH AT HOME

Condition of Fish

The best way of all to tell if fish is fresh is by smelling it, as all fish should be fresh and pleasant. Next come sight and feel. The eyes must be bright and not sunken, the gills clean and free from slime, the scales bright and not easily detached from the skin. The flesh should be firm and elastic to the touch and well attached to the backbone.

Test shellfish for freshness by smell first, and remember it is terribly important not to eat and cook them if there is any doubt as to their freshness. With shrimp types, the outer skin should be firm, crisp and dry, with the segments of the abdomen and limbs intact and shiny. Mollusca with two shells should be tightly closed, or snap shut as soon as they are tapped. In univalves the operculum should be closed. When these hard shelled animals are tapped they should give a clear ring, and when forced open, the flesh should be firm.

The quality of the sea angler's catch is influenced by so many variables; weather, season, tides, and local conditions. Variations occur from year to year for no apparent reason; even the longshoremen cannot account for them. On the whole, though, local advice is the best guide as to where, when and how the fish are running. Listed on page 329 are recommended months for good eating of different species of sea fish, but much depends on location. Herrings, for example, are at their best in Scotland during the summer, and migrate slowly south down the east coast as the water cools until November finds them at their finest in the Dover area. The best crab season on the east coast is during the summer months, starting in May, but in some areas the crabs get thin and watery in August and improve again in September, October. Turbot and Brill may be good at any time of the year, and may also have definite "off" periods.

How to Prepare Fish

Fish for cooking must always be fresh.

CLEANING FISH   Flat fish are cleaned by cutting out the gills, then making a small incision in the stomach, just behind the head, and pulling out the gut. Wash the fish well and, if required, remove the head with a semi-circular cut.

Round fish are cleaned by slitting the stomach from the head towards the tail, and removing the entrails. Wash well and remove the head with a straight cut if required.

SCALING FISH   With the back of a knife, or with a blunt knife, scrape off the scale, working from tail to head.

WASHING FISH   Always wash fish out with cold, strongly salted water, and never soak fish in unsalted water.

SKINNING FISH   Sole should be washed and dried and the fins removed. With the tail facing you cut the skin across just above the tail. Dip your fingers in salt which will help you to grip; then, holding the tail with one hand and the skin with the other, pull the skin hard and quickly towards the head. Other flat fish are skinned after filleting. Lay the fillet down and cut through the flesh only, at the tail end, then work the knife up towards the head, pulling the fillet towards you as you cut.

SPLITTING FISH   Having slit the fish and cleaned it, and removed any roe, place on a board cut side down. Then press the fish firmly down with your hand all along the back-bone. This will then come away from the flesh easily.

FILLETING FISH   Flat fish are filleted thus: Lay the fish on a board and with a sharp pointed knife cut each side of the backbone from head to tail, down to the bone. Start with the left-hand top fillet, and keeping the knife oblique slide it through resting on the bone, taking three or four strokes from head to tail. Pull the fillet off, turn the fish round and repeat, working from tail to head. Turn the fish over and repeat the operation, producing in all four fillets.

Round fish are filleted by placing on a board with the head away from you. With the sharp pointed knife, slit the fish from head to tail, down the backbone. Cut the fillet at the head, and remove. Repeat on the other side, producing in all two fillets.

TRUSSING FISH Whiting are skinned and the tail is drawn through the mouth. Pin the fish thus by passing a skewer through the top of the head, through the tail, and out through the lower jaw. Large Haddock can be trussed in an S shape by passing a long skewer through the centre of the head, through the middle of the body, and through again just above the tail. Tie a piece of tape at each end of the skewer to keep the fish in good shape.

"*Good cooks and good Ash seldom dwell together.*"
FRANCK

Cooking Methods

Any of the following methods may be adapted for your particular purpose.

POACHING If you have a fish kettle it is perfect for poaching fish, but fish wrapped in foil can be poached in the oven. A fish kettle has a perforated plate in the bottom on which the fish rests and with which it can be lifted out and drained without damage. If you have no fish kettle, whole fish can be handled gently and safely by placing a saucer in the bottom of your stewpan and laying a clean cloth on top with the ends hanging out, making a kind of hammock in which the fish can be slung and lifted out when done.

[283]

When cooking trout or salmon a court bouillon (see page 285) is usually prepared first and, when cool, is poured over the fish already in the kettle or pan, never more than just covering the fish. The kettle is placed on a low flame and gradually brought up to simmering point, and cooking is carried out very carefully and quietly indeed. If the fish is to be served cold, let it cool in the kettle before draining.

Coarse-fleshed fish cooked in this way (cod, bream, turbot, etc.) should be placed in just boiling court bouillon. This seals the fish at once and keeps in the flavour.

Times for poaching vary with the fish, but fish is done when it goes opaque and exudes a creamy liquid.

When using a fireproof dish for poaching, the dish is well buttered and the fish laid in it just covered with court bouillon, and the dish is then covered with buttered grease proof, or with aluminium foil, or its own lid.

FRYING FISH   Deep frying is best done in a proper fish fryer with a wire basket, using pure lard. Shallow frying is best done in an ordinary frying pan, in oil or butter. Fish for frying is always coated in some way; either with seasoned flour, batter, or egg and oil and white breadcrumbs. The cleaned, washed, and dried fish should be seasoned with salt and pepper and a little lemon juice, and then dipped in the coating. Test deep fat by dropping in a small piece of bread; if the bread immediately goes crisp and golden the fat is hot enough. If there is no bubbling, heat the fat some more.

Egg and breadcrumb coating is done successfully by beating up egg lightly with a tablespoonful of oil, and seasoning. Put this mixture into a shallow dish and dip the fish into it. Make breadcrumbs by passing stale bread through a coarse sieve. Dip the fish coated with egg mixture into the breadcrumbs, or press the crumbs on with a flat knife. Don't have the fish too wet with egg, nor leave it to soak in the egg; and shake off surplus crumbs before frying.

[284]

Fish fried in shallow fat is usually just dipped in seasoned flour. A teaspoonful of curry powder added to the flour will give an unusual taste.

Batter is best made by putting 4 oz. flour, $\frac{1}{4}$ teaspoonful of salt, and an egg into a bowl, and mixing it to a smooth batter with about $\frac{1}{4}$ pint of milk or water. The fish is dipped into this and dropped immediately into hot fat, without a frying basket.

Some fish such as herrings, mackerel, and sprats, which are naturally oily, are dry fried, by being cooked gently in a frying pan without adding extra fat.

STEAMING FISH Wrap the fish in greaseproof paper after sprinkling it with salt, pepper, and lemon juice. Place it in a steamer and cook for 20 minutes to each pound, and 20 minutes extra for large fish.

GRILLING FISH Thick fish should be scored before grilling, and mackerel and herring split open and grilled open side first. Always preheat the grill and brush over both fish and grill with melted butter before cooking.

BAKING FISH Fish should be baked in a fireproof dish with knobs of butter on the fish, according to the various recipes.

Court Bouillon

Court bouillon should always be prepared before fish is cooked. To add the ingredients to the water in which your fish is cooking does not have the same effect at all.

Equal parts of water and white wine.	Small piece of celery.
	Salt and peppercorns.
1 onion.	A bouquet garni.
1 clove garlic.	2 shallots.
1 carrot.	1 clove.

The water and wine are brought to the boil, and a tablespoonful of vinegar is added to every quart of water. Add

[285]

all the other ingredients and simmer for 1 hour.

Court Bouillon can be made with the wine omitted.

After using, the court bouillon will make the basis of a sauce or a very good fish soup. For this purpose it should be strained and reheated with the addition of macaroni, spaghetti or vermicelli, with some grated cheese added just before serving.

Smoking Fish at Home

Whether you are a successful angler with, as a result, fish disposal and storage problems from time to time, or whether by courtesy of kind people who are anglers you are the recipient of occasional salmon or seatrout or trout, you should give some thought to a simple smoking process.

One can, of course, take or send fish to one of the commercial smoke houses which exist in London and Dublin and elsewhere but since the charge for smoking is expressed as so much per fish—usually about one pound sterling irrespective of size, it can be costly with small salmon and even more so with seatrout. True, these places will apply professional expertise and I have tasted nothing better than salmon smoked in the Hebrides by herring curers handling the salmon along with the kippers. And some salmon, smoked by the use of juniper dust in Norway, are quite superb.

Unnecessary refinements aside, smoking is not a complicated process providing one has or has access to a structure capable of simple adaptation as a smokehouse for large fish. Small fish such as seatrout and brown trout can be treated with lesser facilities—in fact in smoke-boxes.

First, however, the basic needs for the larger unit: these call for a shed, outhouse or other reasonably isolated building of which the dimensions are not critical. Interior measurements giving roughly a six-foot cube will suffice but it matters not at all if one wall is eight feet long and another five— or if the roof is seven feet above floor level. Floor ideally would be concrete and walls of brick or stone. If, however, the structure is timber, one can provide a "fireplace" or fireproof area on floor and on adjacent walls. The smoke-producing fire is not fierce—indeed it must not be and fire risk is minimal with common-sense elementary precautions.

Since the need is for a slowly-smouldering fire producing smoke without flame or appreciable heat, it follows that draught is critical and to provide this two openings 4–6 inches square are called for, one near to floor level and one high up in the opposite wall. Both should be adjustable of aperture by means of hinged or sliding flaps. Some experiment is advisable (before risking precious fish) to determine which aperture setting yields a suitable rate of combustion in the sawdust fuel. Much in this context must depend on the exposure to prevailing wind and consequent draught.

Two simple pieces of equipment complete the installation. First, a small table or shelf on which the fish may be salted with the top preferably at a slight slant so that it will drain and second, a section of ordinary garden wire netting stretched on a light wood frame. The size of the latter must depend on how many fish are likely to be available for smoking at one time but four feet by five will easily take four sides of salmon in the ten- to twelve-pound class. The frame is suspended from the roof on wires and should be about four feet from the floor.

A final point on structure: if the roof is unlined or otherwise uninsulated there will be condensation which may drip onto the fish. The roof should therefore be clad with wall-board, roofing felt or scrap timber nailed up to the underside of the rafters.

All that is required now is a quantity of salt—the cheapest grade will serve, a long-bladed very sharp knife and a supply of dry sawdust—preferably oak. Ordinary sawdust from the sawmill will, however, do although it will probably contain only a small proportion of oak.

Remove head and fins from the fish. Then, starting at the head end and placing the knife close to the backbone slice the fish from end to end—keeping the knife close to the bone all the way. Turn the fish over and repeat the process. You should end with two slabs of fish and the backbone complete with the tail. The small rib bones will be left in the two sides but these can be taken out when the sides are thinly sliced for the table.

Now sprinkle salt liberally over your table, lay the fish on the salted surface and sprinkle again over the fish. Leave for twelve hours and then wash and dry. That done, lay the fish on the suspended wire netting and prepare to smoke. If the floor is earth, stone or concrete and the walls of stone or brick, you can simply light a small paper and twig fire in a corner, feeding it with sawdust till smoking actively. Heap more sawdust round your fire and retreat. You will need to inspect progress to make sure that the sawdust is burning and being consumed at a reasonable rate—i.e. at about two average buckets per twenty-four hours. The aim is to achieve dense smoke and little heat because the fish must not be "cooked". The quietness or otherwise of the fire is of course governed by the draught and some experiment may be indicated here.

Results may vary with different smokehouses but for smoking to average taste, fish from ten to fifteen pounds should take about twenty-four hours, larger fish a few hours longer and small salmon, grilse and seatrout say twelve hours.

The finished fish should be brought indoors to dry in a rather higher atmosphere for about twelve hours before wrapping in greaseproof for keeping in the refrigerator or sealing in polythene for storage in the deep freeze. For the latter purpose meticulous care in sealing is worthwhile if the fish is not to become too dry in the freezer.

Finally, for seatrout and river trout a small smoke-box conforming broadly to the principles set out above for larger structures may be made from two tea-chests, one atop the other—the base of the lower one having been knocked out. The top box should contain a rod or rods on which fish can be hung and both boxes suitably placed draught holes. The burning sawdust can be located on the ground in a shallow metal pan or tray. After gutting and wiping out, small seatrout and brown trout generally can be smoked whole, or simply split open like kippers.

SIDNEY SPENCER

Smoked fish pâté

A delicious recipe for smoked fish pâté using any kind of smoked fish, such as trout, haddock, mackerel or kipper.

¾ lb. smoked fish.

10 oz. cream cheese.

¼ pint cream.

Lemon juice, salt and black pepper to taste.

Flake, bone and poach fish gently in a little milk in low oven until just cooked. Put all ingredients in liquidiser or mixing bowl, and mix until consistency of thick Devonshire cream. Put into dish or individual ramekins and leave in refrigerator until ready to serve with crisp brown toast and butter. This recipe makes enough for approximately 8 people.

DIPPING WITH GRASSHOPPER.

PART THREE

SAUCES FOR GAME AND FISH
HOME FREEZING OF GAME AND FISH

CHAPTER SIXTEEN

SAUCES FOR GAME
AND FISH

Introduction

If you cannot make good sauce, you cannot call yourself a good cook. In these days of packeted everything it is all too easy to succumb to temptation for the sake of ease and speed, even down to making something as simple as breadsauce out of a packet. It is an insult to good game and fish, and if somebody goes to the trouble of presenting you with good food to cook, it is an insult to them not to do the job properly. Strong words these, but good sauces are so easy if you will take a little trouble.

Equipment A good, small, non-stick saucepan is a boon and a blessing for the saucemaker. So is a wooden spoon with a pointed corner to scrape around the pan. A small double saucepan is extremely useful where a sauce contains eggs and must not be boiled. A sieve is useful, just a coarse one for straining, or a finer one for rubbing through; but nowadays most of us have electric blenders, which are, efficient do the job just as well, and much more quickly. Modern electric beaters, liquidisers or fast hand whisks help to resurrect lumpy sauces and make mayonnaise-making a simple job. A pressure cooker is extremely useful for making stock out of carcases, bones, etc. One just puts in a lot more water than usual, and the stock is made in a fraction of the time.

Basic Recipes There are several basic sauces upon which others are based; Sauce Bechamel, Sauce Espagnole (Brown Sauce), Mayonnaise, etc., and one or two basic methods of making sauce. Whatever stock or liquid is being used, sauce must be thickened and this is done in several ways which are mentioned in the recipes. First by using a "roux". This is simply melted butter in which PLAIN flour is cooked for a few moments before the liquid is added, very gradually. The flour is thus cooked in the butter and loses its raw taste, and the resulting sauce should be very smooth. To produce a coloured sauce without adding gravy browning, the roux is cooked until it goes brown. Care must be taken that it does not burn.

Velouté sauces are thickened by the addition of egg yolk to the liquid. If egg yolk is allowed to boil it will curdle, so the sauce must be made in a double saucepan (or one saucepan lodged over water in another slightly bigger one) and stirred all the time until the egg thickens (rather like egg custard).

Other thickeners; ground rice, arrowroot, cornflour, etc., are also used to thicken sauces, and these are usually moistened with a little cold liquid before being added to the gravy or sauce, and stirred until the thickening takes place. When meat is dusted with flour before being cooked, that flour will probably be sufficient to thicken the sauce or gravy without further additions.

Stocks, etc. Always boil up carcases, cooked or uncooked, and bones, to make stock, and use that stock to make sauces and gravy wherever appropriate. If a dish has been cooked in wine and seasonings, that combined with the juices which have been exuded during cooking, should be used for the sauce or gravy. Sauce Espangnole, and glaze (see page 298) are basic for use to make all kinds of sauces especially where there is no residue from cooking, or bone stock to use. I think one has to stick to first principles yet use a little imagination when making sauces. The various recipes given here can be altered and adapted to fit circumstances, but if the main ingredients are used, the type and flavour will remain the same.

Stock cubes are useful, but tend to be very salty, and have no jellying effect. Care must always be taken with salt, especially if any bacon or ham has been used in a recipe.

The residual saltiness may be quite sufficient without adding any more.

Serving sauce   Hot sauce must be served hot and must remain hot. ALWAYS warm the container well, beforehand. If you have a hotplate, keep the sauces and gravy on it for second helpings.

Capsicum (Green Pepper) Sauce

2 tablespoonsful wine vinegar.

¾ pint Sauce Espagnole (see p. 298).

Pinch of red pepper.

1 dessertspoonful French mustard.

1 oz. glaze (see p. 297).

1 tablespoon tomato purée.

3 green peppers.

Seeds from the peppers.

Pinch castor sugar.

1 teaspoonful chutney.

1 dessertspoonful English mustard.

A splendid green pepper and mustard sauce which goes with almost anything, fish, meat, or game, if you like it. Make Sauce Espagnole with a stock cube if you are in a hurry, (see page 298).

Put all the ingredients, EXCEPT the peppers but including the seeds, into a saucepan and simmer together for fifteen minutes. Add the three chopped peppers, reheat, and serve.

Courté Sauce

Juice of 1 lemon and 1 orange.

4 tablespoonsful sauce espagnole (see page 298).

1 wineglassful port wine.

Pinch of castor sugar.

1 wineglassful claret.

2 finely chopped shallots

½ oz. of glaze

An excellent wine sauce to eat with teal, widgeon, pheasant, or other birds, roast, grilled, or braised. The glaze can be omitted, stock cube used for the sauce espagnole, and cheap red wine substituted for the port and claret and you will still have a good sauce, but not up to top standards!

Boil up together the fruit juices, sauce espagnole, glaze and shallots. Skim, add the wine and the castor sugar, reheat and serve very hot.

Meat Glaze

Reduce any quantity of the stock, according to how much glaze you want, until it is brown and treacle thick. If you wish to keep this glaze, pour some melted lard into it, and as it cools and sets this will form an airtight cover. Be sure that when you do use the glaze, none of the fat goes with it.

Demi-glace

Mix together three quarters of a pint of the basic stock, and $\frac{1}{2}$ pint of Sauce Espagnole, and reduce it until the sauce is of the consistency you require. Then add two or three tablespoonsful of Madeira as liked.

The secret of these sauces is the long-drawn-out simmering which by modern standards is time consuming and expensive, but there is no real substitute.

Stock

Now for the classic stock recipe from which the glazes are made.

2 lb. shin of beef cut into large pieces.	
1 knuckle of veal.	Bones from a poultry carcase.
And/or ham bones.	And/or pork bones.
2 chopped onions.	6 oz. red wine.
2 chopped carrots.	Garlic.
Bouquet garni.	Peppercorns.

Fry chopped onions and carrots in lard, and as they cook

and change colour, add the shin. Brown it well and add the wine and all seasonings and herbs; bring back to the boil and transfer it to a much larger pot and put in all the other bones, add enough water to cover and simmer very very slowly, if possible over night on the side of the stove. DO NOT ADD ANY SALT. Strain off the stock.

Sauce Madeira

Ingredients as in Sauce Espagnole printed below, but exclude the sherry and add five ounces of Madeira wine instead. The addition of some sweet herbs (thyme, parsley etc.) would be an improvement.

In an emergency a brown sauce, with the addition of the Madeira would just do.

Sauce Espagnole, Meat Glaze, Demi-glace

Sauce Espagnole or Brown Sauce is one of the basic sauces to which one adds to make all kinds of other sauces. From it also is made meat glaze and "demi-glace", classic ingredients of various sauces and recipes.

1 onion.	1 pint stock made with
1 carrot.	beef stock cube.
2 oz. mushrooms.	Bouquet garni.
2 oz. lean bacon or	6 peppercorns.
raw ham.	1 bay leaf.
2 oz. butter.	2 tablespoonful tomato
2 oz. flour.	purée.

$\frac{1}{8}$ pint sherry.

Slice the vegetables and chop the ham. Melt the butter and fry first the ham, and then, gently, the vegetables until they are golden brown. Add the flour with a sprinkler and stir it in and fry slowly until it is all brown. Add the stock, herbs and spices and stir till the sauce simmers and cook for half an hour. Then add the tomato purée and simmer for another half hour. Rub through a fine sieve or an efficient electric blender, add the sherry, and reheat.

Nabob Sauce

2 large onions.	1 oz. butter.
1 apple.	Juice of 3 lemons.
Bunch of herbs.	1 dessertspoonful tamarinds
Pinch of turmeric.	(if available).
4 red peppers.	Big pinch of ground ginger.
Tablespoonful	Small teaspoonful cumin
chutney.	powder.
2 sliced tomatoes.	1 dessertspoonful ground
$\frac{1}{4}$ pint coconut	rice.
milk.	2 tablespoonsful grated
$\frac{1}{4}$ pint tomato	coconut.
purée.	2 figs.
$\frac{1}{2}$ gill cream.	$\frac{1}{2}$ pint good stock.
1 tablespoonful	1 tablespoonful cooked
cooked turnip.	carrot.

3 green peppers, diced.

A very complicated curry sauce which goes with pheasant and rabbit, anything which will fit with curry really. It is not a hot sauce, but rather highly flavoured, thick and sweet.

Slice one onion and cook it in butter till it is golden. Add the other sliced onion, the apple, juice of one lemon, herbs, tamarinds, turmeric, ginger, red peppers, cumin, chutney, ground rice, tomatoes, grated coconut, coconut milk, and figs. Add tomato purée and stock. Boil for $\frac{1}{2}$ hour, add the cream, and put all through a blender or sieve. Add the carrot, turnip, and peppers, reheat and use.

White Mushroom Sauce

½ lb. button mushrooms.
1 quart white stock (chicken stock or cubes).
Juice of 1 lemon.
Salt.
2 oz. butter.
2 oz. plain flour.
½ wineglassful sherry.
1 gill thick cream.

Creamy white mushroom sauce to go with rabbit, pheasant, etc.

Chop the mushrooms and boil them in the stock with the lemon juice and a pinch of salt, for ½ hour. Skim. Make a roux with the flour and butter and add the stock gradually, stirring all the time. Add the sherry and cream, reheat, and serve.

Brown Mushroom Sauce

¾ pint sauce espagnole.
1 oz. glaze.
2 wineglasses sherry.
2 oz. mushrooms.
2 oz. button mushrooms.

Plain mushroom sauce to go with pheasant.

Boil the ingredients together, reserving the button mushrooms. When the quantity has reduced by half, put through a sieve or blender. Slice the button mushrooms, add them to the sauce, bring to the boil and serve.

Cheese Sauce

2 cupfuls court bouillon.
Yolk of two eggs.
½ cup of cream.
2 tablespoonfuls butter.
Salt and pepper.
½ cupful grated cheese.
3 tablespoonfuls flour.

Reduce the court bouillon by half by boiling. Melt the butter and blend in the flour, then add the court bouillon and cream, stirring constantly. At just below boiling point add the egg yolks, stir well, and add the grated cheese, but do not boil once the egg yolks are in.

Polonaise Sauce

¼ pint thick espagnole sauce.	2 chopped shallots.
1 oz. glaze.	4 chopped mushrooms.
½ pint of champagne.	¼ pint asparagus tips.
	6 cooked and sliced globe artichoke bottoms.

This one really is expensive, and it's one way of serving asparagus and artichokes. Nevertheless it will turn venison (or ham, tongue, or beef) into something very special. Dry cider would do at a pinch instead of champagne.

Boil all the ingredients together except the asparagus and artichokes. Then skim, and when it is quite thick, put it through a sieve or blender. Add the vegetables, reheat, and serve.

Estouffade Sauce

Bones of 2 partridges.	3 mushrooms.
2 wineglasses sherry.	1 onion.
Pepper.	1⅓ pint light stock
8 peppercorns.	(chicken stock cube).
1¼ oz. plain flour.	1¼ oz. butter.
2 large tomatoes, skinned and pulped or 1 tablespoonful tomato purée.	1 oz. grated Parmesan.
	Juice of 1 lemon.
	Sherry sauce for bird entrees.

Put the bones, onion, mushrooms, sherry, peppercorns seasoning and stock into a saucepan and boil slowly for 1 hour. Make a roux with the flour and butter, and strain ¾ pint of the stock on to it gradually, stirring all the time. Add the rest of the ingredients, boil for 15 minutes, skim, and use.

Lucine Sauce

Bird bones.	2 chopped shallots.
1 tablespoonful olive oil.	Bunch of mixed herbs.
	2 tomatoes.
2 mushrooms.	Small bacon bone.
Pepper.	1 oz. glaze.
1 wineglass sherry.	1½ oz. grated Parmesan
1 pint sauce	cheese.
espagnole.	Red pepper.
2 chopped green peppers.	

Tasty cheese and pepper sauce which must be made with the juices from the bird and its bones. Good with any bird.

Stew the bones with shallots, oil, herbs, mushrooms, tomatoes and pepper, in a skillet or frying pan with a lid, for 20 minutes. Add all the rest of the ingredients and cook for ½ hour. Skim, remove the bones, put through a blender, and serve.

Make this same sauce without the cheese and the green peppers, add a few drops of red colouring, and it becomes MAGENTA SAUCE.

Lemon Sauce

1½ oz. butter.	½ pint of the liquid in
1½ oz. flour.	which the fish was
¼ pint thin cream.	cooked.
1 egg yolk.	Seasoning.
2 tablespoonfuls thick cream.	Juice of a lemon.

Heat the butter in a pan and stir in the flour, add the fish stock and thin cream gradually, stirring all the time, and cook until thickened. Whisk in the other ingredients and cook gently for a few minutes longer.

Orange Sauce (1)

¾ pint sauce espagnole.

Juice of a lemon.

3 oranges.

Small teaspoonful castor sugar.

Wineglassful sherry.

½ oz. arrowroot.

Pinch of salt.

Rich orange-flavoured sauce to serve with wild duck.

Reduce the Sauce Espagnole a little, add the lemon juice, orange juice and a little castor sugar and bring to the boil, thicken with arrowroot mixed with the sherry, and give the sauce a good whisk. Cut two oranges into fine slices removing pith and pips and add it to the sauce. Reheat till quite hot.

Then cut the peel of one more orange into little Julienne strips, or match sticks, put them into cold water with a little salt and bring to the boil, strain, rinse in hot water and add to the sauce.

Orange Sauce (2)

¾ pint Sauce Espagnole.   1 Seville orange.

A simpler and less rich orange sauce.

Reduce the Sauce Espagnole by one third. Peel the yellow rind only from the orange and cut it into little strips. Scald them in boiling water for 5 minutes, then add them to the sauce and simmer till the rind is soft (about 10 minutes), add the orange juice and serve.

Sauce Vinaigrette

To three parts of olive oil use one part wine vinegar.

Salt.   Made mustard.

Pinch of sugar.   Pepper.

Mix the seasonings with the vinegar, add the oil little by little whisking well all the time.

[303]

3 oz. chopped pineapple.	2 tablespoonfuls brown sugar.
3 oz. pineapple juice.	1 teaspoonful ground ginger.
½ pint water.	
Salt.	1 teaspoonful dry mustard.
2 teaspoonfuls oil.	½ cupful mayonnaise.
1 tablespoonful soya sauce.	2 tablespoonfuls tarragon vinegar.
1 tablespoonful Worcestershire sauce.	1 tablespoonful tomato paste.
	Pepper.
1 tablespoonful sherry.	1 clove garlic or teaspoonful garlic salt.

2 oz. chopped spring or pickled onions.

Put all ingredients except chopped pineapple and onions into a bowl and whisk till blended. Then add the pineapple and onions and heat all together, stirring constantly. Simmer for 10 minutes before use.

A simpler sweet and sour sauce may be made by omitting the sherry, the Worcestershire sauce, the ginger, the mustard and the mayonnaise, and thickening instead with a dessert-spoonful of cornflour blended in when mixing.

Sauce Hollandaise

1 tablespoonful court bouillon.	4 oz. butter.
	1 tablespoonful lemon juice.
2 egg yolks.	Pepper.

Heat the court bouillon until reduced by half, add a table-spoonful of water and strain on to the beaten yolks. Heat in a double pan until creamy, whisking all the time. Then whisk in the butter, and add lemon juice and pepper just before serving.

Julienne Sauce

1 dessertspoonful olive oil.	2 oz. chopped raw lean bacon.
3 mushrooms.	Bunch of mixed herbs.
Pepper.	1 wineglassful port wine.
6 anchovy fillets.	1 wineglassful claret.
1 pint sauce espagnole.	1 wineglassful sherry.
	3 pickled gherkins.
1 oz. glaze.	3 shredded red chillies.

Serve with fish, or hare or venison.

Another expensive alcoholic sauce, hot, rich, and piquant. Fry the bacon, mushrooms, and herbs in the oil till tender. Add the rest of the ingredients, except the gherkins and chillies, and boil till the quantity is reduced by half. Put through a blender, and then add the gherkins and chillies.

Sauce Tartare

4 small gherkins.	1 tablespoonful capers.
2 shallots.	1 teaspoonful chopped parsley.
2 teaspoonsful tarragon vinegar.	

Made by adding these ingredients to sauce below.

Sauce Mayonnaise

1 yolk of egg.	$\frac{1}{2}$ pint olive oil.
2 tablespoons wine vinegar.	$\frac{1}{2}$ teaspoonful French mustard.

Salt and pepper.

Put the mustard in a bowl and add the egg, whisk lightly. Then, whisking all the time, pour in the oil very gradually. Season and add enough vinegar to make the sauce the consistency you like.

4 oz. butter.	6 peppercorns.
2 egg yolks.	1 tablespoon white stock.
2 tablespoons	Salt.
tarragon vinegar.	1 tablespoon chopped
1 chopped shallot.	tarragon.

Put the peppercorns, shallot and vinegar into a pan and heat until the vinegar is reduced by half. Then strain, add the stock and the beaten egg yolks. Stand in a double saucepan and heat, whisking all the time, until the mixture thickens. Do not boil. Beat in the butter and the chopped tarragon, and add salt to taste.

Shrimp Sauce

Shrimps.	Pepper and salt.
1 oz. plain flour.	The liquor and cream in
1 oz. butter.	which the fish was cooked.

Melt the butter in a pan and blend in the flour, add the liquor slowly stirring all the time. Season as liked. Add the shrimps and continue to cook slowly until they are heated through.

Laver Sauce

Juice of 2 lemons.	1 tablespoonful red-
1 oz. glaze.	currant jelly.
4 tablespoonsful	1 pinch castor sugar.
sauce espagnole.	$\frac{1}{2}$ pint of laver.

An unusual sauce containing laver, the specially prepared seaweed available round our western coasts. Commonly served with mutton, it is also very good with venison.

Boil all ingredients except the laver for 10 minutes, skim, add the laver, put through a blender, reheat, and serve.

Bread Sauce

½ a small white loaf,   Salt and pepper.
without crust.   Knob of butter.
4 cloves.   1 medium onion/2 small
½ pint of milk.   ones.

Standard recipe for breadsauce, to be eaten with all kinds of game and poultry.

Put the bread, broken into pieces, into a non stick saucepan with the salt and pepper, butter and milk. Cut the onion into halves and stick the cloves into the onion pieces and put these into the saucepan. Bring the mixture to the boil and stir it all together. Simmer for 2 minutes, stirring gently. Put aside for at least 1 hour, then reheat, remove the onion and cloves, stir well and serve. This produces a fairly solid bread sauce. If you prefer it smoother and runnier, add more milk, and beat and press the bread with a wooden spoon. To make very smooth breadsauce, use breadcrumbs and not bread pieces. Another method is to put the ingredients as above, with plenty of milk, into a covered fireproof dish and let the whole lot cook at the bottom of the oven, slowly, for an hour before serving.

Imperial Sauce

¾ pint juices from cooking game or venison.
1 wineglass port wine.   1 oz. glaze.
1 wineglass claret.   ½ pint Sauce Espagnole.
1 wineglass sherry.   1 dessertspoonful red-
2 bayleaves.   currant jelly.
Juice of 1 lemon.   Bones from the bird.

A very alcoholic thin sauce for pigeons, game, venison. Use the pan juices from the meat to make the sauce.

Put all the ingredients together and simmer for 15 minutes, after which time remove the bones, skim, strain and serve.

1 small crab.	6 anchovy fillets.
¼ pint thick mayonnaise.	2 tomatoes, skinned or 1 tablespoon tomato purée.
1 tablespoonful tarragon vinegar.	Pepper.

1 tablespoonful finely chopped tarragon and chervil.
Saltspoonful English mustard, the same of French mustard.   1 gill stiff whipped cream.
¼ gill liquid aspic.   ¼ pint double cream.

Very good but very creamy crab sauce to eat with hot or cold fish, salmon, cod, turbot, etc., or with cold roast fowl.

Cook the crab. Shred the claw meat and put aside. Take the white meat from the body and pound it with the anchovies. Then add it to all the other ingredients except the double cream and the shredded claw meat. When all the rest is well blended together, add the double cream and the claw meat, and put in the fridge and chill till required.

Chevet Sauce (Celery)

2 sticks celery.	1 pint Sauce Espagnole.
2 tablespoonsful sherry.	Saltspoonful castor sugar.
1 beef stock cube.	

Rich celery sauce to eat with pheasant or duck.

Cut the celery into shreds and put it into cold water with a sprinkling of salt, bring to the boil, strain, and rinse. Then cook the celery in the pint of stock made with the cube, adding water if it threatens to boil dry, until the celery is tender. Strain off the liquor into the sauce espagnole, add the sherry and the sugar, and simmer for 15 minutes. Then add four large tablespoonsful of the cooked celery, reheat and serve.

Beurre de Montpellier

Special sauce for cold fish

2 finely chopped shallots.	1 tablespoonful chopped capers.
Few pieces of watercress.	2 anchovy fillets.
6 leaves of spinach.	2-3 gherkins.
3 sprigs of tarragon.	2 hardboiled yolks.
3 sprigs of thyme.	2 raw yolks.
4 oz. butter.	1 gill oil.
	Seasoning.

Put the spinach, the cress and the herbs into boiling water and boil for 3 minutes, then add the shallots. Drain, refresh under cold tap, and drain again. Then squeeze dry in a cloth. Pound in a mortar, or pass through a sieve with the gherkins and capers. Work in the softened butter, and the two sieved hardboiled yolks and the raw yolks. Chop the anchovy fillets as finely as possible and add these. Blend well. Lastly add the oil drop by drop, as for mayonnaise. Season well with pepper and a little salt. Allow to harden before serving.

"THE IRIS SYRETT COOKERY BOOK"

Suedoise Sauce

½ pint very thick mayonnaise.	2 tablespoonsful grated horseradish.
2 tablespoonsful chopped cucumber.	1 chopped shallot.
1 teaspoonful chopped capers.	1 oz. chopped smoked salmon.
	¼ pint stiff whipped cream.

Another extravagant but delicious cold sauce for hot or cold fish, grilled or boiled (or artichokes, asparagus).

Mix together all the ingredients, putting in the whipped cream last. Chill in the fridge till wanted.

Tomato Cream Sauce

4 ripe tomatoes.	½ gill aspic jelly.
Red pepper and salt.	1 gill stiffly whipped cream.
1 dessertspoonful tarragon vinegar.	1 teaspoonful chopped capers.
1 chopped shallot.	green tarragon.
2 red chillies.	chervil.
1 tablespoonful grated horseradish.	6 boned anchovy fillets.

Hot tomato sauce, good with cold fish or with cold game.
Put the tomatoes through a blender till they are smooth and then mix them with the aspic, and pepper and salt, whipped cream, vinegar and the rest of the ingredients. Blend the whole lot thoroughly together and chill.

Commodore Sauce

2 wineglassfuls white wine.	1 large mushroom.
	2 bay leaves.
1 chopped shallot.	1 dessertspoonful anchovy essence.
1 ounce of glaze (see page 297).	
	2 tomatoes or 1 tablespoon tomato purée.
1 pint Sauce Espagnole.	1 green pepper, chopped.

1 teaspoonful French mustard.

A rich fruity sauce for fish. Takes a little trouble to make as you need Sauce Espagnole (see page 298). At a pinch, make the Sauce Espagnole with a beef stock cube.

Boil all the ingredients together for 15 minutes and then sieve, or put through an efficient electric blender. Colour with red colouring if liked.

Gironde Sauce

1 pint claret.	1 pint sauce espagnole.
1 pint bruised cherries.	2 tomatoes.
Juice of half a lemon.	Saltspoon castor sugar.
½ oz. arrowroot.	1 teaspoonful Kirsch.

½ oz. glaze.

Marvellous and expensive cherry sauce to eat with game, venison (and other meats and poultry).

Reduce the claret to half by boiling and add the cherries and sauce espagnole, and the other vegetables, and seasoning, and boil for half an hour. Add the kernels from the cherries, bring to the boil again, add the Kirsch and serve.

Mustard Sauce

1 teaspoonful English mustard.	2 tablespoonfuls cream or milk.
1 teaspoonful French mustard.	Salt. Sugar.
2 oz. butter.	½ pint milk.
1 tablespoonful flour.	1 dessertspoonful vinegar.

Melt the butter in a saucepan, and stir in the flour and mustard, then the water and vinegar. Add a seasoning of salt and sugar to taste. Rub through a fine strainer or sieve, or blend with a liquidiser, then put back in the saucepan and rewarm, adding the cream or a little milk.

Browned Lemon Butter

2 oz. butter.	Few drops of
Squeeze of lemon juice	Worcestershire sauce.

Melt the butter in a pan until it goes brown, then add the lemon juice, sauce, and season to taste.

Cold Mousseline Sauce

¾ pint aspic jelly.   ¼ pint thick mayonnaise.
¼ pint whipped   Pinch red pepper.
   cream.   1 dessertspoonful
Pinch castor sugar.   tarragon vinegar.

Savoury cold sauce with any kind of fish (or asparagus or globe artichokes).

Whip the aspic jelly until it is stiff and spongy, and mix all the other ingredients in. Chill and serve.

Sauce Tartare

1 hardboiled egg   1 raw egg yolk.
   yolk, sieved.   Salt and pepper.
½ pint oil.   Mustard.
1 tablespoonful wine   1 dessertspoonful each
   vinegar.   chopped capers and chives
       1 tablespoonful chopped tarragon.

Place the sieved egg in a bowl with the raw yolk. Add the oil very gradually, stirring all the time, then add the vinegar and seasoning, still stirring. Finish with the blanched tarragon, and the chives, and capers.

Albany Sauce

6 anchovy fillets.   ¼ pint thick mayonnaise.
1 tablespoonful   Pinch of pepper.
   tarragon vinegar.   Pinch of castor sugar.
Juice of one lemon.   2 chopped gherkins.
¼ pint whipped cream.   ¼ pint chopped shrimps.

Very thick rich cold sauce of fish, dressed lobster, crab, etc.

Pound the anchovies, and mix with the mayonnaise and all the other ingredients. Mix up well and serve cold.

[312]

Ambassador Sauce

White fish bones.	1 large onion.
Bunch of herbs.	4 peppercorns.
Salt.	2 oz. butter.
1½ oz. plain flour.	2 tablespoonsful.
1 teaspoonful essence	cream.
of anchovy.	Juice of a lemon.

Creamy anchovy sauce to eat with salmon sole, or other white fish.

Put the fish bones into a saucepan with the onions, herbs and salt, cover with cold water and bring to the boil, gently. Skim and simmer for ½ hour. Make a roux with the butter and flour, and add fish stock, half a pint gradually, stirring all the time. Then add the cream, anchovy essence and lemon juice, and a little red colouring if you like. Whisk well together so that the sauce is really smooth.

Clementine Sauce

Fish stock.	Salt.
2 sliced onions.	Thyme, parsley, bayleaf.
Juice of 2	Peppercorns.
lemons.	1½ oz. flour.
1½ oz. butter.	1 oz. grated Parmesan
Pinch red pepper.	cheese.
1 tablespoonful cream.	

Fishy cheese sauce for eating with boiled turbot, boiled soles, salmon, etc.

Simmer the seasonings and onions and lemon juice with the fish stock for 20 minutes. Make a roux with the butter and flour and add half a pint of the skimmed and strained stock, stirring all the time, till the sauce is the right consistency. Then add the cheese and the cream.

Monico Sauce

Bone and head of
a sole.

1 wineglass sherry.

Bunch of herbs.

Pinch of salt.

2 tablespoonsful cream.

1 wineglassful white
wine.

1 sliced onion.

4 black peppercorns.

1¾ oz. plain flour.

1¾ oz. butter.

1 tablespoonful chopped button mushrooms.

Wine and mushroom sauce suitable for any fillets of fish.

Put the fishbones in a pan under enough water just to cover. Add the wine and sherry, the onion, herbs, peppercorns, and salt, and cook gently for 15 minutes. Strain off the stock. Make a roux with the flour and butter, and add the stock gradually, stirring all the time. Then add the cream, the mushrooms, and season to taste, and serve hot.

Marinade Sauce

¾ pint fish stock or
court bouillon.

4 chopped
mushrooms.

Red pepper.

1 tablespoonful
glaze.

3 chopped anchovy
fillets.

2 chopped shallots.

1 tablespoonful
tarragon vinegar.

1 dessertspoonful
anchovy essence.

1 tablespoonful lemon juice.

A sharp anchovy sauce for use with any fish.

Put together the stock, mushrooms, shallots, pepper and anchovies, and boil together. Make a roux with the flour and butter and add the stock mixture gradually, and stir while it reboils and thickens. Then add the vinegar, glaze, anchovy essence and lemon juice.

Put through an efficient electric blender and serve hot.

White Sauce or Sauce Bechamel

1 oz. plain flour.   ½ pint milk.

1 oz. butter.   Pepper and salt.

Melt the butter in a saucepan, remove from heat and add the flour, blending well. Return to the heat and cook for a minute or two, stirring all the time. Then add the milk gradually, still stirring.

Cussy Sauce

½ pint Sauce   1 large mushroom.

    Espagnole.   1 shallot.

Teaspoonful chopped   1 teaspoonful

    parsley.   capers.

Caper sauce for serving with grilled mullet, salmon, etc. Use nasturtium seeds instead of capers if the latter are not available.

Boil all ingredients together for about 40 minutes, skim, and serve hot.

Lobster Cream

2 oz. plain flour.   2 oz. butter.

½ pint fish stock.   1 dessertspoonful

Juice of 1 lemon.   anchovy essence.

Red colouring.   Pinch red pepper.

Meat of half a lobster.   Tablespoonful cream.

Lobster cream sauce for masking any hot fish.

Make a roux with the butter and flour. Add the stock and boil. Then add all other ingredients including the lobster meat cut small. Warm it up in a double saucepan or bain marie, do not boil.

Lobster Sauce

Make in the same way as Crab Sauce, but omit the mustard.

[315]

1 lb. neck or knuckle of veal.	10 peppercorns.
	Blade of mace.
2½ pints cold water.	½ pint white wine.
Salt.	1 bay leaf.
2 oz. gelatine.	1 carrot.
Whites and shells of three eggs.	½ turnip.
	Stick of celery.
¼ pint white vinegar.	1 onion.
Bouquet garni.	4 cloves.

Divide the veal and bones and place in salted water. Simmer for 3 hours then strain and allow to cool. Remove all fat and place stock in saucepan with the gelatine. Stand for 20 minutes to soak the gelatine. Whip the egg whites stiffly and add to the stock together with the egg shells which have been washed and crushed. Add all other ingredients except the wine and bring to the boil whisking all the time. Stop whisking and boil for 2 minutes, then move carefully from the stove and allow to settle for 10 minutes. Remove the bouquet garni and add the white wine. Then strain through a jelly bag and the aspic is ready to be poured over the fish.

Green Mousseline Sauce

1 large green pepper.	2 gherkins.
6 anchovy fillets.	1 teaspoonful capers.
Handful of blanced tarragon and chervil.	
1 shallot.	Tablespoonful chopped parsley.
5 raw egg yolks.	
2 egg whites.	1½ oz. fresh butter.
Juice of one lemon.	Salt and pepper.

A thick rich green sauce to eat with salmon, trout, mullet (or with asparagus, globe artichokes).

Put the chopped pepper, gherkins, anchovies, capers, tarragon, chervil, shallot, parsley and a little green colouring if liked, all together and blend, either by pounding, or through an electric blender. Add the rest of the ingredients, and put all together into the top of a double saucepan. Whip the contents together over boiling water until they thicken.

Bon Homme Sauce

1 tablespoonful strained lemon juice.
2 tablespoonsful mushroom liquor or 1 of mushroom essence.
4 oz. grated Gruyere or Cheddar cheese.
1 teaspoonful   1 teaspoonful English French mustard.   mustard.
$\frac{1}{4}$ pint tomato sauce. $\frac{1}{2}$ wineglassful sherry.
6 anchovy fillets.

Splendid sauce with a mixture of flavours, mushroom, cheese and anchovy, very good with any kind of fish.

Put all the ingredients together and stir till boiling and quite smooth. Put the anchovies through a sieve or blender before cooking.

Napier Sauce

$\frac{3}{4}$ pint good fish stock.   2 oz. plain flour.
$\frac{1}{2}$ pint cleaned cooked   2 oz. butter.
     mussels. $\frac{1}{4}$ pint cream.
1 teaspoonful English   Yolks of two
     mustard.   eggs.

Mussel sauce to eat with filleted fish.

Make a roux with the butter and flour, add the stock gradually, stirring all the time. Add the mussels and the mixed mustard. Mix the raw egg yolks with the cream and add this to the mixture. Put it all in a double saucepan and cook over boiling water till the sauce thickens. Stir all the time.

CHAPTER SEVENTEEN

HOME FREEZING OF GAME AND FISH

The freezer should be maintained at o°F (−18°C) for satis-factory storage. When there is a fast-freeze compartment, this should be used for freezing meat and fish quickly which results in a good texture after thawing. When the frozen food is completely hard, it can be transferred to the main compartment for storage, and the fast-freeze switch returned to normal. If there is no special compartment, be sure fresh food is cool before putting it into the freezer, and freeze it against the floor and/or walls of the freezer for maximum chill.

Game and fish should be carefully labelled with details of the contents of the package, weight, age and date when killed. If you find stocks of game and fish are building up too much, turn some of them into pâtés, pies or casseroles which can be frozen again, but not stored longer than 1–2 months. If you want your frozen game and fish to taste good and retain perfect texture, be sure to thaw slowly in a refrigerator before cooking, not in a warm open kitchen.

GAME

All types of game freeze extremely well, and can be kept from 6–8 months; though cooked game dishes should be stored no longer than 1 month.

It is essential that all game should be hung and prepared for cooking before freezing. Game which is not properly hung before freezing will be tough; also the flesh deteriorates rapidly after freezing and thawing so that it cannot be hung successfully at this stage. Number of days required for hanging depends on how high you like the bird when cooked (see page 155).

It is possible to freeze game before plucking or skinning, but is both difficult and unpleasant to do this when the game has thawed, and is far better to prepare the game ready for cooking before putting it in the freezer.

PREPARING FOR THE FREEZER

Game may be frozen raw or cooked. In general, it is best to freeze raw birds or animals which are young and well shot. Older or badly shot game is best converted into cooked dishes before freezing since badly shot flesh becomes nearly black when plain roasted. It is preferable to roast game after freezing, as cooked roast game which is frozen becomes flabby after thawing out. (The flesh exudes moisture on thawing).

All game for freezing should be kept cool after shooting, and hung for the required time. Shots should be carefully removed if possible, and shot wounds thoroughly cleaned. After plucking and drawing birds, the cavity should be thoroughly washed and drained, and the body wiped with a damp cloth. Particular attention should be paid to the vent to see that no faeces are left. Any giblets which are required should be cleaned and packed separately as their freezer life is very short (1 month). The game can then be packed, cooled, and frozen. Some birds should not be drawn before freezing (see notes on individual types of game).

PACKING

Game is best packed in heavy polythene; birds may be most easily packed in bags, but hare and venison can be wrapped in sheet polythene. Sharp protruding bones should be padded with foil, greaseproof paper or extra polythene sheeting to prevent tearing and breaking packages. Joints, if frozen separately of hare, rabbit or venison may be separated by sheets of foil, Cellophane or polythene.

When the game has been wrapped, air must be drawn out of the package. This is best done by inserting a drinking straw and sucking out surplus air so that the wrapping material adheres closely to the contents or more simply by squeezing air out with hands round packet.

Thawing and Cooking

Game should be thawed in the sealed freezer package. Thawing in a refrigerator is more uniform and gives better results, but will take longer. Allow 1 hour per lb. weight at room temperature, and 5 hours per lb weight in the refrigerator. Start cooking game as soon as it is thawed and still cold, to prevent loss of juices.

Game Birds

Grouse, pheasant, partridge, wild duck and *pigeon* should be plucked and drawn before freezing, together with any *waterfowl fed on fish. Plover, quail, snipe, woodcock* should be plucked but not drawn.

Hares and Rabbits

These should be hung head downwards, with a cup to catch the blood, a plastic cream carton is a good idea. Rabbits can be frozen after bleeding; hare can be hung up to 5 days before freezing, in a cold place. Skin and clean, wiping the cavity well with a damp cloth. These animals may be frozen whole, but are more conveniently cut into joints. Each piece can be wrapped separately, then all packed together in polythene, and a few joints may be extracted for a small recipe. Blood can be frozen separately in a carton.

[320]

VENISON

A carcase of venison should be kept in good condition, with the shot wounds carefully cleaned, and the animal kept as cold as possible. After beheading, the animal should be bled, skinned and cleaned, and the interior washed and wiped. The meat is best hung in a very cool place, just above freezing point, with the belly propped open so air can circulate. Seven to ten days hanging will ensure tender meat; the carcase should be wiped over with milk on alternate days to help keep the meat fresh.

It is best to get a butcher to cut the meat. The best joints can be frozen whole, wrapped in polythene. The rest of the meat can be minced to freeze raw, or can be casseroled or made into pies and frozen in this form.

Venison is a dry meat, and is often marinaded before cooking. This marinade should be poured over the meat while it it thawing.

Venison Marinade

½ pint red wine.   1 large sliced onion.
½ pint vinegar.   Parsley, thyme and bayleaf.

Mix ingredients together and cover frozen venison joint as it thaws, turning meat frequently. Use the marinade for cooking the meat, but for roasting cover the meat with strips of fat bacon before cooking.

COOKED GAME IN THE FREEZER

Any favourite game recipe can be frozen with little adaptation. *Pâté* should be packed in small containers, as it deteriorates quickly after thawing. *Roast game* will be flabby on thawing, since the flesh exudes moisture. *Casseroles* can be made to standard recipes, but cornflour should be substituted for flour as a thickening agent, or the mixture may curdle on thawing. For the same reason, cream should not be added to recipes until the reheating stage. *Pies* will be best if the contents are cooked but the short or flaky pastry left raw; when the pie is cooked after thawing, the pastry will be crisper with better flavour. *Soup* made from game will freeze well, but headspace must be left in the container. No starchy additions such as flour, potatoes, rice, pasta or barley should be frozen in the soup as they will become soggy. Add these when re-heating, if necessary.

HOT WATER CRUST GAME PIES

These are normally eaten cold and can be frozen baked or unbaked, but there are risks attached to freezing them. The pastry is made with hot water, and the pie may be completely baked and cooled before freezing, but without the jelly. This must be added just before the pie is served, and can be done by freezing the stock separately when the pie is made, then heating it and pouring it in through the lid while the pie is thawing (about 4 hours). This will speed up the thawing process but will also accelerate deterioration so don't keep. The pie can also be frozen unbaked, partially thawed, than baked. But this means the uncooked meat will be in contact with the warm uncooked pastry during the making process, and unless the pie is very carefully handled while cooling, there is severe risk of dangerous organisms entering the meat. It is better therefore to make such a pie freshly for use, and this can of course be done with thawed out frozen game.

FISH

Fish freezes well, but should be processed as soon as it is caught, and certainly within 24 hours. Fatty fish (haddock, halibut, herring, mackerel, salmon, trout, turbot) will keep a maximum of 4 months. White fish (cod, plaice, sole, whiting) will keep a maximum of 6 months. Shell fish should be stored no longer than 1 month.

CLEANING

Fish should be killed at once, scaled if necessary, and the fins removed. Small fish can be left whole; large fish should have heads and tails removed, or can be divided into steaks. Flat fish, herring and mackerel are best gutted, and flat fish may be skinned and filleted. Fish should be washed well in salted water during cleaning to remove blood and membranes, but fatty fish should be washed in fresh water.

PACKING AND FREEZING

There are four ways of preparing fish for freezing. The Dry Pack is the easiest method to use.

1. *Dry Pack*   Separate pieces of fish with double thickness of Cellophane, wrap in freezer paper, polythene, or in a carton, seal and freeze. If too much air is left in the pack, the fish will dry out and be tasteless. Fish should be frozen quickly on the floor of the freezer.

2. *Brine Pack*   This should *not* be used for fatty fish, as salt encourages oxidation and rancidity. Dip fish into cold salted water (1 tablespoon salt to 1 quart water), drain, wrap and seal. Do not store longer than 3 months.

3. *Acid Pack*   Citric acid preserves the colour and flavour of fish, and ascorbic acid is an anti-oxidant which stops the development of rancidity. An ascorbic-citric acid powder can be diluted in a proportion of 1 part powder to 100 parts water. Dip fish into this, drain, wrap and seal.

[323]

4. *Solid Ice Pack* Small fish, steaks or fillets can be separated with Cellophane or polythene, then frozen in quantity in refrigerator trays or loaf tins with water. The solid blocks can then be removed from the containers and wrapped in foil for storage. There is no particular advantage in this method.

LARGE WHOLE FISH

If a large fish, such as salmon or salmon trout, is likely to be served whole, it can be protected from wrapping marks and its silver looks preserved by 'glazing'. The fish should be cleaned, then placed without wrapping against the freezer wall in the coldest possible part of the freezer. When the fish is solid, it should be dipped in very cold water so a thin coating of ice will form. After a further hour in the freezer, the fish should be 'dipped' again, and the process repeated until the ice is $\frac{1}{4}$ inch thick. Note: The fish can be stored this way without wrapping for only 2 weeks.

COOKED FISH DISHES

Cooked fish does not really freeze well, as overcooking spoils both flavour and texture and this is difficult to avoid in the reheating process after freezing. Dishes which do not need reheating are worth freezing though, such as potted shrimps or crab, and fish pâtés. Fish cakes and fish pies do not suffer too badly from freezing. They are best prepared up to the final browning or frying stage before being frozen.

SMOKED FISH

Smoked haddock, kippers, trout, mackerel and salmon can all be frozen very well. Rub each fish with a fine film of good salad oil before packing and freezing, as this will save a dried-out surface on thawing.

All fish should be thawed slowly in unopened wrappings. 1 lb. or 1 pint package takes about 3 hours in room temperature or 6 hours in a refrigerator. Complete thawing is not necessary before cooking. Shellfish should be eaten as soon as thawed and still cold.

SHELLFISH

Shellfish of all kinds is best frozen immediately after catching and cooking. Oysters, clams and mussels are sometimes frozen raw after cleaning, but in view of the danger of poisoning, it is preferable to cook them before freezing.

Crab should be cooked, drained and cooled thoroughly. Clean and remove all edible meat, and pack in waxed tubs or polythene bags for freezing. The flesh may also be returned to the well-scrubbed shell for freezing.

Lobster and Crayfish should be cooked while alive. After cooling, they may be frozen whole in a polythene bag. It is also possible to remove all edible meat and pack this into cartons or bags.

Oysters and Clams should be washed and removed from the shells, reserving juice. Boil for 3 minutes in enough juice and water to cover, cool and pack with juice in cartons.

Mussels should be well scrubbed and cleaned, then put into a large saucepan covered with a damp cloth and put over medium heat for about 3 minutes until they open. After cooling in the pan, the mussels can be frozen in their shells, or removed and frozen with their juice in cartons.

Shrimps and Prawns should be cooked slowly so as not to shell and cooled in the cooking water, then shelled and packed in bags or cartons. They can be frozen in their shells with heads removed, but there is little advantage in this method.

MARY NORWAK

[325]

Appendix

SEASONS FOR GAME, FISH AND SHELLFISH

Game Birds

England, Scotland and Wales

Pheasant	October 1 – January 31
Partridge	September 1 – January 31
Grouse	August 12 – December 10
Blackgame	August 20 – December 10
Capercaillie	October 1 – January 31
Ptarmigan	August 12 – December 10
Woodcock (England & Wales)	October 1 – January 31
(Scotland)	September 1 – January 31
Snipe	August 12 – January 31
Wildfowl (inland)	September 1 – January 31
(foreshore)	September 1 – February 20
Wild Geese	September 1 – February 20

Deer
England and Wales

Roe Deer	Buck	No close season but not usually shot between October 2nd and April 30th
	Does	November 1 – February 28-29

Scotland

Red Deer	Stags	July 1 – October 20
	Hinds	October 21 – February 15
Roe Deer	Buck	May 1 – October 20
	Does	October 21 – February 28-29

Fish (*A guide only, dates vary under different district and river boards*)

England and Wales

Salmon	February – October 31 (But varies on different rivers)
Brown Trout	March 1 – September 30
Rainbow Trout	No close season
Sea Trout	March 1 – September 30
Coarse Fish	June 16 – March 14

Scotland

Salmon	January – November (but varies on different rivers)
Sea Trout	
Brown Trout	March 15 – October 6
Rainbow Trout	No close season
Coarse Fish	No close season

Note: The cook should be reminded that fish caught late in the season are not normally regarded as so good for the table

Recommended months for good eating depending on location

Game

Partridge	October – November
Pheasant	November – December
Grouse	August – December
Blackgame	September – October
Ptarmigan	September – December
Capercaillie	September – November
Pigeon	August – November
Wild Duck	September – January
Wild Geese	September – January
Woodcock	October – December
Snipe	August – January
Rook	May
Hare	August – February
Rabbit	August – February
Venison	All months except close seasons

River and Lake Fish

Salmon	February – September
Sea Trout	March – September
Trout	April – August
Char	June – July
Grayling	November
Pike	July – February

Sea Fish

Flounder	February – July
Dab	February – July
Plaice	May – November
Sole	June – November
Halibut	August – March
Turbot	All the year round
Skate	October – May
Brill	All the year round
Cod	October – May
Hake	August – January
Haddock	September – February
Whiting	October – February
Pouting	June – August
Herring	June – December
Mackerel	April – August
Red Mullet	April – October
John Dory	January – March
Whitebait	April – July
Sprats	October – November
Gurnard	August – October
Dogfish	September – December
Pilchard	August – November
Sea Bream	July – December
Conger Eel	August – November

Shellfish

Cockles	June – August
Crawfish	May – July
Shrimps	October – November
Lobster	June – September
Crab	May – September
Scallops	January – February
Mussels	August – February
Oysters	September – April
Crayfish	May – July
Prawns	May – October
Winkles	May – August

INDEX

[331]